THE PSYCHOLOGY OF ANOMALOUS EXPERIENCE

—REVISED EDITION—

Psychology Series

James E. Alcock, Ph.D., Series Editor

Other titles in the series:

**Cognition and Affect: A Developmental
Psychology of the Individual**
Laurence R. Simon, Ph.D.

THE PSYCHOLOGY OF ANOMALOUS EXPERIENCE

A Cognitive Approach

GRAHAM REED

—REVISED EDITION—

PROMETHEUS BOOKS
Buffalo, New York

To the Memory of
George Westby

Published by Prometheus Books
700 East Amherst Street, Buffalo, New York 14215

Library of Congress Catalog Number: 88-61531

ISBN 0-87975-435-4

Printed in the United States of America

FOREWORD TO THE REVISED EDITION

It is fair to say that since this book was first published there has been no major breakthrough or shift in direction in the psychological study of cognition. Indeed, the weight of research findings in the intervening years tends to support the theoretical thrust propounded here—that cognitive processes are selective, dynamic, interactive, and modifiable by expectancies or set.

At the same time, the tendency among psychological writers to ignore or actively avoid anomalous instances continues to prevail. It is as though we psychologists are so concerned to establish 'universal laws' that phenomena which do not readily fit our models are regarded as, at best, messy and inconvenient. Only in the field of visual perception have anomalies continued to be studied in their own right. (In fact, the investigation of optical illusions has, if anything, increased, and has played a major role in the study of visual processes.)

At the other extreme, despite burgeoning research in the area of memory, there have been no major contributions to the examination or explanation of anomalies of recall or recognition. This is surely regrettable, for mnemonic anomalies have the potential to make significant contributions to the development of theoretical models. And at the very least, such models should be shown to be capable of accounting for relatively common anomalous experiences like *déjà vu*.

On the credit side there is a growing professional interest in the phenomenological flavour of experience as opposed to observable behaviour. This, of course, reflects a paradigm shift in psychology, manifested in the humanistic 'third force' thrust.

Outside the professional confines of psychology, there seems to be an increasing interest in anomalous experiences. The precise topics of intrigue vary, of course, like any other fashions. Interest in UFOs and the Bermuda Triangle have diminished, and 'Out of the Body Experiences' are the 'in' thing. Sadly, what remain unchanged are the explanatory constructs used in popular discussions of such beliefs and interpretations. Lay people, however highly educated and technologically sophisticated, tend to make simplistic assumptions about the nature of human information-processing. Commonly, they postulate causal mechanisms *outside* the system (aliens, ghosts, electrical forces, etc.). The main purpose of this book is to suggest that many anomalous experiences may be amenable to examination in terms of normal psychological processes, without recourse to such variables as 'special powers', visitors from outer space, voodoo spells, or toxic substances in the water supply.

CONTENTS

ACKNOWLEDGMENTS

I should like to thank my old friend Professor George Westby who, as editor of the series, asked me to write this book. Professors E. W. Anderson and J. Hoenig opened my eyes to the diagnostic precision of European psychiatry and to the value of the phenomenological method. Jack Kenna, like George Westby, has generously shared with me his erudition, clinical acuity and warm humanity.

Of the many friends and colleagues who read and discussed sections of the manuscript I would particularly like to mention John Warder, Graham Davies, John Shepherd, Tony Marcel, Jan Deregowski and Terry Bloomfield.

Toronto   G.F.R.

INTRODUCTION

The aims of this book are modest, and its level intentionally simple. But its approach is somewhat unusual. First, the book is concerned with *experience*, rather than with behaviour. For the most part it is concerned with subjective phenomena, our knowledge of which is dependent upon introspection and verbal report as opposed to observable responses. In this respect it reflects a swing of the pendulum of psychological interest which has become increasingly evident in recent years. Secondly, it focusses upon *unusual* experiences, upon the irregular or atypical as opposed to the usual. It has been customary, in the study of academic psychology, to focus upon regular or 'normal' behaviour, experience and processes. The consideration of irregularities has in general been avoided, or isolated by encapsulation under the heading of 'abnormal psychology'. This is strange when it is borne in mind that the study of the abnormal has consistently proved of value to studies of normal functioning. Here, the approach is deliberately reductionist and integrative. Thus, thirdly, discussion here is in terms of *normal* psychology. And, fourthly, the emphasis is placed upon *cognitive* processes, as opposed to affective or motivational concepts.

The word 'anomalous' means irregular, disordered or unusual. An experience can be anomalous merely in terms of its infrequency of occurrence. The individual who experiences it does not regard it as abnormal, but as surprising. For instance, many people have occasionally woken up with the false belief that somebody has just called their name. This is not usually regarded as grounds for concern. The individual may react with irritation but he will generally merely laugh it off. On the other hand, the individual may regard as quite rational an experience which is very odd in the eyes of others. Thus, a person may believe that his nose, which appears quite ordinary to everybody else, is extraordinarily long and misshapen. Or he may know that invaders from Mars have established a base camp in his back garden, a fact which is stoutly denied by his family and the neighbours. Again, an experience can be anomalous in the sense that the individual is aware of disorder in himself, although his behaviour appears quite normal to others. He may suffer, for instance, agonies of indecision every morning as he is faced with the choice of wearing black or brown shoes. Or he may be filled with unspeakable terror at the very thought of entering an elevator or crossing a road. An experience may also be anomalous both in the eyes of the individual *and* of others. For instance, a man who reports that he can feel the claws of a large but invisible bird embedded in the back of his neck will be adjudged by his friends as being subject to a most anomalous experience. But he may be pretty disturbed about the matter himself. He may be fully aware of the absurdity of his belief, and his fear of the bird may be overshadowed by the worry caused by that knowledge.

The best documented types of anomalous experience are often those described by psychiatric patients. So this book is necessarily concerned with psychopathology—the signs and symptoms of mental disorder. But in so far as it does refer to psychopathology, its approach is somewhat at variance from that prevalent in textbooks of abnormal psychology. There are several points of difference:

(1) Traditionally, abnormal psychology texts have modelled them-themselves upon manuals of *psychiatry*. They are usually organized around nosology, and concerned with the problems of classification. This is implied by chapter headings such as 'Schizophrenia', 'Hysterical disorders', and so on. Now, diagnostic categorization is central to the study and practice of psychiatry. It is crucial for a number of practical reasons, including administrative requirements, the standardization of case reports and, most important, decisions about appropriate regimes of treatment. But it is not the most central nor the most proper concern of psychologists. This book will examine anomalous experiences themselves, rather than the illnesses with which many of them are associated. It will, for instance, discuss depersonalization and hallucinations, rather than depressive illness and schizophrenia. In other words, the focus of interest will be *psychological phenomena* rather than *psychiatric nosology*.

(2) With certain honourable exceptions, abnormal psychology texts, like psychiatry texts, make little attempt to reconcile their material with the findings of normal psychology. For the most part they tend to be 'dynamically' orientated—that is to say, they depend

upon assumptions drawn from one or the other school of psycho-analysis. Some are 'eclectic', which usually means an uneasy admixture of the above with some brand of learning theory. This book, whilst not discounting the validity of either of these approaches, attempts as far as possible to look at anomalous experiences in the context of normal psychology. The approach taken is that generally called 'cognitive psychology', which is concerned with the ways in which we perceive, interpret, remember and think. Or, to use current terminology—the ways in which information is selected, coded, organized, stored, retrieved and utilized. Such an approach differs on the one hand from 'dynamic' approaches which stress motivation, conflict and defences, and on the other from the behaviouristic ones, with their emphasis on stimulus, response and reinforcement. The present approach will doubtless be criticized by some readers for paying insufficient attention to motivational and affective factors and by others for ignoring learning and the modification of behaviour. But these have been amply explored elsewhere.

(3) The approaches of most 'dynamic' writers can be traced back to the Vienna school of psychoanalysis. This book has been influenced more by the 'main-stream' school of German psychiatry, as exemplified in the work of Karl Jaspers. The latter used the phenomenological method to identify the *formal* qualities of experience. Psychoanalytic workers, on the other hand, have been primarily interested in the *content* of experience. Strangely enough, most abnormal psychology texts have ignored the distinction between form and content altogether. Indeed, many psychologists seem to be unaware that there is any such distinction. This book stresses it.

The study of content of experience affords rich insights into the psychic development of the individual. But analysis at this level provides only ontogenetic, phenotypical evidence. To shed light on psychological functions and malfunctions, analysis of the formal structure of experience is required. One man believes that he is being ruthlessly pursued by Goldfinger, whilst another believes that he is Portnoy's lost twin brother. Such information may give us hints about each man's life history as well as his reading habits. But before we can make any hypotheses about the psychological functions involved, or attempt to generalize the information, it is necessary to examine the *form* of the two experiences. And this will involve considerable phenomenological investigation into the quality of the experiences—do the individuals believe that they correspond to objective reality or are they expressing an 'as if' awareness? Are the beliefs held with unshakable conviction or are they struggled against as unfortunate and ridiculous intrusions?

The chapter titles were originally chosen to emphasize the relation of the various phenomena described to the traditional 'areas' of normal experimental psychology. However, it rapidly became apparent that many of the phenomena could equally well be discussed in the terms suggested by several chapter titles. (The reader will notice that several chapters end by suggesting that the chapter title was not perhaps the most appropriate one after all.) But perhaps this is as it should be. The material of psychology is complex, and highly interactive. Most of the area boundary lines we draw are arbitrary and ill-defined. They serve at best as expository aids which allow a vast amount of material to be artificially broken down into more workable packets. Thus it is to be expected that a phenomenon like *déjà vu* may be discussed in terms of memory disorder, ego disorder or temporal disorder. Or, as here, it can be classified as an 'anomaly of recognition'. There is no one profitable approach to such a phenomenon, no 'right' classification.

I

ANOMALIES OF ATTENTION

'Every one', asserted William James, 'knows what attention is.' Perhaps they do; but, at least as far as psychologists are concerned, the trouble is that their knowings do not match. And dictionary definitions, such as: 'The act of applying one's mind, notice, consideration . . .' (*Pocket Oxford Dictionary*), raise more questions than they answer. So we may profitably start by considering some of the varieties of attention and the ways in which the word is used.

Clearly, a distinction must be made between *passive* and *voluntary* attention. The first of these terms refers to situations where our attention is 'arrested' or 'captured', despite ourselves. This passive attention is a function of the event or stimulus, and many studies have been made to determine the characteristics which make a stimulus attention-gaining. These include size, motion, colour, repetition, contrast and novelty, features which are deliberately employed by advertisers whose aim of course is to attract maximum attention.

Voluntary attention refers to situations where we deliberately focus upon some particular feature or train of events. This may be the most interesting among the whole array of those available for inspection. But it may be only one of many equally arresting items, or indeed something to which we pay attention *despite* the fact that it is dominated or masked by other features or events. At one time, psychologists referred to passive attention as 'primary' or 'unlearned', whereas voluntary attention was termed 'secondary' or 'forced'. Another distinction was made between the latter and attention which was determined by habit or training. This was termed 'derived primary' or 'learned'.

A further distinction, which has not as yet been much studied, is that between attention for discrete events as compared with on-going sequences which involve development and change such as football games, films, lectures or discussions. Psychologists have tended to employ experimental situations which involve the repeated presentation of discrete signals such as lights or tones. Elegant theories derived from such experiments tend to be weakened when sequentially developing signals such as language are employed.

Let us look briefly at some of the ways in which the word 'attention' has been used, and some of the key concepts and terms employed in its study:

(1) Perhaps the most commonly recognized type of attention in everyday life is that where we *concentrate*, with more or less success, upon some particular task. Thus we speak of concentrating upon a textbook, the presentation of an argument, driving a car in heavy traffic or swinging a golf club. Later, the anomalous experience of *absent-mindedness* as related to this type of attention will be considered. Ironically, absent-mindedness is generally taken to involve a lack of concentration, whereas in fact it describes the opposite.

Our level of concentration may be diminished when we are distracted from the task in hand by events irrelevant to the task or simply by our own thoughts or day-dreams as in 'wool-gathering'. This will affect our performance most seriously in unfamiliar tasks or those in which we are relatively unskilled. We may be able to perform habitual activities or ones in which we are highly skilled with minimal conscious attention. The *time-gap experience* will be discussed as an anomaly related to this question of level of skill.

(2) In referring to 'voluntary attention' above it was noted that we can attend to one particular signal or sequence when there are many others equally or more interesting, all competing for our attention. Under the title of *selective attention* this phenomenon has excited the interest of experimental psychologists since the 1950s, after an interval of some forty years during which the whole area of attention had received relatively little examination. The seminal book in this resurgence was Broadbent's (1958) *Perception and Communication*, whilst a most readable up-to-date exposition has been provided by Moray (1969a).

The problem is that the selection of one event or feature involves the exclusion or disregard of the rest. How are we able to *non*-attend to many things whilst attending to a few? Yet we are continually doing just this—we attend to the movement of one person in a crowd, the sound of one instrument amongst those of a whole orchestra or the relevant announcement amongst all the noise at a railway station or airport. In a sense the whole thing is anomalous; as an example, the *tuning-in* phenomenon will be discussed.

(3) A third usage of the word 'attention' is in relation to *arousal*. For instance, when we are frightened, delighted, amazed, curious or sexually aroused, our attention is heightened. We become acutely attentive if we are approached by a belligerent drunk or a provocative and attractive member of the opposite sex. Dependent upon our cultural background, we may exhibit similar attention changes when we are faced with a sonnet by Shakespeare, a Rembrandt etching or a wine bottle whose label lays claim to a particular vintage. Or an unexpected cheque, or a severed hand. . . . In such cases, arousal is associated with intensity of attention. We have mentioned the 'focussing' of attention; this implies differential distribution or *deployment* of attentional resources. Arousal involves the focussing of attention, but crucially it affects the *degree* of attention. Arousal theory states that the activation of the organism varies along a continuum from sleep to drowsiness through optimally effective functioning to diffuse over-excitation. Clearly this is an example of what we have referred to as 'passive' or 'primary' attention because it is involuntary and consequent upon the effects upon us of external events. We are aroused by the situation despite ourselves. Subsequently, of course, we may employ voluntary attention also.

With reference to this type of attention, responses to *stress* are discussed, but later on such experiences as 'possession', which can also be considered from the attentional point of view, are covered.

(4) The cat at the mouse-hole displays highly focussed and intense attention. But she is not attending to the mouse-hole as such. She is waiting for the appearance of the mouse itself. Similarly, the industrial meter-watcher must be highly attentive, not so much to the display currently before him, but in anticipation of occasional *changes* in the display. Study of the decrements in performance of radar operators during World War II initiated a mass of research into this sort of attention, which was termed *vigilance* by Mackworth (1950). No anomalous experience which could be considered as a direct vigilance problem is discussed, but the findings of vigilance studies are relevant to many of the experiences covered.

(5) A crucial element in vigilance is anticipation. One school of thought regards attention in general as being a question of *expectancy*. According to this view, attention may be equated with *perceptual set*, meaning that the organism is 'tuned' to receive certain signals rather than others. Thus, Hebb (1949) defines his use of attention as 'a central facilitation of a perceptual activity' (page 102). In the present author's view, 'set' is a tuning procedure which is *preparatory* to attention. Thus, it is more logically regarded as a

characteristic of attention, rather than as a *type* of attention. The concept of 'set' is of central importance in psychology, however, despite the fact that it has been used in many different ways. It will be called upon in discussion throughout this book. Meanwhile it may be noted that there are several ways in which 'set' may validly be regarded. Hebb's usage is similar to what we mean when we talk of tuning a radio receiver—the dial is 'set' to a particular frequency, so that signals are received when a given station starts to broadcast. Another usage has reference to the attitude of attention evoked, for instance, by the military command 'Att-en-*shun*!' The trained soldier responds with an alert physical posture, associated with a readiness to respond to whatever the next command may be. A related usage is contained in the starter's call: 'Ready?... *Set* ... Go!' Here, the command alerts the runners—they tense up ready to respond, but they know what will come next. Finally (for present purposes) there is the 'set' induced by verbal instructions, such as: 'I want you to press this key every time you see two lights ...'

(6) One of the reasons why the study of attention was neglected for many years was the growing influence of behaviourism. Experimental psychologists became reluctant to depend upon introspection, and most contemporary investigators have studied responses to external stimuli. (Thus, the type of attention we mentioned first—that of mental concentration—has not been a popular area of study in recent years.) But 'attention' can also be used to refer to *the way in which we select or dwell upon our own thoughts and memories*. The word is used in this way by workers in the field of personality, especially those with a psychoanalytic orientation. The 'New Look' psychologists and their successors—the 'cognitive styles' psychologists—use it in both senses, emphasizing that the ways in which an individual perceives the outside world are determined by his personality and reflect unique inner processes and characteristics. So we can study differences between individuals in terms of their *preferred modes of attention*.

Having cleared the way, we shall look at the anomalous experiences mentioned above. We shall then consider individual differences in attentional processes; for what may seem anomalous to one person may not seem so to another because of their differing personality structures. Finally we shall look at anomalous experiences which may be interpreted as reflecting pathology or gross disorder in attentional mechanisms.

ABSENT-MINDEDNESS

The traditional picture of the 'absent-minded professor' (AMP) portrays an unkempt, white-haired figure shambling along the centre of King's Parade, Cambridge, blissfully unaware both of the traffic screaming to a halt around him and of the fact that he is carrying a vacuum cleaner instead of his brief-case.

This sort of behaviour is regarded by the observer as highly anomalous but it is not seen as pathological, despite the fact that it has much in common with lay presumptions about lunatics. Far from being associated with mental illness or intellectual impairment, it is usually cited (with elaborations) as evidence of the eccentricity associated with genius. This is particularly so when the individual behaves in this way so consistently as to suggest that it reflects a relatively stable personality variable rather than temporary aberration.

The true AMP himself is not aware that his behaviour is unusual. Indeed, were he aware, he could not be said to be absent-minded. For the whole point about absent-mindedness is that the individual is so preoccupied with his own thoughts that he closes out much of the external information which is currently available to him. He may engage in many habitual activities such as seizing his brief-case and setting off at the time he usually leaves to deliver his lecture. But he is not responsive to feed-back regarding changes in his routine. Thus, in the way that Henri Bergson asserted was the crux of humour, his actions are machine-like. If the vacuum cleaner happens to be standing where his brief-case usually is, then he seizes that on his way out. Furthermore, he may not regulate the details of his on-going habitual behaviour in accordance with environmental demands. If his goal is the college gates he may make directly for them, regardless of traffic conditions across his route. In short, the AMP's *level* of attentiveness is low for what are to him distracting stimuli. But it must be remembered that not only is he very attentive to his thinking, but he may also attend closely to any external activity related to that thinking. One variant of the AMP is the absent-minded scientist who is so involved in his experiment that he fails to notice that his beard is on fire. Thus, the *level* of his attention is associated with his *deployment* of attentiveness which will be considered in a later section. It may be presumed that absent-mindedness is a threshold phenomenon. The AMP's diminished level and scope of attention to external events are directly but inversely related to the degree of his preoccupation with those events of concern to him. If the competing signals from the environment suddenly increase in intensity or significance it may be anticipated that his general attentiveness will increase to a more appropriate level. Indeed, although there are many stories of AMPs disappearing down uncovered manholes, there are no recorded instances of any who actually failed to skip out of the way at the last moment as the omnibuses bore down upon them. And it is difficult to believe that the classic AMP would remain quite so absent-minded were he to be confronted by an equally absent-minded lady professor sauntering down King's Parade in the nude.

The question of enhanced environmental signals leads directly to something to be discussed later—attentional changes in the face of a stressful situation.

THE 'TIME-GAP' EXPERIENCE

After a long drive the motorist will quite commonly report that at some point in the journey he 'woke up' to realize that he had no awareness of some preceding period of time. People often describe this, with some justification, as a 'gap in time', 'a lost half-hour' or 'a piece out of my life'. The strangeness of the experience springs partly from 'waking up' when one is already awake. But mainly it is due to the knowledge of a blank in one's temporal awareness. Doubtless the uneasiness associated with such a realization is largely culturally determined. For in our culture our everyday lives are sharply structured by time requirements. For most of us there are conventional times for commencing and finishing work, for taking breaks, for eating, sleeping and enjoying leisure pursuits. We talk about 'wasting time' as opposed to 'spending time profitably'. We are continually consulting our watches or turning on the radio to check our subjective estimates of the passage of time, and in many jobs 'clock-watching' has a very real significance. Only when we are on holiday can most of us indulge in the luxury of ceasing to bother about clock time. But furthermore, our consciousness of self is closely related to the sense of *continuity* in the passage of time. To miss a period of time can be very disturbing; it has been used as the theme of several stories and films, as in the alcoholic's 'lost week-end'.

A little reflection will suggest, however, that our experience of time and its passage is determined by *events*, either external or internal. What the time-gapper is reporting is not that a slice of time has vanished, but that he has failed to register a series of events which would normally have functioned as his time-markers. If he is questioned closely he will admit that his 'time-gap' experience did not involve his realization at, say, noon that he had somehow 'lost' half an hour. Rather, the experience consists of 'waking up' at, say, Florence and realizing that he remembers nothing since Bologna. It is now noon, whereas he left Bologna at eleven-thirty. The time-gapper describes his experience in terms of *time*, whereas he could just as well describe it in terms of *distance*. To understand the experience, however, it is best considered in terms of the absence of *events*. If the time-gapper had taken that particular day off, and spent the morning sitting in his garden undisturbed, he might have remembered just as little of the half-hour in question. He might still describe it in terms of lost time, but he would not find the experience unusual or disturbing. For he would point out that he could not remember what took place between eleven-thirty and twelve simply because nothing of note occurred. Doubtless there were many events during that time—clouds moved across the sky, sparrows twittered, leaves fluttered across the lawn. But none of these represented any drastic change in the situation, and none had any alerting significance for our man. Why then is he puzzled about his failure to remember anything between Bologna and Florence? Simply because he knows very well that he has driven his car from one place to the other, which demands continual personal events in the form of on-going skilled activity, which naturally presents a continual shift of visual scene and which normally involves events related to other road-users. But the point is that the time-gap is experienced when a portion of the journey lacks events of significance. There is little traffic, clear visibility, a good road surface, no warning signs and so on. In short, the demands of the task are relatively unchanging.

Now our performance of complex skills involves perfecting the basic elements, the integration of these into a new level of skill, then the further integration of several such levels and so on in a hier-archical progression of *schemata*. Our mastery of the overall skill is facilitated by the fact that, when we have perfected each component or level, its performance becomes 'automatic', in the sense that we can withdraw active attention from that level of activity and concen-trate on the next. We seldom 'attend' to our execution of habitual, life-long skills such as grasping, walking or talking. We become conscious of them only when our functioning is impaired by injury or ill-health. On the other hand, we do have to attend to the ways in which these basic skills must be organized in response to environ-mental demands, particularly when these are stressful or unfamiliar. We may walk for miles along a smooth track without noticing what we are doing. Matters become very different when the track surface deteriorates or the path winds along the edge of a cliff. In the per-formance of more formal activities, much depends upon the amount of change involved in the task. The skilled boxer cannot afford to relax his concentration because, however habitual the *elements* of his performance, his opponent is continually introducing changes which demand the reorganization of these elements. But when the task is relatively 'closed' and strategic reorganization unlikely, then the skilled person can perform it with a minimum of active attention. Thus the experienced knitter can execute a complex activity whilst conversing or watching the television or listening for the baby. The pianist can play familiar music whilst discussing audience reactions with his colleagues and the carpenter can operate a lathe whilst instructing his apprentice.

The relevance of the above to the time-gap experience is obvious. The task of driving is itself highly skilled, but its component activities are over-learned and habitual to the experienced driver. Steering, changing gear, adjusting speed, giving signals and so on all become automatic acts which do not require his conscious attention. Their organization and integration at the tactical level also become habitual within a certain range of requirements. (Indeed, a major danger in motorway driving, where the road is straight, wide and well surfaced and where constant speeds over long distances are possible, is that drivers can afford to diminish their conscious attention to the point where the task becomes boring and they fall asleep.) However, traffic conditions usually demand continual reorganization of skilled responses at the strategic level and this requires constant alertness and conscious attention.

The key to the time-gap experience, then, is the level of organization or schematization required by the situation. But why is it that the driver realizes that he has been driving 'automatically'? Simply that the situation *does* change and events demanding his active attention do intrude. As he approaches Florence, he encounters more traffic, warning signs, traffic lights and so on. His on-going routine activity is now insufficient; the situation suddenly demands responses to new information and feed-back, in the form of continual strategic reorganization of his skills. He must, in fact, 'wake up', relatively speaking. And, in waking up, his reactivated conscious attentiveness enables him to register among many other things that he is now in Florence. In one sense he is correct in describing what has happened as a 'gap'. But the gap is not in time, but in alertness or high conscious attention.

'TUNING-IN'

One of man's most puzzling talents is his ability to follow one on-going activity or information source when there are many others competing for his attention. We can do this even when the physical characteristics of the competing events are more intense—are louder, shriller, bigger, brighter and so on. The ability applies both within and between each of our sensory channels. We can visually follow the performance of just one player in a football game, regardless of all the other players and events around him. We can auditorially follow the tone of the clarinet at a concert, though it is only a tiny part of the rich sound of the symphony orchestra. Similarly, amongst a great deal of tactile input, the football player or the clarinettist can follow the progress of a fly along the back of his neck. And we can do each of these things in the face of other competing input to our other senses.

We are probably most conscious of this ability in the auditory sphere, especially in the following of other people's voices. In this case it is commonly referred to as 'tuning-in'. Thus the lady in a restaurant may say to her husband: 'Sorry dear, what did you say? I wasn't listening—I was tuned-in to that funny-looking couple in the corner.' And it is this aspect of selective attention which, under the title 'the cocktail party problem', fired off a renewed interest in the subject of attention among experimental psychologists and which has attracted active investigation and theorizing for some fifteen years. Clearly there are two sides to this problem coin, either or both of which can be used as points of attack. The first of these is: 'How do we select and attend to one on-going sequence of events, despite everything else that is going on?' The second is: 'How do we exclude or inhibit everything that is going on except that one sequence to which we are attending?' It is this second aspect of the problem which seems to have preoccupied most active researchers in the field. And the answers they have come up with have usually been developments from or modifications of Broadbent's (1958) 'filter theory'.

For present purposes, the original version of Broadbent's well-known model may be summarized as follows:

(1) The nervous system may be regarded as a *single communication channel of limited capacity*. Its capacity is much lower than the combined capacities of the many parallel input channels from the senses. The central processing channel may thus become a sort of bottle-neck.

(2) To prevent overloading of the central channel, input must therefore pass through a *selective filter*. Selection is based on physical features such as intensity, pitch and spatial localization. The filter handles the parallel inputs sequentially.

(3) The likelihood of information being selected and fed through to the central channel is related to such input properties as physical intensity and length of time since the given class of events was sampled.

(4) Input may be held for up to a few seconds in a *short-term store* until the class of events to which it belongs is next selected.

Broadbent's model is neat, elegant and supported by considerable experimental evidence; it has inspired a vast amount of investigation and fruitful controversy (excellently summarized by Moray, 1969b). Unfortunately, as it stands, it just cannot encompass many aspects of the very situation it was designed to explain. The main findings from which Broadbent derived the model were drawn from his investigations of 'dichotic listening' or the 'split-span experiment'. This involves feeding through earphones a different message to each of the subject's ears. The individual signals (digits or words) from one message are paired with those from the other, and the pairs are presented simultaneously, one member to the left ear and one to the right:

LLL
RRR

Broadbent found that, if the subject is instructed to pay attention to the left ear, he will report signals in the order LLL, RRR. Similarly, if he is instructed to attend to the right ear, he will report RRR, LLL. It was this re-ordering of signals that suggested to Broadbent that the non-attended material must be queued and held in store until the 'significant' material had been processed. But the dichotic listening situation became a standard psychological laboratory experiment and a wealth of new information rapidly indicated that, whilst Broadbent's findings were basically correct, a great deal depended upon the type of the signals used. If two messages are presented as follows:

Left – TODAY IS Cambridge
Right – Nearly at THURSDAY

and the subject is instructed to attend to the message entering his left ear, he is very likely to report hearing 'Today is Thursday, nearly at Cambridge'. And if he is presented with:

Left – TO – ly
Right – Near – DAY

he is likely to report hearing 'Today, nearly'. He will, in fact, switch ears according to the *meaningfulness* of the signals. So, clearly, Broadbent's stress on physical characteristics as the criteria for signal selection was too narrow. Psychological attributes may be more or less important according to the nature of the task. And the real cocktail party situation is pre-eminently an example where psychological factors predominate. When we 'tune-in' to a conversation it is the *meaning* of the words used which we are following. Again, whilst shadowing the messages on one channel, the subject may be induced to shift his attention to the other if it introduces a signal of special significance to him. For instance, the sound of his own name on the non-attended channel will attract his attention. To account for all these anomalies, alternatives to Broadbent's model have been proposed which involve some sort of selection *prior to the filter*.

Furthermore, Broadbent's model suggests that the non-attended material is rejected whilst the other is being processed. It is held briefly in the short-term store, but if the processing channel is occupied for more than a matter of seconds the contents of the store dissipate. But in fact signals on the subordinate channel are *not* totally excluded. Gross changes, such as a switch from male to female voices, are noticed. So one modification which was proposed for Broadbent's model was that the filter does not *exclude* irrelevant information but merely *attenuates* it (Treisman, 1960). And a related problem that raises difficulties for the filter model is that subjects notice the cessation of signals on the non-attended channel and can thus report *non-signals*.

Finally, the filter model cannot explain selective attention to one's own thoughts. Absent-mindedness is an example of tuning-in to what is going on inside our own heads. When we concentrate upon our own thoughts our thresholds for other signals are heightened, just as they are when we tune in to a conversation at a party.

In short, Broadbent's original model was not sufficiently dynamic to account for the facts. And the alternatives which have been suggested involve filters which only attenuate input, pre-filter filtering, filters which are further into the system and filters which themselves process information. One may be forgiven for detecting a certain tautologous development here. For in order to make Broadbent's neat model workable, subsequent theorists have had to postulate filters functioning at a level which is almost as complex as that of the central mechanism itself. The concept of 'filtering' is attractive and useful, and we shall be using it in general terms later in this book. But an acceptable outline has still to be presented of the functioning of filters, whether they work in series or parallel, their levels of activity and their organization.

CHANGES IN ATTENTION AS RESPONSE TO STRESS

Absent-mindedness reflects the failure of signals from the environment to engage attention. What happens when signals are maximally attention-gaining? Let us take the example of a stressful situation, where signals have heightened impact because of their fear- or anxiety-provoking significance. Just as danger signals elicit bodily changes which are accompanied by changes in performance, so are our *cognitive* processes modified in characteristic ways.

First of all, our attention becomes heightened and relatively restricted. As our muscles gird themselves for maximal activity, so we tend to *focus* awareness in a way which must originally have had clear survival value. In physically dangerous situations the threatening features demand all our attention, and other matters are put to one side. Up to a point, this is most appropriate; we are harnessing all our resources in preparation for action. But there is for each of us a breaking point. Either our attention becomes so narrowed that we 'freeze' (physically and mentally) or our behaviour disintegrates and we panic. When a driver sees another car skidding towards' him, he immediately experiences several cognitive changes. A moment before he may have been driving automatically, his mind far away. Suddenly, he is very conscious of himself, the controls, his speed, the road ahead. This necessarily involves the submergence of his previous train of thought as well as the normal balance of his physical control over his vehicle. He is now very conscious of his own position in space and time relative to the approaching car. Similarly, he acquires a sort of 'tunnel vision'—he perceives only the other vehicle and the area between. What was a global field is suddenly articulated. What was an interrelated overall pattern of road, sky, hedgerows, houses and hills breaks down. Just as his earlier stream of thought has been ousted, so the general visual scene is blurred into what the Gestalt psychologists described as 'ground' totally dominated by the relevant 'figure' of threat.

Now in civilized urban life we rarely meet actual physical danger. Stress is more usually related to social demands and intra-psychic conflict. In other words, we provide our own danger signals, which are usually the product of the ways in which we construe our own behaviour and the situations in which we find ourselves. And our construing is the product of our interpretations of and predictions about any given situation and our learned standards, aspirations, self-images and so on. But whether these signals are external and refer to actual danger or are internal and spring from our 'state of mind', our cognitive responses tend to be the same.

Not only do we differ radically according to our individual kinds of learning and previous experiences, but we vary in our degrees of autonomic reactivity. Some autonomic nervous systems are more reactive than others; so some people's emergency response thresholds are lower than others and can be triggered off more easily. When such people are also liable to be over-sensitive in their construing of situations, they are continually vulnerable to anxiety and impaired performance. This leads to further tension and doubts, so that a vicious circle is set up. When the person no longer feels able to cope he may seek psychiatric help; he may well now be termed 'neurotic' and diagnosed as suffering from an 'anxiety state'.

The psychiatrist will try to help his neurotic patient in a number of ways. He will try to muffle his autonomic reactivity by prescribing sedatives. He will suggest (to the patient, his family or even his employers) ways in which the number of threatening situations in the patient's life may be reduced. And he will attempt to modify the ways in which the patient construes those situations. Thus he may persuade the patient to change his job to one more commensurate with his talents. At the same time he may urge the patient's wife to be more supportive, to build up his confidence. And meanwhile, by exhortation and parable he will try to prevail upon the patient to view himself more positively.

INDIVIDUAL DIFFERENCES IN MODES OF ATTENTION

The attentional changes noted as occurring in stressful situations are common to all of us, though in varying degrees. But each person probably has his individual attention pattern which is sufficiently consistent to allow it to be given the status of a personality characteristic.

Earlier, the Gestaltist differentiation between 'figure' and 'ground' in a visual field was referred to. The same sort of differentiation can be made with regard to other modalities. Currently, experimental psychologists make a similar distinction when they speak of the 'signal' as opposed to the 'noise', terms which were borrowed from telecommunication engineering, and which were first applied in psychology to auditory tasks. When we are conversing with a friend at a party, his voice is the figure or signal, and the general hubbub is the ground or noise. People vary in their ability to differentiate between perceptually significant and non-significant features of the environment in this way. A number of 'cognitive style' researchers such as Witkin and his associates (1962) have demonstrated that both children and adults show individual consistencies in their degree of 'field articulation'. There seems to be a continuum, ranging from 'global' perceivers, who make relatively little discrimination among elements, because they do not seem to break the field down sufficiently, to 'articulated' perceivers whose perceiving is sharply discriminative. Global subjects are reported to be passive in their processing of input, whereas articulated subjects are actively analytic in their processing and structuring of the field. Thus global perceivers have relative difficulty in perceptual tasks which demand segmentalization and an analytic approach. An example is the 'embedded figures' type of test, where geometric shapes are 'hidden' by being set against a complex ground. The subject's task here is to isolate and identify the 'camouflaged' figures.

Of considerable interest is the fact that an individual's degree of success in articulating his perceptual field is paralleled by his level of performance in intellectual tasks such as problem-solving. Indeed, the use of the term 'cognitive style' is related to the finding that the global/articulated dimension seems to apply throughout the range of any individual's cognitive functioning, and is not restricted to visuo-perceptual activity.

The Witkin group's investigations began with studies of what they termed 'field-dependence/independence'. They discovered that sub-jects differed in their ability to adjust their bodies in space in the presence of misleading visual cues. This ability was examined by using the now well-known 'tilting-chair/tilting-room', an apparatus which consists of a tiltable chair (which can be adjusted by the sub-ject) in a tiltable room (adjusted by the experimenter). The subject sits in the chair and tries to adjust its tilt until his trunk is upright. To succeed, he must discount the false visual cues of 'verticality' provided by the room. Some subjects can ignore these, and adjust their position correctly by reference to the cues (kinaesthetic and vestibular) provided by their bodies. Others do not seem so able to discount environmental cues. They align themselves to correspond with the 'verticals' of the room and then presume that they are upright, even though they may be tilted up to 35° away from the true vertical. The first group are termed 'field-independent' and the second 'field-dependent'; the two are presumed to be at different points on a continuum of field-dependence/independence. Field-dependence is one aspect of the global type of perceptual response, and field-independence one of the articulated type.

So far, we have been considering the individual's *differentiation* between elements in his perceptual field. This field, however, repre-sents only a selection of everything in the environment. Another aspect of attention is the degree to which people sample the range of signals available to them at any given time, i.e. the *deployment* of attention.

In discussing changes during stress, we noted that attention becomes narrowed. Now what for one person may be a response only in the face of emergency may for another be habitual behaviour. There is ample evidence not only that such differences do exist between individuals, but that each individual is *consistent* in the attentional mode he employs. Such investigators as Gardner (1959) and his associates refer to modes of attention as 'cognitive controls' which share in the organization of personality. The Gardner group have differentiated two attentional strategies—scanning and focussing. Scanners are people who deploy their attention over the visual field, whilst focussers limit their attention to one narrow area.

The term 'focus' invites the analogy of a camera or a searchlight. Imagine a searchlight in use as part of the defences of an isolated military outpost in constant danger of night attack from guerrilla forces. To explore the surrounding terrain the searchlight may be focussed upon one particular area which can then be observed in detail. Or it may be swept across the field, enabling only snap observations of each area to be made, but allowing for coverage of many such areas. But another feature of the searchlight is the *width* of its beam. A wide-beamed light may throw diffused light over much of the field without much movement. On the other hand, the light may throw a very narrow beam, but be shifted continually from area to area. As Wachtel (1967) points out, there has been some confusion as to whether students of attention have used the word 'narrow' to mean *lack of movement* of the metaphorical light or with reference to the *breadth of its beam*. Obsessional persons could be said to deploy their attention with a very narrow beam but with a wide range of coverage. They go to great pains, for instance, to examine many facets of a situation or problem, but fail to interrelate and synthesize all the details they consider. Typically, they are unable to see the wood for the trees. On the other hand, such breaking up of the field allows for the defence mechanism of 'isolation' to come into play. Freud postulated that the obsessional individual can hold potentially disturbing ideas at a conscious level, but defends himself from anxiety by encapsulating and isolating them from associated emotion. He focusses his attention upon ideas, objective data or abstract formulations, but avoids consideration of their affective implications.

To return to a problem mentioned earlier: the fearful or anxious individual displays narrowed attention in the sense that he limits his attention to crucial features of the situation and ignores others, especially those on the periphery of the field. This sort of behaviour, as noted above, would originally have biological survival value. The man facing physical danger concentrates on what is most threatening and ignores the rest, which for the time being is irrelevant. However, beyond a certain point of extreme anxiety—when panic sets in—his attention becomes diffuse, because he is over-reactive and thus distractable. This can be interpreted on the searchlight metaphor by realizing that both dimensions may be involved. At first the light-beam narrows as the light is focussed on the area of threat. The narrowing may become so extreme that the man can no longer interpret the whole field, because the significance of segmental figures is lost if they are deprived of their context. The subject thus becomes confused, and his behaviour begins to disintegrate. His attention now becomes 'narrow' in the other sense. It is due, not to the width of the light-beam, but to the consequent disorganized 'wandering' of the beam over the field. In the first stage there is a failure of synthesis because the narrow area under examination is divorced from its setting. In the second stage there is a failure of integration because many narrow areas are being revealed but in such a hasty and unconnected way that the result is kaleidoscopic disarray.

The psychological 'defence mechanisms' postulated by Freud and his followers can also be approached in terms of selective attention used in one of the ways described in the introductory section. Just as we respond to danger by limiting our attention to certain features of the situation, so we may respond in a like way to disturbing or threatening ideas and memories. They may preoccupy us to the exclusion of everything else. But we can cope with such inner threats by deploying our attention in several other ways. A given individual's personality may be studied in terms of which particular mode of defence he employs most consistently. Thus the obsessional individual may be regarded as one who focusses his attention upon a number of very circumscribed elements of his experience. He ruminates about particular problems, is preoccupied with pedantic details and is 'hung up' with indecision because he fails to see matters in perspective. The hysteric individual, on the other hand, is one whose attention is diffuse and superficial. He can avoid disturbance by encapsulating threatening material and then ignoring it.

Thus we can study changes in attention as responses to threatening situations. Or we can study individuals whose thresholds of response to input are abnormal as in schizophrenia.

PATHOLOGY OF ATTENTIONAL MECHANISMS

We have seen how people's behaviour and experiences change when they are exposed to excessive stimulation from the environment. It would appear that when our receptors are over-loaded our central nervous systems become unable to cope with the input. Beyond a certain point the inhibitory mechanisms which enable us to discount irrelevant information fail to function effectively. In other words, our filtering mechanisms begin to break down. Without the initial 'sorting' carried out by some such filtering device we would find it impossible to focus our attention voluntarily; we would be overwhelmed by what William James called 'The blooming, buzzing confusion of sensation *sans* organization'.

A state of excessive stimulation is not, of course, the only situation in which the results of impaired filtering may be observed. When we are very fatigued we find it difficult to attend to what we are doing, and petty features which we can usually discount begin to irritate or distract us. The tired student burning the midnight oil becomes increasingly unable to concentrate on his books, and more and more uncomfortably aware of the hardness of his chair, the brightness of the light and the temperature of the room. Many an exhausted walker has missed the turning which would have led him to supper and a hot bath and thus condemned himself to a wet night in the heather.

Subjects intoxicated by LSD (lysergic acid diethylamide) or mescaline report experiences with similar characteristics. Their perceptions are 'heightened', in the sense that colours seem more vivid and textures more pronounced. Meanwhile, they are unable to focus their attention; they become passively receptive to the impact of surging, shifting impressions.

Again, there is evidence from laboratory experiments of changes in performance under conditions of stress or induced fatigue, which may be regarded as due to the same sort of process.

Now we may take it (and there is evidence to support this) that individuals vary in the degree of efficiency of their filtering mechanisms. Some people are more disturbed by sensory 'overloading' than others. The stage at which behaviour is impaired and the degree to which it is impaired vary from person to person. So, as well as observing how people in general react to unusually strong stimulation, one may well enquire how people with unusually weak filters react to everyday stimulation. This line of approach has proved to be particularly fruitful in the experimental study of schizophrenia.

It is generally accepted that schizophrenia is a term which covers many disorders or combinations of disorders, all of which present considerable complexity. But certainly young people suffering from *acute* schizophrenia of *non-paranoid* types often complain that what chiefly disturbs them at the beginning of their illness is the feeling that everything seems painfully intense, to a point where they can no longer cope. Several surveys of such accounts (e.g. McGhie and Chapman, 1961) have reported descriptions such as the following: '. . . noises all seem to be louder to me than they were before. It's as if someone had turned up the volume. . . .' 'The colours of things seem much more clearer and brighter. . . .' 'It's as if I'm too wide awake—very, very alert. . . . Everything seems to go through me. . . .'

The apparent *intensity* of input level described above can most easily be explained in terms of 'filtering'. If the filter is too 'open' it will allow through more signals or stimulus features than the organism can handle. It will be recalled that the Broadbent type of model presupposes that at the input stage our cognitive processes are comparable to a single-channel communication system. This implies that items of incoming information must queue up in a short-term store because there are fixed limits to the number of items that can be in the channel for processing at any one time. The function of the filter stage is to help in regulating the input. If it begins to break down, the queuing system will break down and the channel becomes overloaded. Generally we attend only to certain features of the many around us, and we may register only certain attributes. As we cross the street we attend perhaps only to the nearest car, and even so we do not usually notice its number or the precise design of its radiator grille. As we glance in the direction of the bus stop we are likely to notice only the figure of a friend amongst the people in the queue, and possibly that of some unusually attractive girl. And even within that narrow sample of the total visual field we may notice only our friend's red hair and the girl's legs. These 'dominant details' have relative intensity by comparison with the rest of the field. Now imagine some impairment in our filtering system which leaves us unable to limit our attention to dominant details and to inhibit irrelevant or uninformative features. Clearly the situation would be overwhelming; we should be unable to pattern or process the input. Everything would have become equally dominant, and we should be faced with a drastic increase in overall intensity. The effect might be comparable to that due to removing one's sun-glasses on a Mediterranean beach. But it would be infinitely severe. Sun-glasses modify only visual input, whereas a Broadbent-type inner filter applies to all modalities. Again, sun-glasses filter out only one dimension of the visual input—i.e. certain frequencies of light. Our inner filters are concerned with all the physical properties of the input, including form and movement. And finally, our inner filters are intimately related to other levels of cognitive activity—they must be 'tuned' to our on-going activity. Their range of functioning is largely determined by our expectancies and the features to which we are voluntarily 'paying attention'; in brief, they come under central control.

Neuro-physiological evidence for central control over peripheral input was reported in a celebrated paper by Galambos (1956), who discovered efferent fibres which allowed the higher centres to inhibit cochlear activity in the cat. By tapping the cat's auditory nerve and amplifying the impulses, Galambos was able to make direct recordings of the signals passing from the ear to the brain as the cat heard a metronome ticking. The cat was then shown a mouse and the auditory signals were immediately inhibited. The cat had found something much more interesting to pay attention to, and was literally turning a deaf ear to the irrelevant metronome.

For the acute schizophrenic, therefore, not only is the input more intense and less perceptually discriminable, but his ability to 'pay attention' is impaired. He is unable, as it were, to see the mouse for the metronome. In communication terms, as the 'noise' is radically increased the 'signal' becomes less determinable. It becomes more difficult to separate the relevant from the irrelevant. So that in tasks where the schizophrenic is required to attend and respond to a given cue he will be more vulnerable than normal people to *distraction*. Such a prediction is readily testable, and there is abundant experimental evidence which supports it, at least in the performance of relatively simple perceptual motor tasks. Another way of describing such distractibility is to say that the schizophrenic has difficulty in maintaining his preparedness to respond appropriately and swiftly. Shakow (1962), who has conducted relevant experiments with schizophrenics for over thirty years, refers to this as the maintenance of a 'major set'. One prediction that can be derived from this hypothesis is that schizophrenics' reaction times will be longer than those of other people. In the classical reaction-time task the subject receives a warning signal, followed by a preparatory interval before the signal to which he must respond. The first signal warns him to hold himself in readiness for the required action. It serves the same function as the starter's call of 'Ready? . . . Set! . . .' before the starting pistol. The sprinter comes forward and braces himself, ready for an immediate and maximally propulsive action in response to the pistol. He has, literally, to maintain the 'set'. Exactly the same sort of demand is made upon the subject performing a reaction-time experiment. During the preparatory interval he must bear the instructions in mind and hold himself ready for prompt response. According to the 'major set' argument, the schizophrenic will be unable to maintain the set during the interval, so that when the action signal appears he will be slow to react. The longer the preparatory interval the more difficulty will he find in maintaining the set and the slower will be his reaction.

If schizophrenics are disturbed by stimulation, and their ability to 'pay attention' is unduly affected by distractions, irrelevancies or changes, can they be helped by limiting the number of distracting features and by routinizing the situation? The answer seems to be: Yes—up to a point. There is some evidence that they perform better on standard intelligence tests if conditions are muted—i.e. if the test is conducted in a quiet, barely furnished and dimly illuminated room. Similarly, there have been reports that 'sensory deprivation' conditions afford temporary therapeutic benefits to schizophrenics, including some improvement in cognitive performance and a reduction in the vividness of hallucinations.

If schizophrenics find difficulty in identifying and responding to signals can they be helped by accentuating the signals? There have been several studies which suggest that this is so, including some which were designed to test other approaches. It has been shown that, if an additional stimulus such as white noise accompanies the signal, schizophrenics' performance improves relatively more than that of normals. In some cases their reaction times have decreased to within normal limits. This improvement has been attributed to the extra emphasis given to the signals by the additional stimulation. The accentuation helps the patient to pay attention. This seems plausible, but it may be argued that such findings do not offer quite the support for the major set theory that is usually claimed. It is difficult to see why the failure to hold the set during the preparatory interval should be rectified by modifications in the experimental situation which takes place *after* the interval. However, the findings are not irreconcilable with the set approach. Clearly both factors—set-maintenance and distinctiveness of signal—may be of high relevance.

2

ANOMALIES OF IMAGERY AND

PERCEPTION: I

During the early years of scientific psychology, the topic of imagery attracted a great deal of investigation. But after the advent of behaviourism interest waned until quite recently. Among the reasons for this decline the one most often cited has been that the study of imagery necessarily relies upon introspective reports. A more fundamental reason, however, is that it is difficult to assimilate the phenomenon in the classical stimulus-response (S-R) paradigm. Imagery is not an external stimulus, but nor is it usually a response to such a stimulus. The crucial problem, of course, is that the classical S-R approach does not readily account for autonomous activity within the organism. Yet our central nervous systems engage in constant activity, even in unchanging or neutral environments where no stimulus can be identified.

Imagery is usually defined as an experience which revives or copies a previous perceptual experience in the absence of the original sensory stimulation—in other words it is quasi-perceptual. The objection to this sort of definition is that it may be taken to imply that 'perceiving' and 'imagery' are two quite discrete processes, one of which may, however, ape the other. Furthermore it may suggest that perception is somehow objectively 'right', which would imply that it consists of an isomorphic reflection of external events. Most cognitive psychologists would deny that perceiving functions in such a passive, mirror-like manner. On the contrary, the current view would be that perceiving is an active process of construction and reconstruction which involves the matching of selected inputs with stored experiences. So it could be argued that when we are aware of imagery what we are experiencing are samples of what in perceiving would function as 'match' material. On this view perceiving is a complex process which involves imaging.

Imagery itself can scarcely be regarded as being anomalous. When we speak of anomalies of imagery we are not referring to the images or the imaging. The unusual quality of the experience is usually a function of the situation in which the individual is aware of his imaging, or is attributable to his assessment of it. For instance, when one falls victim to an illusion, it is not the image which is faulty but the level of match accepted.

Warren defines an 'illusion' as 'a misinterpretation of certain elements in a given experience, such that the experience does not represent the objective situation, present or recalled'.

In one sense, therefore, all illusions are anomalous. But the word 'illusion' is conventionally applied to a variety of phenomena. At the one extreme are idiosyncratic experiences which are regarded as unusual both by the people experiencing them and by those to whom the experiences are recounted. These experiences are usually related to the individual's expectancies or to pathological states. At the other extreme are experiences or interpretations of events which are shared by most people. Such experiences may reflect the normal functioning of our sensory and perceptual systems, and are orderly and predictable. This group would include certain of the classical 'optical illusions' which have always preoccupied experimental psychologists. Then there are those 'illusions' which may be surprising to the naive observer, but do reflect an appropriate assessment of objective physical feature of the environment. This group would include desert mirages. It might well be argued that neither of these types of experiences should technically qualify as an 'illusion' at all, inasmuch as they do not really involve 'faulty' interpretation. Whether this be so or not, we shall concern ourselves here with some more illusive types of illusion.

THE EFFECTS OF DIMINISHED INPUT

Earlier, we discussed absent-mindedness, which involves a diminished reception of signals from the environment. What happens when there is a diminution of the signals themselves? This may take the form of an overall *lowering* of input. Or it may be a question of absence of *change* in the input. An everyday example of the first case is that of lying in bed before going to sleep—this is usually accompanied by low levels of illumination and noise. An example of the second case is that of being engaged in a monotonous task—there are plenty of things to attend to, but they are repetitive and relatively unchanging.

How do we respond to such situations? Most people would agree that we tend to become drowsy. In the first example, of course, that is the object of the exercise; in the second, we refer to ourselves as 'fighting to keep awake'. For present purposes, the important aspect is that our increasing drowsiness is accompanied by 'day-dreaming'— a free-ranging flow of experience springing from within. And this usually involves imagery of some type, although the images are diffuse and not necessarily in the visual modality.

Most of us have not experienced prolonged subjection to conditions of lowered or unchanging environmental input. But many possible examples spring to mind, including some types of aviation, watch-keeping, solitary imprisonment, deep-sea diving and lone survival at sea, in the desert or in polar conditions. The recorded observations of explorers, prisoners and survivors tend to support the argument we have drawn from mundane examples. In general, the longer people are exposed to stimulus-deprived conditions, the more intrusive and intense their imagery becomes. For instance, the lone sailor Joshua Slocum was smitten with sea-sickness in the middle of the South Atlantic and could not leave his cabin for several hours. When a storm blew up a phantom helmsman appeared and took control of the vessel. Slocum had a long conversation with him, and was told that his visitor was the pilot of one of Christopher Columbus' ships. Similarly, Admiral Byrd voluntarily isolated himself in the Antarctic for six months in search of peace and quiet. But the silence, gloom and monotony of his environment had a very different effect. For much of his time, Byrd lay on his bed, apathetic and inactive, the victim of nightmarish hallucinations.

However, many experiences of the kinds described are complicated by physical and emotional factors such as malnutrition, fever, fear and loneliness. Most of them also demand activity of some kind, so that the individual himself imposes changes upon his immediate environment. So it would be imprudent to attribute the increase and intensity of imagery to the diminution of input alone. However, there is also a wealth of evidence available from experimental, controlled studies, where the intensity, meaningfulness and changeability of input have been systematically reduced.

'Sensory deprivation' (SD) is the rather ill-chosen title for an area of psychological research which captured the interest of the public as well as that of workers in a number of non-psychological disciplines. This is perhaps because the early reports in the field were not only dramatic but seemed to have relevance for two highly publicized topics—'brain-washing' and space travel. Subsequent reports were not so dramatic, but the waning of lay interest has probably been associated with the fact that it became clear that 'sensory deprivation' was not a crucial consideration for either political indoctrination or space travel.

Sensory deprivation studies are concerned with how we react to severely diminished or monotonous and unpatterned sensory input. Hebb had hypothesized that for optional functioning the central nervous system requires constant stimulation and changing input. He predicted that exposure over a prolonged period to an excessively monotonous environment would result in cognitive disorganization. So it was no coincidence that the pioneer work on sensory deprivation was carried out in his laboratory at McGill University in Montreal.

The first public reports, which appeared in 1953–4 (e.g. Heron *et al.*, 1953), described experiments using a small, dimly illuminated, semi-soundproof observation cubicle. The subjects were college students (male) who were paid to lie in bed alone in the cubicle for as long as they could. This was usually for a period of two to four days, during which they were allowed out only to eat and to go to the toilet. Meanwhile, sensory input was restricted in several ways. The subjects wore translucent goggles which admitted diffuse light but prevented the perception of forms. They wore cotton gloves and cardboard cuffs which extended beyond their finger-tips and thus restricted tactile sensation. Auditory stimulation was limited by masking noise—amplifier hum in ear-phones and constant noise from the air-conditioner and extractor fan.

As might be expected, subjects reacted to these unusual conditions initially by going to sleep. As each experiment continued, however, they slept less and began to be extremely bored, to the point of hungering for stimulation. Most of them found the experience increasingly unpleasant; they began to show emotional lability and irritation. After release from the experimental situation subjects were confused, dizzy and fatigued. Most of them showed deterioration of performance on a number of perceptual and other cognitive tests, such as size constancy, spatial orientation, form perception, number series completion and symbol substitution.

But the findings which aroused most interest and speculation were those which reported the occurrence of 'hallucinations'. The investigators identified several levels of 'hallucinatory' phenomena. The simpler forms were experienced by all subjects; these included flashes and dots of light, lines or simple patterning. The majority of subjects also experienced a more complex level developing from the first; this was described as 'wallpaper patterns'. A few subjects reported that they had perceived fully integrated scenes. Several subjects also reported auditory, kinaesthetic or somaesthetic hallucinations, whilst one or two reported that their bodies had felt 'strange' or displaced.

Unfortunately it seems likely that some of the early investigators were neither sufficiently strict in their definition of 'hallucination', nor was the interviewing of subjects intensive enough to determine whether their experiences had been hallucinatory or not. What constitutes a hallucinatory experience is considered in the next chapter. Meanwhile, it is fair to say at least that sensory deprivation subjects do report an unusual awareness of imagery, often in several modalities. This fits well with the view outlined in the introduction to this section. Perceptual processes involve a dynamic process of selection, emphasis and match-testing. Furthermore, our central nervous systems are continuously active, although the *level* of activation varies according to environmental demands, our physical state and so on. We do not 'switch off' between perceptions. Thus a reduction of signals at the input stage does not decrease activity in the rest of the system. It may adjust to input diminution by compensatory activity at other stages. It will certainly accept lower levels of match, partly because there is less information to work upon, and partly because feed-back is lacking. At the same time the subject *notices* his experiences because there is nothing else to divert his attention, and he *reports* them to the experimenter because he is asked to do so. We probably experience many of the classical 'SD effects' every day of our lives. But we fail to attend to them because we are bombarded with more interesting or pressing information, and if we do notice them we seldom report them.

HYPNAGOGIC AND HYPNOPOMPIC IMAGERY

The drowsiness experienced as one falls asleep, and again as one wakes up, is often accompanied by pronounced imagery, as mentioned earlier. The intermediate state between wakefulness and sleep is referred to as *hypnagogic*; that which precedes full wakefulness after sleep is termed *hypnopompic*.

McKellar (1957) found that of 182 students 115, or 63·18 per cent, reported hypnagogic imagery, whilst 39, or 21·42 per cent, reported hypnopompic imagery. Of those subjects who had had such imagery about two-thirds reported that they had occurred only occasionally; but a few subjects experienced them regularly.

Both hypnagogic and hypnopompic images are notably autonomous, in the sense that they occur suddenly and are not under voluntary control. Very often they are vivid and realistic, although their content may be bizarre.

Hypnagogic images can occur in any sense modality, but auditory and visual images are the most common. Perhaps the most familiar experience in the auditory modality is that of 'hearing' one's name called; the individual's name has arousal characteristics for him, so that this piece of imagery often succeeds in bringing him back to full wakefulness. Many people 'hear' snatches of music; sometimes this may be a recognizable composition 'played' by a full orchestra. Several of McKellar's subjects reported that this image was so 'real' that they had dragged themselves out of bed and gone downstairs, thinking that they must have left the radio on. Sometimes the musical content appears to be original. Indeed, Wagner developed part of the overture to *Das Rheingold* from hypnagogic imagery.

The most common type of hypnagogic visual imagery is probably the 'faces in the dark' which often terrify children as they are falling asleep, and which are also reported by some adults. The 'faces' are often distorted in size and shape, and may be in bright but unnatural colours. Other hypnagogic visions also are commonly in colour, and often have a surrealistic quality. They are of short duration and may flash on one after another, so that they have been compared to lantern slides. Unlike dream images, they appear in a sequence which seems to be quite illogical and disjointed. Furthermore, they seem to be unrelated to the subject's on-going cognitive experience. Many of McKellar's subjects reported that they were able to think whilst their hypnagogic images appeared like irrelevant illustrations. McKellar likens the imagery to the projection of slides which have been mixed up, but which were in any case designed to accompany a different lecture. The content of these visual images is of infinite variety. It ranges from simple images such as 'flickering points of flame', through patterns which may be identified as geometric shapes to complex, meaningful images. The latter include single objects such as 'a purple pine tree', integrated scenes such as 'a sort of Grand Prix event—the cars hurtling away into the far distance', and elaborate fantasies such as 'a green alligator goose-stepping past a miniature Blackpool Tower in a yellow snow-storm'.

Among McKellar's subjects, *kinaesthetic* hypnagogic imagery appeared third in order of frequency. One of his subjects reported imagery related to hunting on horseback: '. . . can feel myself bracing to take jumps, check my horse, urge him on, etc.' After long periods of travel by car, especially at the high and consistent speeds associated with motorway driving, drivers often feel that they are 'still driving' before they go to sleep. In fact, the demands of their imaged driving may wake them up. When they start to drop off again the imagery may return, thus beginning a sort of vicious insomniac circle. But this experience, like the well-known 'rolling deck' felt by ships' passengers after they come ashore, may well be regarded as having more in common with after-imagery than with hypnagogic imagery.

Olfactory and *tactile* hypnagogic imagery seem to be less common, but rare individuals have reported the 'smell' of wood smoke, scent,

cooking and cigars. Others have felt that they were holding someone's hand or were in contact with 'a smooth, flat surface, like glass
. . .'

Hypnopompic imagery seems to present no radical differences from
the hypnagogic variety, although it is reported less frequently. It is
possible, of course, that hypnopompic experiences are not recalled
so readily because they are dispelled or submerged by the press of
activity which for most of us follows only too soon after wakening.
When they are recalled, hypnopompic images are sometimes contin-
uations of dreams. But more commonly they anticipate the demands
of workaday life. Thus, many people become accustomed to waking
at a particular time. They may experience imagery of a bell ringing,
before the alarm clock actually goes off. Or they may hear a knock
at the front door or the mail dropping through the letter box before
the postman arrives. A fairly common image of this type is that of
hearing some other member of the household calling to say that it is
time to get up. These 'habit' images clearly have a useful function,
but they can be vexing during holidays. People have complained
bitterly of leaping out of bed in response to such imagery, and com-
pleting their toilets before realizing that everybody else in the house
was still in bed, and that they too had promised themselves a 'long
lie-in'.

It has been noted how hypnagogic images may be invested with
fear-provoking qualities. They may also be attributed to supernatural
causes or to telepathy. Subjects who are interested in spiritualism,
ghosts or witchcraft may interpret their images as representing the
attempts of spirit contacts to 'come through'. Those who are interested in ESP (extra-sensory perception) may credit themselves as
being 'percipients'; their images are then interpreted as telepathic
communications. Ironically enough, experiments in telepathy have
often required subjects to maintain 'watch' late at night, preferably
at bedtime, on the grounds that they are more likely to 'receive'
communications when they are relaxed and unlikely to be distracted.
Furthermore, the 'messages' in such experiments often take the form
of coloured geometric shapes such as yellow diamonds or blue
squares. Approximations to geometric shapes or patterns are amongst
the most common types of hypnagogic images, and as we have seen
these are usually coloured. Again, as noted earlier, hypnopompic
images often have reference to the subject's anticipations about his
forthcoming day. So it is not surprising that they are often interpreted
as examples of *precognition* by those who are interested in ESP, or as
premonitions by the superstitious. Hypnagogic imagery may also be
interpreted as a pathological phenomenon by adolescents and by
persons who are worried about their mental health. Several of

McKellar's subjects had sought medical help because they presumed
that their hypnagogic imagery had psychiatric implications. As
McKellar observes, the study of normal personality has benefited
from the examination of abnormal phenomena. In hypnagogic
imagery we may have a normal phenomenon the study of which may
shed light on abnormal experiences.

The reader will probably have noticed several points of similarity between hypnagogic imagery and the experiences of SD subjects which
initially aroused such excitement. It now seems highly likely that
many experiences which were described as 'hallucinatory' were really
hypnagogic. They were probably reported with such frequency
because sensory deprivation is naturally a very boring situation in
the early stages of which drowsiness is readily induced. Far from
indicating that SD conditions may evoke abnormal experiences, the
subjects' reports often merely suggest that they were continually
nodding off to sleep.

There has been little experimental examination of hypnagogic/
hypnopompic imagery or its connotations. But Foulkes, Spear and
Symonds (1966) reported an experiment in which the subjects' level
of sleepiness was assessed by EEG; at an early stage they were
wakened and asked to report what had been going through their
minds. These reports were then rated for their degree of hypnagogic
imagery, and associations were found between the ratings and personality measures. High imagers were found to have significantly
more favourable personality attributes than low imagers. They were
less rigid, more self-accepting, more socially poised and more creative. Low imagers were rigid, conventional and intolerant. The
hypnagogic imagery ratings did not correlate with similar dream
ratings arrived at by obtaining reports from the same subjects when
they were awakened from deep sleep. High dream fantasy ratings
were found to be associated with concern regarding the control of
impulses. The experimenters suggest that the *absence* of hypnagogic
imagery is related to the possession of rigid defences against impulse.
Rigidly defensive subjects tend to prevent the emergence of inner
thoughts and feelings. In deep sleep these overwhelm the ego's
defences, whereas in the hypnagogic state some degree of ego control
is retained.

ILLUSIONS

In experimental psychology it has become conventional to use the
term 'illusion' to refer to perceptions which do not correspond to the
objective physical properties of a display, usually a visual one. Standard examples are the Müller-Lyer and the Ames distorted room. The

illusions we experience outside the laboratory do not seem to involve quite the same psychological processes. Let us look at a few of the 'real life' situations in which we experience illusion. Perhaps the most common one is the 'waiting to meet a friend' situation. The scene may be set in a railway station; we have arranged to meet a friend, but are not sure which train he will be arriving on. We feel some excitement at the imminent reunion, coupled with impatience and a certain anxiety lest we miss each other in the crowd. We trot from platform to platform, craning our necks to scan the bustling throng. How many of us have not caught a glimpse of our friend at the other side of the concourse and rushed after him, only to find ourselves slapping the back of a complete stranger? A mundane parallel is that of waiting to be called to a meal. Having been warned that lunch is nearly ready, we are mowing the lawn, mouths watering in anticipation. We hear the call and rush indoors—to find that what we had heard was only the dog barking or the coalman addressing the lady next door. Most people have also had the experience, especially as children, of walking along a lonely lane at night and having the illusion that they can see somebody or 'something' waiting to spring out at them from behind the next tree. Given that the individual in this situation can summon the courage to go any further, he usually discovers that the cause of his trepidation is a bush or a fence-post. Perhaps the most well-known illusions are those performed by stage magicians—rabbits are brought out of hats, billiard balls out of stooges' ears, playing cards and yards of bunting out of thin air.

What do such experiences have in common? They are all due to *misinterpretation*, which itself is based on (1) the individual's *set*—his predisposition to a certain kind of interpretative response related to his current preoccupation, and (2) the the ambiguity or lack of definition of the situation or stimulus. The stimulus, in fact, is open to a variety of interpretations and the perceiver tends to employ the one which most fits with his expectations. Perception is a hypothesis-testing activity, and the 'hypotheses' most readily available for testing are determined by our subjective probabilities about the likelihood of occurrence of any given event. We *expect* to see our friend on the railway station, i.e. there is subjectively a very high probability of his imminent appearance. And, as well as setting up a subjectively highly probable hypothesis the victim of illusion is prevented from 'testing' it adequately, because the objective evidence is indeterminate in some way. Thus, in clear daylight, the bush would be perceived as just that. In the dark, but in reassuring, lively company, it might have been perceived as merely an unidentifiable object. In either case it is quite possible that the individual would not have paid it any attention. Firstly, he would not have set up particular hypotheses.

Secondly, his threshold of response would have been higher because of social distraction. On his own in the dark his threshold would be lower because of his emotional state. But heightened emotion or stress are not necessary conditions for experiencing illusions, although they are often related, as in the bush example, to the development of the set.

Strictly speaking, we should discriminate between *misinterpretation* and *misidentification*. It is possible to identify an object, person or scene correctly but mistake its attributes and thus be led into misinterpretation. Many phenomenologists would claim that the term 'illusion' is correctly applied only to this situation and not to simple misidentification. However, the same psychological processes probably underlie both types of experience, so the differentiation will not be pursued here.

In information-processing terms it could be said that an illusion is experienced when the observer, working in accordance with set-induced subjective probabilities, sets up a comparator or criterion. Because of his response bias, coupled with the indeterminacy of the event itself, he is then liable to accept poor levels of match with the criterion, the result being that he will pass mis-matches.

Traditionally, phenomenological psychiatrists also class under the heading of illusions, misinterpretations due to *inattention*. Thus, in correctly perceiving a whole we may fail to notice irregularities or omissions of detail. The gestalt psychologists have provided us with a wealth of experimental evidence related to this sort of cognitive error, which they explained in terms of 'closure' and the tendency towards the perception of symmetry and balance. A favourite everyday example is the way we tend to ignore misprints in a text. In grasping the overall sense of a sentence we may overlook a misspelling or the omission of a conjunction. This is related to our saccadic eye movements. We do not in fact look at each word in a sentence, nor at each letter in a word—our eyes jump from one chunk of print to another. Furthermore, once we are over the stage of learning to read, we take in larger and larger 'chunks' at a time. The faster and more experienced the reader, the fewer words he *needs* to perceive to grasp the meaning of a sentence. This is what forms the basis of many 'speed-reading' systems.

The professional proof-reader has to train himself to segmentalize his print-perception, to break down the gestalt activity most of us acquire in learning to read. Indeed, he must un-learn meaningful reading. He must be able to scan a sentence *without* responding to its sense. He must be able to assess its meaning, of course, so that he can indicate any failures of communication to the sub-editor. Similarly, he may note stylistic or syntactic errors. But his primary task is to ensure that the type has been set up in exact reproduction of the manuscript. Thus proof-reading is a very exacting task which requires close and unflagging visual attention, and involves the ability to suspend at will the highest level of application of a complex and over-learned skill. The proof-reader is unlikely to experience illusions due to inattention, but only because of his special training. For the most part, effective perception probably often demands errors of the type described above.

Pareidolia

Most people with strong visual imagery have seen pictures in the fire or in clouds. They would probably describe this activity as day-dreaming or imagining. But strictly speaking it involves misperception of an external stimulus, and so is classed as an illusion, the technical term for which is *pareidolia*. It does not involve conscious effort or any particular set, nor can it be explained as the result of any intense emotional state. On the contrary, people engage in pareidolia as they do in day-dreaming, sun-bathing or flicking pebbles into pools. All are tranquil, fantasy-indulging ways of passing the time. Perhaps they will become less common as the transistor radio and the television set are allowed to provide a continuous time-passing backcloth.

Pareidolic illusions do not disappear when attention is heightened. This is because the 'stimulus' is so diffuse and ambiguous; it has little structure and no objective 'meaning'. In one sense, indeed, the illusion is not really a misinterpretation because there is no objectively appropriate interpretation. Hebb (1949) suggested that a report of what one sees tachistoscopically is rather like trying to reconstruct early man from a tooth and a rib. We might apply this palaeontological analogy to pareidolia by saying that here it is as though the perceiver is idly sifting through the rubble of an archaeological dig, picking out the odd fragment at random and saying: 'Well, I know it didn't—but this *could* have come from a . . .' The little girl who sees a camel in the clouds knows that there isn't really a camel there. She is picking features out of a diffuse and inchoate field and 'filling in the gaps' to construct a picture of a camel. But an interesting point is that once she has constructed the picture she may not always be able to demolish it voluntarily. She may look away from the cloud, but when she looks again, if its shape has not changed radically, the camel is still there. If she attends to the cloud more closely, the camel may merely become more distinct. She is still doing a perceptual construction job.

THE SENSE OF PRESENCE

Possibly the same sort of process is involved in the phenomenon known as *the sense of presence*. This refers to the feeling that one is not alone, although nobody else is physically present. The feeling is not supported by visual, auditory or other sensory cues—or, at least, the subject is unable to define such cues. Severe forms are usually classified by psychiatrists as hallucinations, and the phenomenon has been reported in cases of schizophrenia, hysteria and organic states. But it is also frequently experienced by normal, healthy people under certain conditions. Thus, when walking alone on dark nights many people may 'sense' that someone is following them. They may reassure themselves that this is highly unlikely, or reprimand themselves for letting their imagination run riot. But they usually look round just to make sure . . . The experience is most common in strange surroundings, especially ones with eery or sinister connotations. Witness the evident relief with which people emerge into open daylight after exploring murky castle ruins. Such situations encourage heightened suggestibility and an appropriate set, especially in timid or imaginative people. Some natural stimulus such as a draught or an echo may lend itself to misinterpretation, without the subject realizing it. He then provides content related to his set. The fact that no visual illusion has been experienced only adds to the vague sense of unease. An invisible 'presence' may suggest a 'being' rather than another human.

Exhaustion can often disturb our capacity for logical appraisal and weaken our ego controls so that we may become more vulnerable to suggestion, illusions or hallucinations. Fatigue coupled with loneliness in the face of Nature probably accounts for the experiences occasionally reported by normally hard-headed and physically fit walkers and mountaineers. Such a report may establish a legend related to a particular forest, gully or peak. And the legend will provide a set for the suggestibilities of subsequent visitors to the spot. Legends of this kind sometimes refer to the ghosts of individual humans or animals. More often, the phenomena are attributed to atavistic forces, faceless spectres or enormous beings. A good example is the 'giant spectre' which haunts Ben Macdhui (4296 feet), the highest of the Cairngorm peaks in Scotland. This particular legend is of quite recent origin, dating back only to the late 1920s when a story related by a veteran climber and respected scientist reached the newspapers. Professor N. J. Collie, F.R.S., had recalled that on one occasion he had been alone on the summit of Macdhui when he felt he could 'hear' footsteps in the snow as though somebody or 'something' was accompanying him. The feeling became so overwhelming that he fled from the peak. Since then the invisible 'thing' has stalked many lonely walkers over the snowy, featureless top of Macdhui and among its vast cliffs and desolate lochans.

It is an interesting point that children often go through a phase when they are loth to go upstairs to bed unless they can hear their parents' voices, the radio or other familiar noises. Similarly, adults often keep up their spirits when they are alone at night by whistling or humming. It may be that such auditory accompaniment is reassuring because it fulfils two functions. Firstly, it masks tiny sounds which could be misinterpreted. Secondly, it provides a familiar focus for attention. Silence can be peaceful or disturbing, according to one's set and arousal level. The very absence of meaningful stimuli allows free play for interpretations which reflect one's 'state of mind'. Silence offers an unstructured field which may act as a screen upon which one can, as it were, project one's uneasiness, by allowing diffuse fears to become conscious.

3

ANOMALIES OF IMAGERY AND
PERCEPTION: II

So far various types of imagery and illusion have been discussed, experiences which occur quite commonly in normal as well as disturbed people. A related phenomenon is *hallucination* which is traditionally associated with mental disorder. The hallucinatory experience was originally defined by Esquirol as *a perception without an object*. In other words, a person may be said to be hallucinating if, for example, he 'sees' something which is not there. Now visual imagery also involves 'seeing' something which is not there. But most imagery does not possess the characteristics of perceptions of the outside world—it is not experienced as being substantial and 'out there'. The imager usually experiences his images as being inside his head and realizes that what he 'sees' is the product of his imagination—he does not interpret it as a direct reflection of external objective reality. The hallucinator, on the other hand, is not aware that what he is 'seeing' originates in himself. He accepts it as referring to external reality, and believes that his visual experience is one of normal perception. Again, hallucination is not a question of misidentification or misinterpretation of stimuli. True hallucinations are not determined by perceptions of external events, although they may coexist.

Esquirol's definition has the merit of being succinct; but as it stands it would apply equally well to dreams and to hypnagogic/hypnopompic imagery. Indeed, some authorities accept the latter as types of hallucination, but not the former, whilst others accept both. Jaspers' (1962) definition of hallucinations distinguished sharply between them and illusions, and was deliberately formulated to exclude dreams and imagery. 'Hallucinations proper are actual false perceptions which are not in any way distortions of real perceptions but spring up on their own as something quite new and occur simultaneously with and alongside real perceptions.' Jaspers maintained that hallucinations are a discrete category of experience, quite separate from imagery. This was because he differentiated between 'perceptions' and 'images', a distinction which is probably valid from the phenomenological point of view. In other words, the two types of experience are usually felt to be different by the subject. Jaspers listed their respective characteristics as follows:

(1) Perceptions are taken to have reference to concrete reality and have an *objective* quality, whereas images have a *subjective* quality.

(2) Perceptions appear in *external objective space* (i.e. they are felt to be 'out there') whereas images appear in *inner subjective space* (i.e. they are felt to be 'inside oneself').

(3) Perceptions are clearly defined and detailed, whereas images are diffuse and incomplete.

(4) The 'sensory elements' of perceptions are vivid, full and fresh by comparison with those of images. For example, images are not usually experienced as being brightly coloured.

(5) Perceptions are constant whereas images dissipate.

(6) Perceptions are involuntary; they cannot be deliberately changed and subjectively are accepted passively. Images are under voluntary control; they can be conjured up or modified at will. Subjectively, their production involves deliberate activity.

Jaspers emphasized, as have most subsequent authorities, that hallucinations possess *perceptual* characteristics (as listed above) but in the absence of external stimulus. And conventionally, psychiatry and psychology textbooks consider hallucinations under the general heading of 'disturbances of perception'. Jaspers' definition, taken along with his definitions of what constitutes perceptual experience, satisfactorily excludes dreams, illusions and many types of imagery. But it still leaves a number of loopholes. For instance, it fails to exclude eidetic imagery which, as we shall see, possesses almost all the characteristics of 'perceptions' listed above. But it may be that any definition along his lines would prove unsatisfactory, however many qualifying clauses were introduced. Jaspers was attempting to force psychological phenomena into categories determined by his own presuppositions, and these would now be regarded by cognitive psychologists as being outdated. But, as suggested above, this does not invalidate his phenomenological analysis. The crucial point about true hallucination is that the subject *feels* that his experience has reference to external reality although objectively it has not; and he will describe the experience in terms similar to those classified by Jaspers as characteristic of 'perceptions'. We shall return to this

question in the final discussion, after examining hallucinatory
phenomena and allied experiences in more detail.

So far we have been discussing the *form* of hallucinations. Their
content, of course, is practically limitless because it may include anything previously experienced by the individual as well as reconstruc-
tions and syntheses of experience. It reflects the individual's needs,
problems and preoccupations, which is why it is of crucial interest to
workers of a psychoanalytical orientation. And as the individual is in
part a product of his society, the content of hallucinations, like that
of other psychological phenomena, also reflects cultural characteristics. In our society, hallucinatory content is usually concerned
with the fears and conflicts which would be expected from people
who are suffering from mental disorder or delirium due to physical
illness. In some cultures, however, certain hallucinatory experiences
are regarded as desirable or necessary. Individuals deliberately seek
hallucination by exhausting themselves or inducing toxic conditions.
Understandably, when they succeed, the content of their experience
is related to the social prescriptions. Among the Crow Indians, the
courage of a brave was determined by the assistance of his guardian
spirit. If the latter was prepared to cooperate, he would appear at
some time during the brave's youth. In order to ensure this, the
young man would go out alone into the wilderness and submit himself to fasting, physical fatigue and self-torture. Both his status among
his fellows and his hopes for his future achievements necessitated not
only that he should hallucinate, but that the content of the hallucination should be appropriate—to wit, the appearance of the spirit. The
same applies among sub-cultures even in our own society. Thus, in
certain religious cults, the hallucinator can obtain status within the
cult and ensure a rosy future after death, so long as the content of his
hallucinations involves contact with some member of a spiritual
hierarchy. To achieve this end, he will prepare himself by strict
training, contemplation and the renouncing of fleshly desires such as
food. In other words, he builds up a preparatory set for the requisite
experience and for the content in question, whilst inducing a physical
condition where hallucination is possible. Appropriate physical conditions would include exhaustion, severe malnutrition and delirium
associated with infectious illnesses, exposure or toxic states. The last
of these is readily attained by the ingestion of certain drugs, and
again in our society as well as in many eastern and South American
cultures hallucinatory experience with prescribed content is deliberately striven for by the use of drugs.

Hallucinatory content may thus reflect individual suffering or cultural objectives. Furthermore, it may be simple and fragmentary or complex and continuous. It is conventional to attempt to categorize the varieties of the experience, however, and this can most conveniently be done in terms of the sensory modalities in which they occur. It should be remembered that they can occur in several modalities concurrently, and may coexist with other forms of unusual experience.

(1) *Visual hallucinations*

Visual hallucinations range from primitive flickers, flashes and 'stars' to organized, lifelike apparitions and scenes. One patient was disturbed by a 'threatening light' which bobbed around his room. Another could see 'a sort of rocky cliff, with a path coming down', along which advanced 'a thing like a giant woman with a yellow skull where her head should have been'. In our culture visual hallucinations are characteristic of acute organic states with clouding of consciousness. In delirium tremens, patients are often terrified by hallucinatory animals and insects. These are usually in full colour, mobile but of unnatural size. The famous 'pink elephants' originated in alcoholic hallucinations of this type, whilst other patients have reported monster crabs, snakes and spiders. Some patients suffer from *micropsia*, seeing 'Lilliputian hallucinations'. These involve tiny people whose appearance usually provides the patient with pleasure or amusement. One patient was entertained for hours by a tiny troupe of circus acrobats and trapeze artists who performed on her bed-rail.

True visual hallucinations usually have 'substance'—they appear to be three-dimensional and solid. They throw shadows, and their movements and positions relate naturally to objectively real features of the environment. For example, a hallucinatory visitor walks on the floor, through open doors, round the furniture rather than through it, may be partially or totally concealed by real objects and so on. Less frequently, the hallucinations may be less lifelike and possess fewer objective physical properties. They may be diminished in size, as we have noted, or be semi-transparent. It is often difficult to obtain clear descriptions in any case, because the visually hallucinating patient is usually suffering from clouding of consciousness.

(2) *Auditory hallucinations*

These range from primitive noises, such as bangs and whistles, to organized, meaningful sounds such as speech and music. Most common are voices uttering short but comprehensible phrases. The voices may be identifiable in terms of age and sex, whether or not

they are of the same nationality as the subject and whether or not
their owners are known to him. There may be several voices conversing, but more usually only one voice is heard. The *source* of the
voice can often be located with precision—it may come from the
next room, a tree, the roof or the ground under the house foundations.
Sometimes voices seem to emanate from animals, birds, objects or
from parts of the patient's own body. Patients attribute such voices
to very different *origins*. They may believe them to belong to relatives
or acquaintances, alive or dead, or to celebrities or historical per-
sonages such as the Queen, the Pope, Hitler, St Paul or Elizabeth
Taylor. More commonly, their origins are unknown and mysterious
—strangers, doctors, agents, conspirators or omniscient commenta-
tors. Associated with this anonymous group are non-human agencies,
the product of atomic radiation, witchcraft, spirits, radio or outer
space. Attributions of this kind are usually connected with delusional
beliefs.

Auditory hallucinations are characteristic of schizophrenia and
chronic organic states. A common type of schizophrenic 'voice' is
one which refers to him in the third person, usually in a critical,
denigratory or abusive manner. The comments have reference to his
moral or intellectual weaknesses, and are often couched in obscene
terms, e.g. 'He's got pox—he's rotting', 'She's a dirty tart', 'He's no
wit, he's a shitty shit'. Sometimes the voice will provide a continual
running commentary on the patient's actions and thoughts. Some
schizophrenics can hear a number of voices whispering together. The
words cannot be made out, but are presumed to be critical or
condemnatory.

In organic states, especially where the patient is delirious, the voice
may issue commands (the *imperative hallucination*). This sometimes
occurs also in depressive illnesses, where, for example, the voice may
urge the patient to kill herself or her children.

Echo de pensées is a type of auditory hallucination specific to
schizophrenia. The patient 'hears' his own thoughts 'being spoken
aloud'. This can be very annoying to him, as it suggests that people
around him can eavesdrop on everything he thinks.

(3) *Olfactory hallucinations*

Hallucinations of smell occur in schizophrenia, epilepsy and depressive illnesses. The most commonly reported example is that of
middle-aged schizophrenics who claim to 'smell' poison gas which is
usually being pumped into their living quarters by their enemies.
Epileptic attacks are often preceded by unpleasant hallucinatory
smells, such as those of burning rubber, rancid fat or rotting veg-
etables.

Depressives and schizophrenics may complain that they themselves emit smells. Other people's denials of this are taken to be deceitful, reflecting either well-meant but misapplied kindness, or hostile cunning designed to encourage the perpetuation of the condition.

(4) *Tactile hallucinations*

The most common type of touch hallucination is the *cocain bug*—the sensation that insects are crawling on or under the patient's skin. This is characteristic of acute organic states, especially in drug-induced conditions.

Some patients feel cold winds, vibrations, electric shocks and sexual sensations. Schizophrenics attribute these to outside agencies such as radiation or electronic devices. Patients may complain of sexual assault. Males may feel that somebody is caressing their genitals in order to embarrass them by provoking them to have erections and orgasms in public. Females are troubled by covert ravishings. One woman could feel her family doctor's penis intruding into her anus, although she could not see the doctor himself. Another could feel a colleague's damp fingers continually exploring her breasts, despite the fact that he was in another part of the building.

(5) *Gustatory hallucinations*

Gustatory hallucinations are most commonly experienced by schizo-phrenics who believe that their food has a peculiar taste. This is often associated with the delusional belief that somebody is trying to poison them. Hallucinations of taste are also experienced in epilepsy, where they may usher in a temporal lobe attack.

(6) *Somatic hallucinations*

A number of hallucinations relate to bodily experiences but are not specifically to do with touch. They refer to pain, proprioceptive and kinaesthetic sensations, or to sensations regarding the inside of the body or head. Hallucinations of this kind seem to be largely restricted to chronic schizophrenia and some organic states.

Schizophrenic patients may complain of painful tugging, twisting or tearing sensations. These may be described in terms of activity, so that 'things have happened' or 'are happening' to their bodies. More deteriorated patients may insist that they have been disembowelled, their livers eaten away, flesh stripped from beneath their skin, the marrow sucked from their bones and so on.

An uncommon variety of bodily hallucination is *delusional zoopathy*, where the patient knows that his body has been infested or invaded by an animal. He cannot see this animal but he can feel it, and can usually describe it in detail. In some cases the animal crawls about its host's skin; here, tactile hallucinations are involved. In other cases the animal lives inside the host's body. It may be a bee, a wasp or a beetle which wanders about inside. Or it may be a slug, worm, snake or other reptile which lurks in some particular area. Thus, the snake may be coiled around the gut, the slug may be esconsed just beneath the heart, a toad may be lodged in the rectum. Sometimes tiny worms are believed to be burrowing through the brain.

SOME SPECIAL HALLUCINATORY PHENOMENA AND ALLIED EXPERIENCES

In this section four phenomena which deserve special attention are considered. The first two of these—*negative hallucinations* and *doppelgänger*—are true hallucinations of particular interest. The other two might be termed intermediate experiences or bridges between hallucinations, imagery and illusions. *Pseudo-hallucinations* seem to be halfway between true hallucinations and imagery, whilst *functional hallucinations* possess the characteristics of both hallucinations and illusions.

(1) *Negative hallucinations*
In ordinary visual hallucinations the subject 'sees' something which is not there; in negative visual hallucinations he apparently does not 'see' something which is. Clearly the term 'negative hallucination' expresses this neatly, but its psychological implications are perplexing, to say the least. Theoretically, there is no reason why imagery should not involve inhibition as well as creation. But there seems to be no parallel in normal imagery. The nearest equivalent is probably the counter-suggestion given to a hypnotized subject, who may be told, for instance, that there is no other person in the room or that he has no trousers on. But his subsequent behaviour is very much an 'as if' or acted-out activity. He does not attempt, for instance, to walk through the other person. To the individual with positive hallucinations these are real; he will retreat from his animal, duck to avoid a blow from some threatening figure and carefully walk round hallucinated objects. The negative hallucinator, like the hypnotic subject, seems to fail to perceive the object, but does not behave as though its absence were real. It is possible, therefore, that the experience has more in common with suggestibility than true hallucination.

(2) *Doppelgänger*
Earlier the 'sense of presence' was discussed, which is not uncommonly experienced by normal people, given some suggestibility and

an appropriately eery situation. Under such conditions it may be regarded as a form of illusion because the subject is usually aware of the fact that he is alone, and very often reproves himself for being 'over-imaginative'. In its pure form the experience consists of an incorrect 'awareness'; it is not a visual hallucination because the 'other' person is not 'seen'. Nor is he 'heard' or 'touched'. However, the experience is sometimes elaborated by psychiatric patients, who can describe the 'other' person in detail even when 'he' is behind them. Sometimes they may be unable to describe 'him', but can locate 'him' with precision: 'He follows me all the time. He keeps a yard behind me and a little to the left.' Such a patient may well believe that there really is someone there. In these severe cases then, the 'sense of presence' is a hallucinatory experience.

An interesting variation is *doppelgänger*, or *autoscopy*, a visual hallucination in which the 'other' person is recognized as being one-self. The concept of the phantom 'double' seems to have perturbed mankind since ancient times. It figures in folk-lore and fairy stories throughout the world, and is still prevalent in the religious beliefs of many primitive societies. Shamans and witches cultivate and control their spirit doubles. The shaman double may be despatched to round up the erring spirit of a patient, or to bring back news of events in New York or on the moon. The witch's double may be sent to represent her at covern meetings, a particularly convenient arrangement when the meeting is to be held at a distance, or during inclement weather. In many primitive religions a man's double is his soul, but in others the relationship is more complicated. Some Australian aborigines believe that a man's soul leaves his body after his death, and then joins the double in the ancestral cave. In either case, the actual appearance of one's double is clearly more likely when one's end is in sight; it is only a small step to complete the circle by presuming that the double is a harbinger of doom. This may explain, for instance, the German folk-belief that *doppelgänger* is a portent of imminent death. But such a belief may also be related to the fact that the experience is associated with conditions such as brain damage or dangerous infectious diseases which often prove fatal. So that, like many old wives' tales, this belief probably had a pragmatic basis, despite its superstitious interpretation.

The idea of meeting one's double has had a morbid fascination for many creative artists, and it seems to have inspired the same gloom in sophisticated intellectuals as in primitive people. It has often figured in literary works, and almost without exception has been presented in a setting of approaching tragedy or disintegration. The list of distinguished writers who have described autoscopic phenomena in this way includes de Maupassant, Oscar Wilde, Jean Paul

Richter, Kafka, Edgar Allan Poe, Steinbeck and, notably, Dostoievsky. It seems likely that the subject fascinated and perturbed many of these because they had personal experience of it; several of them suffered from epilepsy, cerebral disorder or psychiatric illnesses. Other famous writers are known to have experienced *doppelgänger* personally. Goethe, a man of monumental stability, once met himself on the road riding a horse. Shelley, a much less balanced individual, was out walking near Pisa when he was approached by a figure in a long cloak whose face was concealed by a hood. The figure advanced to within a few feet of the poet before raising the hood, when Shelley was terrified to find that it was himself. '*Siete sodisfatto?*' enquired his double, 'Are you satisfied?'

Doppelgänger has received relatively little scientific attention. Perhaps the first 'case report' on record is attributed to Aristotle; it describes a man who could not go out for a walk without meeting his double. But the phenomenon was not discussed in the medical literature until the end of the nineteenth century. Since then, although several European studies have appeared, there have been few by British or American authorities.

Usually the *doppelgänger* apparition appears without warning and takes the form of a mirror-image of the viewer, facing him and just beyond arm's reach. It is life-sized, but very often only the face or the head and trunk are 'seen'. Details are very clear, but colours are either dull or absent. Generally the image is transparent; some people have described it as being 'jelly-like' or as though projected onto glass. In most cases the double imitates the subject's movements and facial expressions in mirror-imagery, as though it were his reflection in a glass.

The subject not only thinks that he can see his double but knows that it is himself, which suggests that somatic and kinaesthetic, as well as visual, hallucinations are operating. Indeed, many subjects have reported that they could 'feel' and sometimes 'hear' their doubles. An intriguing aspect of this is that as the subject knows that the double is himself, he may regard it as a part of himself, and thus feel that he knows what it feels like. Usually he believes that it feels cold, sad and weary, a belief which is presumably determined by our cultural traditions. The stereotype ghost in western cultures is seldom cheerful; he is usually too preoccupied with his chains, the seaweed in his hair or the fact that he is a lost soul.

Doppelgänger experiences occur most commonly late at night or at dawn, and last only a few seconds. A given individual may have only one such experience during his lifetime. But a few cases have been reported where the person's double followed him around permanently, like a shadow. The experiences reported by normal people have been isolated episodes of short duration, which have occurred during stress or fatigue and in conjunction with disturbances of consciousness. But the experience is more common among epileptics (where it may be an attack 'equivalent'), in patients suffering acute delirium or in those with brain damage in the parieto-occipital regions.

Presumably the form of the *doppelgänger* experience can be considered in the same way as any other hallucination. The fact that its content is the individual himself could be interpreted in terms of his needs or as a symbolic representation of his preoccupation with himself. But why does it appear as a mirror-image? Perhaps the key to this is that it seems to be a *multi-modal hallucination*. Nothing can involve the intimate use of so many sense modalities as one's own body. Perhaps the *doppelgänger* is a literal body-image externalized. Recall Sir Henry Head's concept of the body schema—a plastic and isomorphic representation of one's body which must be incorporated in our nervous systems if we are to account for our constant awareness of our posture and position in space. The provocative possibility arises that the *doppelgänger* experience may in some way be a displacement or projection of that internal model.

(3) *Pseudo-hallucinations*

Pseudo-hallucinations, like true hallucinations, are perceptions without objective stimuli. But phenomenological differences have beer identified. The phenomenon has caused much controversy among psychiatrists, so that it is not surprising that several eminent psychologists have confused it with true hallucination, and thereby been misled in their consideration of the latter. The classical description of pseudo-hallucination propounded by Jaspers was that they possessed all the characteristics of 'perceptions' which were listed earlier, except that:

(a) They lack the substantiality of perceived external stimuli, and
(b) appear in inner subjective space.

On the grounds that these two features are not characteristic of normal perception, Jaspers argued that pseudo-hallucinations should not be considered as hallucinations at all, but as a special type of imagery. However, he admitted that the phenomenon was not clear-cut; not all the other characteristics of perception might be present, and the experience might shift over into, or be combined with, true hallucination. To complicate matters, other psychiatrists have stressed that pseudo-hallucinations do have the substantiality of external stimuli, are projected into outer space and are not seen by the 'inner eye' but experienced as if through the sense organs. However, and this seems to be their main definitive characteristic, they do have a *subjective quality*. Although they may have the clarity of normal perceptions and, for instance, blot out the background, the subject is not deceived. He knows that they do not correspond to external objective reality, and realizes that they are the products of his imagination. Thus people do not usually describe their pseudo-hallucinations as being actual scenes or people. They generally refer to them as 'visions'.

Pseudo-hallucinations are experienced when the subject is wide awake, with his eyes open or closed. They are usually visual or auditory, but may occur in other modalities. They are psychologically meaningful, being related to the subject's situation, and their content is generally to do with people. For example, the subject may 'see' jeering faces or 'hear' the voice of his dead wife. It may well be that the experience is related to the subject's level of suggestibility, so that it is not surprising that, although it can occur in any mental disorder, it is commonly reported by hysterics. Several of the features mentioned above—the subject's acceptance of the phenomenon, the fact that it occurs spontaneously, the fact that it is psychologically meaningful and therefore implies an appropriate expectancy set and some degree of suggestibility—would suggest that some of the visions, revelations and visitations reported by devout people could well be termed 'pseudo-hallucination'. Whether such a person is then regarded as a mystic or as a hysteric will depend on the views prevailing in his culture at that time. But if he also claims to *believe* in the objective reality of his experience the question may now become one of whether he is a saint or a schizophrenic. For if he does not recognize the subjective quality of his experience, he is reporting not a pseudo-hallucination but a true hallucination. The position is rather clearer with mediums and clairvoyants. They do not claim that their apparitions and voices are 'objective'. The 'phenomena' are avowedly subjective because they exist only through the medium's personal 'unusual powers'. Indeed she would hotly contest any suggestion that her experience could be shared by the ungifted. In this case, given that she is offering an honest report, she is experiencing a pseudo-hallucination.

(4) *Functional hallucinations*

This is the term given to the experience reported by some chronic schizophrenic patients whose hallucinations seem to parallel objective and appropriately perceived external stimuli. Thus, the patient may hear voices whilst the bath tap is running. They stop when the tap is turned off, but start immediately when it is turned on again.

The crucial point here is that the patient hears the tap running *at the same time* as he 'hears' the voices. Another patient may hear the sighs of dead relatives every time the sparrows twitter outside his bedroom window; but he hears the birds as well. A patient known to the author heard obscene and threatening comments whenever the river fog sirens sounded. He could hear the fog warnings and knew very well what they were. He was unable to explain why the mysterious comments were made only as the sirens sounded, but clearly regarded their concurrence as being far from accidental.

Pseudo-hallucinations and functional hallucinations were referred to above as 'bridges' between true hallucinations and imagery on the one hand and illusions on the other. Whether they should be regarded as truncations or types of hallucination or as exaggerations of imagery and illusion is open to debate, but is not a question of particular importance. However, the identification of the phenomena is of importance, which is why they have been discussed here. Firstly, they do represent different sorts of experience which can be phenomenologically determined. Secondly, there is the pragmatic reason that precise differentiation between such phenomena may have important clinical consequences. Take the hypothetical example of a young man who complains that he can hear people talking about him upstairs, when in fact the house is empty. When pressed for a more detailed description of his experience he may say that he knows nobody else is in the house; it is merely that he feels as if there could be. On consideration the strange voices might well be the wind in the eaves, or the creaking of a bedroom window. It might fairly be concluded that we are dealing with a nervous young man with a lively imagination. On the other hand, he may reply that he can definitely hear voices quite clearly; he can hear them, whether anybody else is in the house or not. This sounds like true hallucination, in which case the possibility arises that our man is suffering from a serious psychotic illness. Again, further discussion may reveal that, when he says that he can 'hear' the voices, he means that they are as clear as real voices—but he is aware that they are in his head. This would suggest a pseudohallucinatory experience; we might conclude that our man is highly suggestible but not necessarily seriously disordered. Again, the first answer about the wind might be amplified. It might be that what he meant there was that the voices came on when the wind whistled, and that he could hear both. This would suggest a functional hallucination, and again a very serious view of our young man's condition would be indicated.

EXPERIMENTAL STUDIES OF HALLUCINATION

Hallucinations have excited interest for thousands of years, and remain something of a puzzle to this day. But, despite their clinical and theoretical interest, psychologists have conducted relatively few experimental examinations of the phenomena. The few productive studies fall neatly into three groups:

(1) Those concerned with the deliberate experimental elicitation of responses to 'hallucinatory' stimuli.

(2) Those where 'hallucinatory' experiences have been reported among the effects of some experimental situation.

(3) Those which have considered the cognitive characteristics of people who confuse their imagery with external reality.

(1) *The experimental elicitation of 'hallucinatory' responses*

(a) *The effects of suggestion.* As long ago as 1895 Seashore demonstrated that subjects who were led to expect a signal would respond even when the signal was not presented. Thus, subjects were told to walk along a corridor until a light flashed. In fact, the light never flashed, but nevertheless some subjects would duly halt. According to the original definition of hallucination as 'perception without an object', these subjects could be claimed to be hallucinating, however mundane the situation. Other early studies involved the use of impressive apparatus for the controlled production of sensory stimuli such as electric shock, warmth or odours. After demonstrating such a machine to the subject, the experimenter would proceed to 'test' him—without, however, actually producing any stimulus. In one such study, up to 90 per cent of the subjects reported 'perception' in the belief that a stimulus was being presented. The same response is readily elicited when victims are exposed to the shock coils beloved by schoolboys and clinical psychologists. The victim is persuaded to grip two metal rods connected to a battery and induction coil. He will usually jump or squeal as soon as the operator switches on—even when the circuit is not completed or the shock is well below his sensory threshold.

(b) *'Sensory conditioning'.* In experimental tasks involving a series of rapid responses to a stimulus (e.g. pressing a key when a light flashes, in order to avoid a shock) it has often been observed that the subject will make one or more responses after the stimulus series has finished. Ellson (1941) examined various relevant variables and found that the conditions most productive of 'hallucinatory' responses of this kind involved:

(i) Difficulty of discrimination between the presence and absence of the objective stimulus (i.e. an intensity just above the subject's threshold).

(ii) Motivation of the subjects (i.e. they must *wish* to perceive the stimulus).

Ellson required his subjects to press a key as soon as they could hear a very faint tone, releasing the key when they could no longer hear it. The intensity of the tone was brought up to the subject's threshold and then decreased; on each trial it was preceded by a light signal. The subjects in the experimental group received 60 such 'conditioning' trials, followed by 10 'test' trials in which the tone was absent. Of the 40 experimental subjects, 32 gave one or more responses to 'hallucinatory' tone signals during their test trials. Of the 60 subjects in one control group which received only the test trials, 12 showed such responses. This implies that, despite attempts to avoid *suggestion* in the instructions, this was playing some part.

In both types of study described above, subjects responded to a stimulus in its absence, a stimulus which they perceived as being 'out there' and over which they had no voluntary control. Their responding indicates that they believed they had perceived rather than imagined the stimulus. Thus, however simple the situations, the subjects were technically hallucinating.

What psychological mechanisms are involved in such situations? In both types it would appear that the subject has a clearly defined *expectancy*. He is 'set' to register and respond to a certain simple event. Furthermore, the experimental condition limits the number of events which are to be attended to. Basically, the subject is required to anticipate one of only two possibilities; the stimulus is either there or not. Lastly, discrimination between these two eventualities is deliberately made difficult. The signal is so weak that the subject is always in some doubt about his ability to identify it. In communication terms, the situation is one of noise versus signal plus noise, where the signal/noise ratio is low. If in Seashore's experiment the subjects had been instructed to halt only when a searchlight was switched on or a cannon fired, it is difficult to believe that any of them would have obliged without the signal.

It may be argued then that experiments of this kind offer support for a 'hypothesis' view of perception. The subject's subjective probabilities regarding the occurrence of an event are manipulated. In the Seashore type of experiment he is 'set' by direct or implicit suggestion to expect that the event will occur—either during the time it takes him to walk down the corridor or immediately after the experimenter 'switches on' his apparatus. In the Ellson type of experiment he is similarly 'set' to expect the event to occur soon after the presentation of its paired signal. Now let us suppose that in another situation the subject finds that the event occurs either only occasionally or not at all. His subjective probability of its occurrence will become very low. He will be 'set' not to expect it during subsequent trials and is thus less ready to respond. So that it may be that instead of responding when there is no signal he may fail to respond when there is. And, indeed, there is ample evidence that this is exactly what does happen. During prolonged watches, radar operators begin to miss signals. The longer the period during which no event occurs, the more likely the operator is to miss the next signal. Ironically enough, it does not seem to have been pointed out that, if the findings of the Ellson type of study are to be classified as 'hallucinations', then the findings from a mass of vigilance studies may equally well be offered as examples of 'negative hallucination'.

The misperceptions induced in experiments like those described above may at first sight be technically defined as hallucinations, which is how they are classified in the literature. But of course they are different in several ways from the pathological hallucinations experienced by mentally disturbed people. Firstly, they are much less complex. Secondly, they are not really spontaneous, for the subject is trained or instructed, not only to expect them, but the precise form they will take (a flash of light, a faint tone, etc.). The patient is not consciously aware of what his hallucinations will be before he experiences them, nor does he know when or if they will occur. Generally he has no expectations regarding the phenomenon. Thirdly, the experimentally induced experiences lack the affective significance of pathological hallucinations, which are often interpretable in terms of the patient's fears, his emotional needs or his preoccupations. In other words, their very simplicity bars them from symbolic loading; but in any case they are imposed from without. They may have hallucinatory *form*, but they have no *content*. Lastly, they lack the phenomenological *flavour* of pathological hallucinations, which often strike patients as being uncanny, doom-laden or otherwise loaded with significance. In fact, these experimentally induced phenomena, with their basis in the individual's 'set', seem to have much more in common with *misidentification* as discussed in a previous section, than with true hallucinations. For, as we have seen, although they involve 'perception' of an absent stimulus, they are not spontaneous; the stimulus is defined by the experimental conditions and the subject is 'set' to expect its presence. And they occur only when differentiation between absence and presence is deliberately made difficult, so that the subject's task is essentially one of identification.

(2) 'Hallucinatory' experiences as effects of controlled conditions

During the last two decades psychologists have found considerable interest in reports that hallucinations figure among the effects produced by certain experimentally controlled conditions. Attempts are still being made to use these conditions for the experimental inculcation of 'model psychoses', and a great deal of fascinating information has come out of such studies. But as far as our present interest is concerned, the findings are of dubious validity; for it has still to be convincingly demonstrated that the perceptual experiences reported can be validly classified as hallucinations at all. For this reason our discussion of this area will be brief and critical.

The two conditions which have attracted most attention as productive of 'hallucinations' are sensory deprivation and the ingestion of so-called 'hallucinogenic' drugs such as lysergic acid diethylamide (LSD), mescalin, hashish and psilocybin. In both types of condition, subjects have reported vivid imagery at several levels of complexity. The most common experience is that of imagery at the most primitive level; the subject is aware of flashes, spots and lines of light, streaks of colour and so on. At the next level of complexity he 'sees' repetitive patterns and geometric shapes. Then there appear isolated pictorial elements, objects without backgrounds, moving creatures and faces. Finally, a few subjects report integrated but dream-like scenes.

Clearly, both conditions facilitate the production and/or the report of heightened imagery. The question is whether it is valid to classify the experiences as hallucinations. In the SD condition, subjects do not usually attribute their experiences to external sources, and seldom regard them as correlates of external reality. They are almost always aware that their visual experiences are forms of imagery, and are seldom misled by auditory experiences. They are less sure in their assessment of tactile, kinaesthetic and proprioceptive experiences, perhaps because in general we tend to rely upon visual check when we become aware of unusual bodily sensations. When SD subjects are tempted to regard their images as 'real' they are not *convinced* of this; subsequently they readily accept the experimenter's assurances that no changes had in fact been introduced into the experimental environment. Furthermore, there is growing doubt as to whether SD imagery is the result of the SD conditions *per se*. It has proved very difficult to disentangle all the possible factors contributing to SD experiences, but certainly personality variables, expectations and suggestion all play a part. And it seems likely that one reason why SD subjects report imagery is that they have nothing else to do but observe their inner experiences. A crucial feature of the SD situation, and one which is relatively novel for urban man, is that the subject is required to lie still for long periods in a featureless and undistracting environment. Once he has run through his stock of current problems and reflections he is left with day-dreams, free associations and self-observation. Perhaps if we had the time and the inclination to do this in everyday life most of us would start to notice imagery. Again, the monotony of the SD situation is naturally conducive to drowsiness and sleep, at least in the early stages. Thus, as we noted earlier, it seems highly likely that the complex phenomena reported are hypnagogic or hypnopompic images.

In the drug condition the same sorts of consideration apply. The experimental subject does not usually believe that his images are 'real'; if he does, he will abandon the belief readily when he recovers from the effects of the drug. In non-experimental situations, on the other hand, the drug user may well express belief, but this is due to 'set' related to social prescriptions.

In both conditions the images are most commonly of the primitive level. When integrated scenes appear, they have been preceded by less complex imagery. True hallucinations, on the other hand, do not show development of this type; typically, they appear suddenly and fully formed, without progression to further levels of organization.

Again, in both conditions, the imagery is unusual and incomprehensible. True hallucinations are more 'meaningful'—they are associated with the hallucinator's preoccupations, fears or hopes. In the case of schizophrenic hallucinations, they are usually related to the patient's delusions. Similarly, they bear some relation to his emotional state, which is not the case with SD and drug imagery under controlled conditions. And whereas psychotics react to their hallucinations with heightened emotion, SD subjects usually react to their imagery merely with surprise, interest and sometimes appreciation of the relief from monotony. Experimental drug subjects react with vague wonderment, or amusement.

Finally, true hallucinations are superimposed upon or coexist with normal perceptions. This is not possible in the SD condition, where the perceptual field is deliberately diminished and patternless, and it does not usually apply in the drug condition, where in any case imagery is more readily produced with the eyes closed.

In short, investigations of SD and 'hallucinogenic' drug conditions have provided a rich supply of descriptions of imagery and pseudo-hallucinations. But it is doubtful whether they can be said to have contributed much to the study of true hallucinations.

(3) *Imagers and hallucinators*

A number of workers have examined their subjects' imagery characteristics in ways which allow inferences to be drawn regarding hallucinators. Others have studied certain cognitive characteristics of hallucinators as opposed to non-hallucinators. Answers to a number of obvious questions about hallucinations and hallucinators now seem to be available.

(a) *Do people who readily experience imagery find difficulty in discriminating between their images and perceptions of external reality?* A technique which allows for the study of this question was introduced by Perky (1910). The subject is required to image an object, such as a banana, whilst looking at a fixation point on a screen. Without his knowledge, a slide of the object is then back-projected onto the screen and its intensity of illumination slowly increased from below his threshold. Segal and Nathan (1964) examined individual differences in response to the Perky situation among normal university students. They found that the subjects who could most easily produce images were also most clear about what were images and what were not. Thus they could readily distinguish their images from external reality and were quick to identify the Perky experience as a 'perception', even at very low intensities. The experimenters concluded that subjects who are 'easy' imagers tend to be 'familiar with their internal experiences'.

(b) *Are hallucinators unusually vivid imagers?* A plausible and long-standing suggestion about hallucinations is that they are particularly vivid images whose very intensity misleads the imager into ascribing perceptual status to them. Thus it is argued that hallucinators may be people whose imagery is in general exceptionally vivid. Seitz and Molholm (1947) compared the results on a test of concrete imagery of groups of auditorily hallucinating schizophrenics, non-hallucinating schizophrenics, patients who had recently recovered from alcoholic hallucinosis and normals. The hallucinatory schizophrenics and the alcoholics proved to have a *lower* mean percentage of auditory imagery than the non-hallucinating schizophrenics and the normals. This study is not the only one to suggest that the answer to our question is that, not only are hallucinators *not* vivid imagers, they are on the contrary relatively weak imagers. But this immediately raises some doubt; for hallucinations themselves are undoubtedly vivid images. A closer consideration of both the answer to our question and the question itself seems to be indicated. What do we mean by a 'vivid imager'? In practice we mean somebody who is *aware* of the vividness of his imagery and is prepared to communicate that awareness. Seitz and Molholm interpreted their results as indicating that relatively deficient auditory imagery is one of the factors responsible for auditory hallucinations. But it seems much more likely that the findings are indicative not so much of any deficiency of imagery as of the hallucinatory patients' relative inability to *identify their imagery* as such. This would fit in neatly with the answer to our first question. Perhaps the hallucinator is insufficiently 'familiar with his internal experiences' and is thus less able to distinguish his images from external reality. So that, whilst Segal and Nathan's 'easy imagers' could readily identify the perception of an external stimulus as a non-image, the hallucinator finds it difficult to identify his image as a non-percept. This leads directly to a further question:

(c) *Do hallucinators find it difficult to discriminate in general between internal and external signals?* Considerable light has been shed upon individual differences in this respect by the work of Witkin and his associates which we discussed earlier. As we have seen, the 'field-dependent' individual seems to be dominated by cues from the environment, and finds it difficult to keep them separate from his inner cues. As we shall see in a later chapter, the concept of field-dependence/independence provides us with one way of examining the 'weakening of ego boundaries' which is regarded as characteristic of schizophrenic illness. And the Witkin group have specifically claimed that hallucinatory psychotics are more field-dependent than non-hallucinatory psychotics. Other investigations, reviewed by Fisher (1962), have emphasized the loss of 'body image boundaries' as a factor in the development of hallucinations in schizophrenic patients.

This evidence all points to an affirmative answer to our question. And further confirmation is afforded if we re-phrase the question: Are field-dependent people liable to experience hallucinations? In other words, do normal people who are field-dependent experience their imagery in a way which might allow it to be described as hallu-cinatory? There is a certain amount of evidence which suggests that this might be so. As we have seen, the experiences of sensory depri-vation subjects have seldom been examined in sufficient phenomeno-logical detail to provide clear indications as to the occurrence of hallucinations in SD. However, several studies suggest that, whilst both field-dependent and field-independent subjects report imagery, the former are more likely to attribute their imagery to external sources.

There seems little doubt that hallucination is a distinct variety of experience. But as we saw in the introductory section it has proved difficult to formulate a definition which would not also apply to other, less abnormal experiences. It was suggested in that section that this difficulty was probably related to the presumption that 'percep-tions' and 'images' are separate psychological phenomena or pro-cesses. Let us consider what is wrong with this presumption.

As we have seen, it is not particularly unusual for people to 'see' things which are not there, to 'hear' things in the absence of sounds and so on. There are variations in the type and intensity of imagery experienced by different individuals. But all of us can produce imagery of some kind under certain conditions. The fact that some people's imagery is sufficiently vivid to stand comparison with perceptions of the external world is perplexing only if one regards perception as a passive reflection of external stimuli. Obviously, any study of perceptual processes must include consideration of the direct relationship between external events and our peripheral receptors. Our sense organs can be analysed in terms of their mechanical and chemical functioning. But visual perception, for example, can scarcely be likened to the functioning of a couple of cameras. Even at the level of analysis of how sensory input is handled, our visual systems are infinitely more complex and interactive. What happens peripherally may be relatively straightforward. Of much greater interest to psychologists is what is going on centrally. Our perceptual processes are selective and dynamic; they include the filtering, sorting, coding and processing of information. What we 'see' or 'hear' represents only a fraction of all the possible signals in our environment. The selection is determined by our attentional processes which themselves are related to our current set and on-going cognitions. The filtered signals are interpretable only by a sort of active problem-solving process which involves the setting up of possible comparators and the search for 'matches'. This serial construction and reconstruction depends upon the material already available and the manner in which it is organized. So perception involves selection, matching and creative synthesis. It is a function, not only of what is coming in, but of what is already there.

Jaspers clearly regarded normal 'perceptions' as having a simple one-to-one or photographic relationship to external reality. His firm differentiation between this and imagery (what is already there) cannot be sustained in the light of modern cognitive psychology. But he may have been right, despite his insistence on the wrong reasons. As we noted earlier, his phenomenological analysis has not been seriously disputed. Subjects with hallucinations *do* experience them as being 'out there', as having objective reality, substance and so on. They regard their experiences as being perceptions of the outside world. Most types of imagery, on the other hand, are not presumed to be 'real'. (In cases such as hypnagogic/hypnopompic images, the initial experience is that they are 'real', but this is fleeting. As soon as the subject becomes fully alert, he becomes capable of assessing the situation objectively.) Jaspers' error was that in attempting to support this difference in psychological terms he selected the wrong line of attack. He chose to assert that 'perception' can be divorced from 'imagery', whereas, as we have seen, both of these are dependent upon pre-existing cognitive organization, and both involve the same processes but with different types of interactive matching. They may be regarded, in fact, as different levels of the same function. In psychological terms it could be said that:

(1) imagery involves the perceptual reconstruction of stored material,

(2) illusion involves the misinterpretation of input in terms of its synthesis with stored material, and

(3) hallucination involves the perceptual reconstruction of stored material and its misinterpretation in terms of input.

There are, of course, many reasons why the topic of hallucinations has proved to be thorny and controversial in the literature. Many of these are related to the misunderstanding discussed above, but others are due to mis-diagnosis or to misuse of the term itself. Hallucinations can occur alongside, or be triggered off by, normal perceptions. They may alternate with normal perceptions or merge with illusions. So that it is not surprising that the term 'hallucination' is often misapplied. Lay people (and many psychologists) often use the term loosely with reference to illusions or imagery. We may use it in a perjorative sense, by applying it to reports with which we disagree. Or we may use it to express scepticism when friends tell us of unusual experiences, or ones whose validity we have reason to doubt. But quite apart from its everyday conversational misusages, the term is commonly incorrectly applied in its technical sense by clinicians themselves. Sometimes this is because a loose definition is being applied; more commonly it is because insufficient care has been taken to elicit a detailed phenomenological description of the experience in question. Both these strictures may well apply to the claims that subjects in early studies of sensory deprivation experienced 'hallucinations'.

However, when strict criteria are employed to determine whether a given experience is or is not a hallucination, two features become increasingly clear. Firstly, hallucinations involve the same mechanisms as other cognitive experiences. In other words, we are not dealing with some unique, pathological device, an aberrant intruder into the cognitive system. Hallucinations border on imagery, pseudo-hallucinations and illusion on the one hand, and unusual schematic categorization on the other. They may be regarded as occupying a position on a number of cognitive continua.

Secondly, the only characteristic of what we call hallucinations which can be sustained as a criterial attribute is that of *conviction*. During the time that he is undergoing the experience, the hallucinator believes in its reality, and subsequently he may be loth to abandon his conviction. The day-dreamer may be happily conducting the Hallé orchestra; if he has good visual imagery he may 'see' the strings banked along the sofa and the brass atop the sideboard. But the question of their reality does not arise. Even the most indulgent day-dreamer does not 'believe' that this is an actual concert. Let the front door bang and he will hastily revert to such mundane duties as filling the kettle. The hallucinating patient, on the other hand, does not recognize that he is the victim of self-deception. He accepts the reality of the animals on his bedroom wall or the voices from the roof. Far from indulging himself, the organic patient may be terrified by his visual hallucinations, and the schizophrenic bitterly annoyed by his voices. Despite Jaspers' contentions, there is no clear line between image and percept. The difference between imagery and hallucination cannot be defined in terms of stimulus or perceptual characteristics, but only in terms of *whether the experience is believed to have an external correlate in objective existence*. In other words, hallucination is crucially a question of *reality-testing*. And hallucinators are usually in no condition to do this effectively. Reality-testing may be regarded as a process of setting up hypotheses and checking them. The normal person who is exhausted or sleepy has access to a number of appropriate and reasonable hypotheses but is temporarily incapable of carrying out the check-tests. The schizophrenic may or may not be capable of check-testing. But many of his hypotheses are bizarre or irrational, which is why he was diagnosed as mentally ill in the first place. The delirious patient can neither assemble relevant hypotheses nor test them.

Thus the question arises as to whether hallucinations should be examined primarily as *perceptual* phenomena at all. Indeed, some typically schizophrenic experiences which are technically classified as hallucinatory may have reference to external correlates which the individual has never perceived, or which are in fact not perceptible. For instance, it has been pointed out that a patient may claim to taste arsenic in his food; this is classifiable as a gustatory hallucination. But in the first place he is unlikely to have ever ingested arsenic. In the second place, arsenic is tasteless. Other patients come face to face with men from Mars. But they have no way of knowing what form Martians take, and, as far as we know, no such persons exist. A quaintly circular example of this sort was afforded to the author by an elderly lady who was very disturbed by the smell of the poison gas being pumped into her parlour by a neighbour. When it was pointed out that nobody else had managed to smell the gas, the old lady slyly retorted that this merely demonstrated her neighbour's evil ingenuity. He had perfected an *odourless* gas!

The crucial point of such experiences is not that they are 'percepts without external stimulus', or any other kind of percept, but that they are projections of the individual's ideas. In information-theory terms, they have reference to anomalous storage characteristics rather than to anomalous functioning at the input stage. It is possible indeed that the hallucinating patient is not 'perceiving' anything anomalous in the conventional sense, but is forced to talk in perceptual terms to express his experience.

Whether or not this change of emphasis is valid, it seems that hallucinations are most readily experienced by field-dependent individuals who are normally unused to identifying their imagery. It is also evident that hallucinations reflect unusual thoughts and beliefs in conjunction with the weakening of reality-based judgment. In other words, for a time at least, the hallucinator has given free rein to some very funny ideas. Once this has been said, the focus of attention has been shifted away from hallucinations as anomalies of perception or imagery to the consideration of false beliefs, which are discussed in Chapter 7.

4

ANOMALIES OF RECALL

Man has always speculated about memory and the subject still offers a major challenge to psychologists. Before anomalies in the field can be discussed, what 'memory' involves must be clarified and some ways of thinking about it outlined.

The first difficulty is that memory is conventionally regarded as a discrete area of study and investigation or even as a discrete phenomenon. But clearly it subsumes, or at least involves, almost all the other traditional areas of psychology. For instance, if we were memory-less how could we be said to perceive, conceptualize, imagine or reminisce? How could we plan, deduce, solve problems or think logically? How could we engage in learning, develop new skills and habits or retain old ones? How could we form social relationships, attitudes or personality attributes? Indeed, without memory, how could we acquire the primitive responses which enable us to survive? So it could be argued that the topic of 'memory' encompasses so many other psychological phenomena and functions that it is no more amenable to examination than 'psychology' itself. Let us leave it that in academic psychology the term has been restricted to the study of certain component activities and performance on certain types of task. In this book anomalies of *registration*, of *recall* and of *recognition* are discussed—three topic titles which themselves are somewhat arbitrary, inasmuch as they refer to highly interdependent phenomena. But at least this allows emphasis of certain subsidiary components rather than the intricacies of the whole.

It can be taken that memory processes include the following:

(1) The *reception of information*. This involves *attention*, which we

discussed earlier. It includes some form of filtering, ordering and selection.

(2) *Short-term storage* of the sort considered earlier.

(3) *Long-term storage* (or 'retention').

(4) *Retrieval* (or 'recall') of information when desired. This involves searching through the store in some way.

(5) *Recognition*. This is discussed later, but for the moment suffice it to say that we must be able to recognize what we retrieve as being that for which we were searching.

What seems to have been the main stumbling-block for students of memory is the question of the nature of our storage system. Models such as Broadbent's have offered a way of discriminating between short-term and long-term storage and we can reasonably regard the short-term aspect simply as what Neisser (1967) has termed 'echoic memory'. The main problem is still how the long-term store works. Of the various explanatory approaches possible, several competitors are still actively supported by different psychologists:

(a) *The 'cupboard' or 'tank' approach.* This is the naive and mechanistic view that our 'memories' are receptacles containing a hotch-potch of all the items of information we have taken in.

(b) *The 'slate' approach.* This suggests that successive experiences are recorded on our memories. With the passage of time, earlier writings become faded or blurred and are thus more difficult to read. And for various reasons they may disappear entirely.

(c) *The 'tombstone' approach.* This is similar to the 'slate' approach, but it suggests that information is engraved or incised. It may be concealed by dust or incrustations of grime—but it is still there. The problem is that as time rolls by the surface of the stone deteriorates and the inscriptions therefore become harder to decipher.

(d) *The 'dictionary' approach.* On this view, information is coded and catalogued in some way. This allows it to be stored in some sort of order. Thus retrieval is facilitated, because only relevant sections of the store need to be searched for any given item.

Several points must be made about these approaches:

(i) First of all, they are all *static* models. They imply that long-term memory is either a *container* of some kind into which items of information are dropped, or a recording device. On this basis it is difficult to explain why our recollections can differ profoundly from the original information (experience).

(ii) Neither the 'cupboard' nor the 'dictionary' approach explains why we *forget* things—why items of information may elude retrieval, or be retrieved in an abbreviated or deteriorated form.

(iii) The 'slate' and 'tombstone' approaches do attempt to cover forgetting—in fact, they emphasize the possibilities of loss or deterioration (though not the *distortions* mentioned in (i)). But, like the 'cupboard' approach, they can explain nothing about retrieval because they do not allow for the *organization* of input. It is scarcely likely that, in order to retrieve a particular item of information, we must run through everything in the store by 'reading' the total recordings of a lifetime.

(iv) The 'dictionary' approach does go some way to solving this last difficulty, because it stresses organization. But it is scarcely likely that organization of the sort postulated can account for what goes on as we try to recall something. Indeed, if we are trying to recall a word but cannot remember its initial letter, then a dictionary will be of little help to us.

(v) Finally, none of these approaches can account for the *personal* quality of memory. We have spoken here of 'items of information', which has a deliberately neutral tone. But in fact only *'logical'* or rote-learned memories are neutral. The square root of 16 or the length of the River Nile are examples of such factual information. But many of the individual's recollections are *'reminiscent'*—they have particular connotations for him, having acquired personal significance.

The view taken here is that memory, at least as far as its long-term characteristics are concerned, is not a receptacle, nor a recording nor a catalogue, but an *active process*. Firstly, it must involve *dynamic organization* and continual reorganization. Secondly, it must involve *matching* procedures of a flexible kind. Thirdly, it must involve the modification and subsequent *reconstruction* of input. The approach most readily reconcilable with these requirements is that put forward in Sir Frederic Bartlett's classical work, *Remembering* (1932).

Bartlett conducted a series of simple yet ingenious experiments which demonstrated that changes such as distortion and condensation are characteristic in the recall of information which is more complex than simple letters, words and digits. This led him to discard the view that recall merely involves the re-excitation or reproduction of 'traces' of individual events. Rather, he emphasized serial changes in recall, and that 'the past operates as an organized mass rather than as a group of elements . . .' (page 197). And to emphasize the *active* nature of recall processes he deliberately used the word 'remembering' rather than 'memory'. In developing his theory, Bartlett utilized a concept introduced by Sir Henry Head, the distinguished neurologist. Head had studied the relationship between our interpretation of impulses from peripheral nerves and our awareness of postural change. It had been assumed that each bodily movement produced a separate cortical image or trace which had a simple chain relationship with any succeeding movement. But Head had pointed out that patients with certain cortical lesions lose the capacity to relate serial movement. They can image the various positions of their arms, for example, and can localize the sensation quite accurately when they are touched. But unless they can see their limbs they cannot identify their current positions. Head's solution was to propose that incoming sensory impulses are assimilated into a constantly changing postural model. In other words, instead of being processed as a discrete entity, each afferent signal is organized in relation to what has gone before. And this dynamic organization Head had called a '*schema*'. Bartlett applied the idea of schemata to remembering, arguing that recall does not involve reactivation but *reconstruction*. We do not revive inert items of information, or draw them intact from some storehouse. We reconstruct them by drawing upon appropriate schemata—the cognitive structures into which the items were originally assimilated. We do not recall the original items themselves at all. What we recall are the relevant cognitive frameworks or organizations from which we can reconstruct facsimiles of the original items. The schemata, of course, are themselves the dynamic integration of items of information. But what is of significance is their interrelationship—the organization as opposed to the items which are organized. Furthermore, Bartlett stressed the effects of *attitudes*. He referred to the processing of input as being related to an 'active, organized setting'. The word 'setting' immediately reminds us of our discussion of the selectivity of attentional processes. Just as our attention is related to our 'set' or expectancies, so our recall of input is partially determined by current 'settings' of the activated schemata. And these settings must be tuned to our personal attitudes. Remembering, like attending and perceiving, has a problem-solving quality which involves the setting up of 'hypotheses'. So that it is not surprising that recall is commonly patchy and distorted, involving both condensation and elaboration. To put it naively, what we remember is to some extent what we think we ought to remember.

THE MNESTIC SYNDROME

There is a vintage jest about a man anxiously describing his condition to the psychiatrist.

'It's my memory, Doctor,' he complained. 'It's become so bad that I can't remember anything from one minute to the next.'

'Very distressing. And how long have you had this problem?' asked the psychiatrist.

'Problem?' repeated the man, blankly. '*What* problem?'

Such a condition is not quite so fanciful as might be thought, and similar cases are met in clinical practice. There is a well-known test of non-verbal reasoning which consists of a booklet on each page of which is an incomplete pattern. The subject's task is to select 'the piece that is missing' from a number of alternatives beneath the pattern. This is useful as a group test; the tester reads through the instructions with the subjects, checks their answers to a couple of examples, and leaves them to work through the rest of the book on their own. A colleague was giving the test individually to a highly intelligent and cooperative patient, a professional man suffering from severe memory disorder. The patient readily understood the instructions and completed the examples immediately. Then the psychologist turned over the page to the next patterns, saying:

'Now, will you do these in the same way as you did the others, please?'

'Certainly,' assented the patient briskly. Then, after a pause: 'Er . . . *which* others? Do you mean I've done something like this before?'

The patient achieved a very good score. But each time a page was turned the instructions had to be repeated afresh. As far as he was concerned, he was faced on each occasion by a situation which was new to him. This is called *anterograde amnesia*.

Such cases are relatively rare, but must have been encountered by many clinical psychologists. They belong to one of a mixed group of chronic disorders which has been termed the '*mnestic syndrome*' (Hoenig *et al.*, 1962). The term is applied to conditions in which memory disturbances are the dominant clinical problem. The disturbances may be of various kinds—amnesia, dysmnesia or hypermnesia. In the mnestic syndrome they are due to organic damage (which is specific rather than generalized, and usually involves lesions in the hippocampal or the mamillary bodies). This may have been catastrophic (e.g. due to violent concussion, carbon monoxide poisoning or severe asphyxia) or the outcome of cumulative 'cerebral insults' (e.g. chronic alcoholism, cerebral arteriosclerosis or continual fight knock-outs).

Patients suffering from some varieties of mnestic syndrome show associated intellectual impairments. They may have clouding of consciousness, a loss of abstract reasoning ability or periods of mental confusion. The interesting points about the type of disorder experienced by the patient mentioned above (and, we may presume, by the apocryphal protagonist of the classic joke) were as follows:

(1) He showed no disturbance of consciousness.

(2) His reasoning ability and powers of abstraction were unimpaired. (So long as the tester allowed for his memory problem he achieved an IQ of 130 on individual tests.)

(3) Although he showed some confusion of personal reminiscence for events prior to the onset of his illness, his rote and logical memories seemed to be relatively unimpaired. He retained, for instance, the specialist technical knowledge associated with his profession.

In fact, the problem for such patients is fairly circumscribed. The central difficulty is simply that they are unable to retain new experiences for more than a very short period. (Recall spans reported range from a few minutes down to 1·2 seconds. Much depends on the type of test employed and the patient's degree of cooperation.) Their disorder may not be apparent to the casual observer. Indeed, patients suffering from the mnestic syndrome may be intelligent, articulate people who manage to disguise their difficulties in a number of ways. They will evade direct questioning as to recent events or, if pressed, will improvise with fictional detail. This is not to say that their stratagems are deliberately employed, in a sort of reverse malingering. A saddening thing about mnestic patients is that very often they do not seem to be aware of their defect. But this may be readily highlighted. For instance, if after a long conversation the interviewer leaves the room, but immediately returns, the patient will respond as to a stranger, and reintroductions have to be effected. Other such patients may recognize the interviewer on his return but be unable to recall when they last met, and greet him as a long-lost friend.

As noted above, the difficulty itself is circumscribed—but its consequences are tragically handicapping, largely because the patient is disorientated in place and time. He is unable to find his way about, because he is unable to recall how he got where he is. He may even feel 'lost' in his own bedroom, because if he turns round he is facing what is, for him, strange territory. Similarly, his lack of sequential experience deprives him of the cues which enable most of us to judge the passage of time. He is literally living from minute to minute. As an exercise in phenomenological method, the reader is urged to attempt to think himself into such a condition for five minutes.

So far, what has been described is similar to the best-known type of mnestic syndrome—*Korsakoff's psychosis*. Korsakoff was a Russian doctor who over 80 years ago published an article describing a 'psychic disorder' displayed by a group of his patients who were mainly chronic alcoholics. He stressed that they were not demented and apparently in full possession of their faculties. They were quite capable of carrying on a lively conversation and playing cards or chess. It may be noted, however, that the symptoms described by Korsakoff were not limited to the mnestic characteristics, but included associated neurological changes. Korsakoff's psychosis is often one stage in a steady course of deterioration into dementia.

Let us look at some of the problems posed for theoretical psychology by the mnestic syndrome. The crucial difficulty is that of identifying what psychological functions are affected by the disorder. Firstly, it is not a *generalized memory defect*. Patients remember not only language and social skills but information, personal experiences, abstract material and so on. Their memory *store* for experiences up to the commencement of the illness is usually relatively intact. Nor is the problem one of *retrieval* from long-term store; in fact, it is only because they can demonstrate retrieval that we infer that the store is intact. It can be argued that they have a retrieval difficulty, but only with new material. But this would suggest that we have different retrieval processes for material acquired at different times, which would be a very uneconomical arrangement.

Strictly speaking, the difficulty is not one of impairment of *short-term memory*. This is usually taken to refer to our immediate memory span—our ability to hold information momentarily (i.e. long enough for current consideration and possible action) without necessarily retaining it subsequently. The most well-known example is our ability to hold a telephone number long enough to dial it. The classical test for this function is the digit-span test, where subjects are required to listen to, and then repeat a string of digits. Now in general, mnestic patients have not been reported to show any gross deterioration on this type of test, although presumably any individual's ability is related to his time-span. (As mentioned above, patients have been reported with time-spans of down to one second.) But in any case, the fact that these patients can carry on protracted conversations, follow instructions and play games such as chess, suggests that they can have no serious defect in this respect.

The syndrome is often referred to by psychiatrists as a failure in *registration*. It may be taken that registration refers to the central coding and organization of perceptual input. In that case the disorder cannot unequivocally be termed one of registration. For coding and organization may be inferred from the fact that the patients can, for example, solve problems, read and write and follow logical arguments. Nearer the mark, perhaps, are those psychologists who have regarded it as a defect of *learning*. This may be regarded as subsuming registration, inasmuch as it refers to changes in performance related to experience. In this general sense, the mnestic syndrome clearly does involve defective learning. But it has been shown that *some* learning can take place. Using the 'saving method', psychologists have shown that the performance of mnestic patients on the paired associate test shows improvement over a series of trials. But one patient required 69 repetitions before he learned 8 association words—a task which normal subjects can achieve with between 8 and 18 repetitions. What is interesting here is that such patients may not be aware that they have experienced the test before, despite the long series of repetitions. Thus they are not *aware* of changes in their performance—they do not realize that they are learning, as do normal subjects.

Similarly, *some* recognition occurs, however distorted. Mnestic patients do recognize places and faces after repeated experiences of them. But they differ from most people inasmuch as their recognitions are not supported by any conviction, and they are usually unable to say where and when they have encountered these places and faces before. Their response to a person who should be quite familiar (e.g. the nurse who attends them every day) seems to be similar to what most of us feel when we are confronted by somebody we have met only once, some time before and in a different setting—'I think I have met this character before somewhere—or somebody very like him.'

Several possibilities seem to emerge:

(1) Registration occurs, but spasmodically. However, as we noted above, there is no evidence that registration *per se* is faulty.

(2) Retrieval processes have been damaged. But, as we have observed, this would presuppose different retrieval mechanisms for new, as opposed to old, storage.

(3) Fresh material is registered and stored appropriately, but is not 'stamped in' or consolidated.

(4) Freshly stored material is not organized in a way which facilitates retrieval.

(5) Some mechanism involved in learning and storage, which was functioning normally prior to the illness and thus helped to establish all the old stored information, is not now functioning effectively.

As we have seen, there are arguments against the first two of these possibilities. The other three are all plausible; furthermore, it is possible that they coexist. Perhaps old schemata are available currently but are no longer modifiable. In Piagetian terms, accommodation and assimilation can no longer occur. This would suggest that new experiences may be registered, but cannot be organized appropriately, and therefore are not effectively consolidated in a manner which allows for optimal retrieval. Furthermore, their lack of organization may leave them available to interfere with the retrieval of subsequent input. A crude analogy might be that of a filing cabinet whilst the records clerk is away ill. All the documents received prior to the clerk's absence have been efficiently cross-indexed and filed; they are still readily available. Since the clerk has been away, the office boy has merely thrown all incoming documents into the bottom of the cabinet. No new individual document can now be retrieved or referred to. At the same time the files remain static, and cross-indexing has ceased. Whilst the office boy is holding the new documents in his hand they can be consulted and related to any of the files. Once he throws them into the bottom drawer, however, it is no easier to find the newest batch than any of the others. They *can* be found, but only after a prolonged search, and even then they can only be related to an out-of-date file. The analogy is crude for a number of reasons related to the fact that our mnemonic processes are dynamic; experiences are not just stored away like documents— they undergo modifications, assimilation and synthesis. But the analogy points up the fact that any system of storage and retrieval requires the work of a 'records clerk' if it is to function efficiently. It demands on-going organization and integration. And it is this that seems to be impaired in the mnestic syndrome.

PSYCHOGENIC AMNESIA

'When I went into the examination room I had it all pat. But as soon as I looked at the question papers my mind went a complete blank. . . .'

How often has the reader heard this plaintive tale—or, indeed, experienced something like it himself? Sometimes, admittedly, it is proffered as a cover story. But there is no doubt that during highly emotional stress most of us can find it impossible to call to mind information which, under normal conditions, we would have no difficulty in recalling. When we are personally involved in dangerous situations or exposed to the shock of an accident, we tend to forget the obvious measures that should be taken or their most appropriate order. When a fire breaks out suddenly in places of work, it is not uncommon for some employees to forget their fire drill or the locations of alarms and emergency exits. Participants in road accidents often confuse their priorities, remembering to take some emergency action but forgetting that it should be preceded by another. Road accidents have been reported where, after a collision in the dark, survivors have rushed off to telephone for medical aid for an injured friend. An appropriate action, but not before removing the victim from the centre of the road and/or putting out warning signs. More than one accident has been reported where, under these circumstances, the helpless victim has been promptly run over and killed by oncoming traffic.

Even in non-traumatic situations, excitement may have the same effect. During boat-drills on passenger liners there are always some people who are unable to remember their life-boat station, or the appropriate route to it. It is for this reason that we are encouraged to *over-learn* certain responses. Few of us are likely to forget, for instance, the telephone number to be rung in case of emergency. But this is only because for years we have been subject to programmes of mass education aimed at stamping in '999' as an automatic response. And this is why members of the Forces, the police, firemen, medical staffs, aircrew and so on are trained in emergency procedures until they become second nature. The point is that ordinary learning is not sufficient where the information in question will be called upon under stress. We may remember everything about our disaster-drill in all sorts of situations—except that of the disaster itself.

One of the key differences between the good amateur and the professional in most skilled activities is that the latter is more capable of withstanding 'competition nerves'. Under the stress of competitive play or public performance most of us cannot remember all that we have learned. The good amateur golfer may well equal the professional under stress-free conditions. But in competition play his performance is less consistent—tension not only affects his motor co-ordination but his judgment. He finds himself unable to recall all the factors which must be taken into account for optimal performance. The best-known example of this, of course, is stage-fright—the bane of every amateur actor, musician and entertainer (and not a few professionals too). Like our blank-minded examinee, the victim of stage-fright may feel confident that he has mastered the words, material or skill that he is about to display. He may feel a precarious confidence before he steps out into the footlights. And then— nothing happens—his lines have completely gone.

Technically speaking, the misfortunes outlined above are classifiable as forms of *psychogenic amnesia*. In psychological terms they are due to transient disturbance in recall. Storage is unimpaired, because subsequently the examinee, sportsman or performer, much to his chagrin, can recall the appropriate material or actions with ease. Neither does recognition seem to be affected. If his lines are thrust into the mute actor's hands he immediately recognizes them as what he should be saying.

Presumably retrieval is ineffective here because, as we saw earlier, arousal narrows down the subject's attention drastically; his anxiety or excitement impairs his performance by restricting the cues and schematic organization which would normally facilitate recall. So that in a sense it is not so much that his retrieval mechanisms are not functioning well, but that they are not functioning at all—they are not being utilized. His stress state interferes with the subject's apprehension of the total situation, and thus prevents him from producing the desired response—that of starting the serial process of recall.

A similar interpretation applies to another and much more extreme form of psychogenic forgetting associated with emotion—*hysterical* or *dissociative amnesia*. But here the recall is *not* the 'desired response'. On the contrary, hysterical amnesia occurs when the individual is trying to avoid the recollection or acceptance of some painful, threatening or humiliating situation. The amnesia provides, for certain personalities, a resolution of conflict by evasion.

Hysterical amnesia involves an apparent loss of identity, inasmuch as the individual can remember nothing about his life to date, even the bare facts of his name, age and address. He is usually described as having 'lost his memory', but this is not so. He cannot retrieve personal reminiscences, but in other respects his memory is unimpaired. His abilities and personality are unchanged. He has no loss of recall for language, formal learning, logical memories or social skills, and he is quite capable of looking after himself and working for his living. (This provides a sharp comparison with the patient whose amnesia is attributable to brain injury or disease; he is usually completely unable to care for himself.)

FUGUE STATES

Hysterical amnesia often follows or is associated with a *fugue* (literally, a flight), where the patient not only escapes from himself by shedding his identity, but also physically flees from the routines and pressures of his everyday life for a while. During this time, he is in a state of disturbed consciousness, although his behaviour may not appear out of the ordinary to the casual observer. Very often such patients will wander about the streets without any particular goal, until they collapse or are picked up by the authorities. Others take to the road, sleeping rough and tramping for days on end. Others make straight for some objective, or travel about in style until their money runs out.

When they come out of the trance state, some patients have
retrograde amnesia for the period of the fugue, but recover their
identity and associated reminiscences. They can return home and
carry on as before, though they are aware that there has been a gap
in their life. Others, after a fugue, display the amnesia described
above; they claim neither to know how they got where they are, nor
to have any idea who they are. If they can be identified they are
returned to their homes, but appear to have no, or only patchy,
recollections of their family, friends and home environment. A few
assume a new identity and start a new life. These are the cases
of so-called *'dual personality'* which at one time excited much
medical interest, and still provide material for thrillers and novels of
suspense.

A classical example of hysterical amnesia and dual personality is
the story of the Reverend Ansel Bourne, which has appeared in many
textbooks. The Reverend Bourne is reported to have disappeared
from his home in Providence, USA. Two months later, 200 miles
away in Norristown, a small shopkeeper called A. J. Brown woke up
one morning to find, to his bewilderment, that he did not know where
he was or how he had got there. He was perfectly well aware that he
was the Reverend Ansel Bourne of Providence. He had never heard
of A. J. Brown or his existence in a sweet shop in Norristown. It
seems somewhat suspicious that, shortly before his disappearance, he
had drawn much of his money out of the bank. It seems likely that
his disappearance was associated with some problem and his recov-
ery with its resolution. Fish (1967) has mischievously suggested the
possibility that during the 'lost' two months some pregnant Sunday
school teacher had aborted.

There is always the problem in considering hysterical amnesia that
the patient may be malingering, particularly as when cases are investigated closely their precipitating problem often turns out to be
associated with criminal activity such as embezzlement. However,
there is no need to assume that because the condition provides a
cover story or escape in such cases, that it was deliberately faked.
There is no clear line between voluntary histrionics and hysterical
behaviour, because there is no distinct line between conscious and
unconscious motivation. Because a man *wants* to forget something
does not necessarily mean that his subsequent forgetting is assumed.
On the contrary, the fact that he is motivated to forget it heightens
the likelihood that he will in fact forget. Most of us tend to remember
the situations in which we shine and forget those in which we show
up badly. Alternatively, we reduce cognitive dissonance by recon-
structing the latter type of situation during continued reminiscence
so that we show up less badly. In the end we may recall such a situa-

tion as one in which we showed up rather well—other things being considered or, more usually, not considered. This involves the involuntary distortion and reconstruction of remembered material, coupled with differential forgetting. The hysterical amnesic may be regarded as doing something similar but more wholesale. Instead of forgetting only certain aspects or portions of the situation, he is making a clean sweep by forgetting the lot, including himself.

PSEUDOLOGIA PHANTASTICA

The everyday distortion of recall referred to above has a direct pathological parallel or extension. This is *pseudologia phantastica*, the fabrication by hysterical individuals of 'experiences' which are intrinsically improbable or readily disprovable. On subsequent retailing of such tall stories further details and elaborations are added, particularly if doubt has been expressed by earlier audiences. Each addition becomes progressively more fantastic, so that the implausibility of the original tale is reinforced. The motivation for this sort of behaviour is a need to attract respect, sympathy or merely attention, a need which is the characterizing feature of the hysterical personality.

The author was once due to test a young lady who arrived at the clinic rather late, giving the impression of one who is distraught but bravely fighting back the tears. After sitting down, she requested time to compose herself because: 'I feel a bit shaken. You see, I'm afraid something has just happened that rather upset me.' After a show of decent reluctance, she then explained that she had caught her bus to the clinic in good time. Her lateness was due to the fact that, as she was about to alight, the conductor had brutally ravished her. The author agreed that this was conduct unbecoming to a municipal employee, and remarked that it was particularly unusual in mid-afternoon, on a main road in the city centre and in the setting of a crowded bus. He enquired whether she had reported the outrage to the police, to which the young lady replied, with wide-eyed sincerity, that she had not yet done so because: 'That would have made me late for my appointment here.' The author's scepticism was confirmed after the session, when he took the young lady back to the waiting room. For there was her mother, who had accompanied her to the clinic that afternoon and had noticed nothing untoward during the journey. The young lady was not at all disconcerted by her mother's amazed denials of her story. The rape, she explained, had taken place as she was about to follow her mother down the bus stairs. She had not mentioned the matter as they walked from the bus stop to the clinic, because the conductor had also tried to strangle her with his ticket-punch strap, so that she was temporarily unable to speak.

The rape tale above may reasonably be interpreted as a hastily invented excuse which got out of hand, coupled with a more general need to gain attention. The young lady in question was physically ill-favoured, and lacking in sparkle. It could be that if she had had enough wit to make up a better story she would not have required such attention-seeking devices in the first place. But this is not necessarily so, because the problem is one of self-evaluation. It is not uncommon for individuals who *are* attractive and (at least initially) interesting to others to regard themselves nevertheless as social nonentities.

The *direction* taken by such attention-seeking fabrications natur-ally also reflects individual wish-fulfilment. The male equivalent of our young lady is that man who haunts most clubs and 'locals'. According·to him he is, to all intents and purposes, in hiding from a veritable legion of love-crazed women. Oddly enough, these are for the most part film stars, prima ballerinas, Italian countesses or the glamorous wives of eminent men. Every hint of doubt from the listener merely elicits more colourful details and additional persona. But the content of pseudologia phantastica is of course not restricted to sexual exploits. Heroism, martyrdom, distinguished origins, scientific invention, financial coups or social fame—all are grist to the mill. Very often the claimant becomes the butt of his fellows, who discover that in the face of scepticism or interrogation he is spurred to even giddier heights of implausibility.

In other instances, however, the fictional character of the 'remini-scences' may not be appreciated by the audience. It is ironic to realize that the term 'pseudologia phantastica' is applied generally to the behaviour of patients merely because their reports are demon-strably untrue. There must be many people who are not under psychiatric treatment because their reports have *not* been recognized as untrue. Hysterics are notorious for their histrionic talents and for their apparent sincerity. On superficial acquaintance they tend to be very convincing, so it is likely that for every patient under treatment there are many non-patients whose equally fantastic reminiscences are accepted as genuine. Presumably the successful confidence trickster comes from the same mould as the psychiatric patient, as do those who appear before the courts for masquerading as high-ranking officers or peers of the realm. Less mischievous but probably of the same ilk are the people who are triggered off by events appearing in newspaper headlines. Thus, reports of unsolved murders result in numbers of people who claim to be the murderer and are quite prepared to support their 'confession' with circumstantial but readily falsifiable details. Every time one person is reported as having seen a ghost or a flying saucer, a crowd of others suddenly 'remember' that they too witnessed the phenomenon.

When children engage in the sort of behaviour recounted above, adults regard them with amused tolerance. Most of us accept that in childhood the boundaries between fantasy and reality are blurred, and the concepts of 'truth' and 'falsehood' are slow to develop. In adults, however, such behaviour is judged in moral terms. The alternative term for pseudologia phantastica is 'pathological lying', which immediately suggests reprehensible behaviour rather than a symptom of personality disorder. Adults are presumed to know the difference between fact and fancy, truth and falsehood, and in our culture to mix the two during verbal report is to be guilty of lying. This is defined as the intentional making of false statements, usually with the purpose of misleading others. It is presupposed that the liar is fully aware of what is true and what is false, and that he is consciously imparting the latter with deliberate intention of deceiving. This is doubtless a fair description of much braggadocio and tall story-telling. We may invent stories to avoid reproach, to impress, to denigrate our enemies or to further our ambitions. More innocuously, we may do so merely to amuse our listeners or even to avoid hurting their feelings. We know what we are doing and, if required, can immediately disavow our stories or modify them in accordance with fact. But for many people the situation is not so simple. We all 'remember' by selective reconstruction. If the discrepancies between what we recall and what actually occurred can be brought to our notice, we do not then accuse ourselves of having lied, but merely of having misremembered. Similarly, we do not regard the amnesic patient's confabulations as lies. We realize that he is filling in the gaps in his memory with fragments of earlier memories. It seems reasonable to suggest that hysterical confabulation involves the same process. In hysterical amnesia the patient's problems are solved at one level by the inaccessibility of much stored information, including that which has disturbed or threatened him. His experience may be interpreted as the reflection of a negative type of defence. Pseudologia phantastica may be regarded as the obverse of this, utilizing a similar process in the opposite direction. Instead of the under-employment of retrieval mechanisms, they are over-employed but in an unduly associative and flexible manner. In the first case, certain schemata are isolated; in the second they are too readily related.

THE 'TIP OF THE TONGUE' EXPERIENCE

A significant feature of recall is that it is not an on-off or 'all or nothing' experience. At the one extreme we may succeed in recalling an item of information and recognize it quite clearly as that which we were trying to remember. We are immediately and confidently aware that we have found what we were searching for. At the other extreme, after a period of brain-racking, we can be equally sure not only that we have not recalled the item but that we have found no clues either. We may experience the flat certainty that further search would be pointless—we know that we have forgotten. But between these two extremes are a number of recall experiences which probably lie on several continua. For instance, we may recall the elusive item but with varying degrees of certainty as to whether what we have re-recalled is in fact what we were searching for. We may come up with an item which can be confirmed as correct and yet be one which we fail to recognize with conviction as the item in question. But the most frustrating in-between experience is that of failing to recall the item and yet somehow feeling sure that we *almost* have it. We say: 'I've got it, but I just can't put a name to it. It's on the tip of my tongue.' Usually the more desperately one now strives to remember the item, the more elusive it becomes. Indeed, a popular piece of advice is to *stop trying to remember it* at this stage, in the hope that it will subsequently 'pop into your mind'. Associated with the 'tip of the tongue' (TOT) stage is the fact that the frustrated recaller will bring up a number of near-miss items. He knows that these are incorrect but may subsequently realize that they were associated in various ways with the target item.

Recently the author jotted down his attempts to recall the name of a much-recommended restaurant. Fragmentary clues were provided by his wife. Both experienced pronounced TOT states. The script (abbreviated) is presented here, and the reader is encouraged to trace associations, with or without the aid of Freud's *Psychopathology of everyday life*:

Clue: 'Out in the country. Supposed to do excellent dinners.'
       No idea. Could be anything.
Clue: 'Stands by itself. Not in a village.'
       Rings a bell. But lots of places like that.
Clue: 'Kurt mentioned it to us. It's about half an hour's drive away.'
       Got it! Just can't think of name. But it's more than a half-hour's drive away. More like an hour.
Clue: 'Due north of here.'

No—north-west. The Globe Hotel—no, nothing like that.
Clue: 'Two words in the name.'
Right. The Copper Kettle—no, the Blue Vase. No, wrong
number of syllables. Copper Kettle was wrong, but has the
right sort of ring.
Clue: 'Mentioned on TV once.'
Right. It's not an Indian restaurant. Why did I think that—
nobody suggested it *was*. Ah yes, the name sounds like The
Calcutta Restaurant. But wrong number of words *and*
syllables. Calcutta Cottage. Ridiculous.
Clue: 'Olde Worldy place.'
Cottage again. World—Globe—Sphere. Kurt said it stood
in a fold of the hills. Isn't it called after the hills? Yes, but
makes it more difficult—silly name for hills. More to do with
a model of hills. No, a *painting* of hills. Hills and cottage
walls.
Earth. Colour.
Got it! *The Terra Cotta Inn!*

A key question is whether the subjective knowledge that one has
almost remembered something has any validity. The frustrated
recaller may feel that he has 'almost got it'—but is he really any
nearer than when he began? Some ingenious experimentation has
suggested that there is a basis in fact for the TOT experience. In a
well-known study by Brown and McNeill (1966) the experience was
elicited by presenting subjects with definitions of uncommon words
and asking them to supply the words. Among 56 subjects, 360 cases
of the TOT state were reported. When they experienced TOT, the
subjects were asked to state as much as they could remember about
the word in question in terms of number of syllables, syllabic stress,
initial letter, suffixes and so on. Analysis of these data showed
accuracy of 'generic recall', prior to recall of the words themselves.
That is to say, both the descriptions of the *form* of the unrecalled
word (number of syllables, location of stress) and *partial descriptions*
(letters) tended to be correct. For instance, subjects were presented
with the following definition among others: 'A navigational instrument used in measuring angular distances, especially the altitude of
sun, moon, and stars at sea.' Nine of the 56 subjects experienced TOT
during their attempts to find the word defined. Some became sure
that they were searching for a two-syllable word, for one that began
with an S or had the initial and final letters 'S . . . T'. They produced
words of similar *sound* (e.g. sexton, secant, sextet) or similar *meaning*
(e.g. protractor, astrolabe, compass). In short, subjects experiencing
TOT were very near the mark on a number of counts. They were

engaging, at some level, in the setting up of criteria and running
through series of possible multiple matches. But they were unable
to define *all* the required criteria although they would recognize
a total correct match if they managed to bring it forward for
review.

At first sight, the paradox of the TOT experience is that it seems
to suggest that we can recognize that we have remembered something
correctly before that something itself is actually available for recognition. We shall be discussing the problem of recognition in a later
chapter. But meanwhile we may take TOT as reconcilable with the
constructive view of remembering. Except for items over-learned by
rote, information is not stored as discrete snippets. It is coded and
assimilated into schemata. Thus recall involves not the retrieval of
the original items, but the activation of the appropriate schemata.
From these, modifications of the items may be reconstructed. The
TOT experience suggests that we have activated one or more schemata correctly and that reconstruction is taking place. There is a good
basis for our conviction that we have captured our item, even though
it has not yet crystallized.

PHOTOGRAPHIC MEMORY

One often hears about (but, ironically, seldom meets) people who are
gifted with 'photographic memories'. The implication is that they can
evoke memory images—of events, scenes, pages of print—which have
the same objective exactitude, clarity and detail as a photograph.
Such a gift could, indeed, be extremely convenient, and its supposed
possessors are usually referred to not only with awe but with envy.
Students in particular often attribute the relative success of those
higher in examination lists to their fortunate possession of the talent.
And certainly there is no lack of supportive anecdotal evidence in
this connection. For instance there is the hoary tale, which appears
in several forms, of the student (usually a mysterious Indian) at a
noted medical school (usually Glasgow) who was suspected of
cheating in a major examination. The examiner felt that there was
something decidedly familiar about the student's paper. Upon
checking, he discovered that it was taken word for word from a textbook (usually Gray's *Anatomy*). The student was promptly hauled
before the Dean and accused of smuggling the book into the examination hall. Whereupon he discountenanced his accusers by mildly
requesting that they select any chapter from the massive tome in
question, and thereupon proceeding to recite the whole thing! The
presumption which often underlies this sort of story is that the
student was the happy possessor of a photographic memory. Having

once read the book in question he could thenceforth image every page and 'read it off' as though the actual book was before him.

Now the approach to memory outlined in the introduction to this chapter suggests that recall is not photographic—it is not inclusive, clear, detailed and exact. If photographic memory exists, how is it reconcilable with our 'reconstructive' approach? First of all, let us be clear about what we are discussing. The basic assumption about photographic memory is that certain individuals can function like a camera. They look at the scene or the page and—hey presto!—a perceptual shutter is released and an objective simulacrum is recorded, as on a photographic film. This is printed and stored, ready for subsequent examination. The 'reconstruction' approach would deny that this is how mnemonic processes function. It does not, of course, deny that material can be learned to some criterion, actively rehearsed and subsequently recalled correctly. In fact, this is probably the explanation for the factual events upon which stories like the one above are based. The prototype of our mysterious Indian student was probably an obsessionally anxious person who merely doggedly learned his mass of material by rote. But such an explanation is too mundane to be attractive in anecdotage. The photographic memory claim invokes instantaneous recording as in a snapshot, not the wearisome repetition and correction of rote learning. So before we can examine our first question we must ask a number of others. Are there in fact cases where the 'memory' consists of a visual image which is objectively correct and detailed? Can such images be projected at will? And if so, over what period of time?

As far as adults are concerned, there have been several studies published of 'memory men' and 'lightning calculators'. Some of these have examined the nature of the visual imagery which often facilitates the remarkable skills of such people. For example, the calculating virtuoso Salo Finkelstein was found to image key numbers and the results of certain calculations whilst he continued to calculate. He could hold these images long enough to refer back to them, thus leaving himself free to concentrate on further stages of calculation. The images could be evoked voluntarily over a period of hours. They were projected at a convenient reading distance from his eyes. But such images were not 'photographic', for subsequent learning could adversely affect the accuracy of the image of earlier material (retroactive interference). Furthermore he did not acquire an image of visually presented material by any instant 'snap-shot'. He seems to have learned digits by actively organizing and interrelating them in certain practised combinations. Finally, his visual images did not take the form of the original presentations. They appeared to him as though written in chalk on a freshly washed blackboard *in his own handwriting.* The Russian mnemonist, S. V. Shereshevskii ('S'), utilized voluntary visual imagery as a basic method in his astonishing displays of recall over many years (Luria, 1969). The material imaged included not only series of digits and written material, but scenes and personal situations. But although his images do not seem to have involved distortions, they were certainly not error-free 'photographs'. Firstly, they were often *incomplete.* The omissions were not the result of faulty recall but of initial perception. If he failed to attend to some feature of the initial event it did not appear in subsequent imaging. Secondly, he described 'building up' his images by associations. And thirdly the images were inextricably fused with impressions in other modalities, which might heighten or blur the visual image itself.

The phenomenon closest to the concept of photographic memory is *'eidetic imagery'*, which excited considerable interest among psychologists in the 1920s and early 1930s. It seems to be relatively common amongst children (estimates of incidence range from 8 per cent to 60 per cent) but very rare after about eleven years of age (estimates range from 1 per cent to 10 per cent). The eidetic image is reported to have several distinguishing characteristics which are very close to those presumed for photographic memory:

(1) The image (which is almost always visual) is remarkably clear and detailed.

(2) It can be a surprisingly accurate reproduction of the original material, which in most studies has been a picture, presented for about half a minute. Indeed, it has been claimed that the image is identical to the original, as though it were some type of prolonged retinal after-image.

(3) It is localized externally, whereas most images are experienced as being inside the imager's head. For this and other reasons, the eidetic image has been described as 'percept-like', although the eidetiker is always aware of his image's subjective nature and can control it voluntarily. The image is usually 'projected' on to a wall or other surface, rather like a slide or film. And again as with a film, if the projection surface is angled or bent, so is the image. The vividness of the latter, incidentally, is so intense that it tends to blot out the background against which it is projected.

(4) The external localization of the image is complemented by the fact that the eidetiker can 'read it off'—his eyes actually rove over the projection surface as he describes details of the image. In this respect also, the eidetic image is similar to a film and unlike an after-image.

(5) The eidetiker can 'turn on' his image over a considerable period of time. In many experiments the subjects have been required to report upon details of their images for up to half an hour after

seeing the original material, and it has been reported that they can be voluntarily recovered weeks or even years later.

(6) Eidetikers apparently differentiate between their memory images and 'ordinary remembering'. They can correct their descriptions given from memory by subsequently projecting eidetic images and checking the details of their earlier reports.

These characteristics of eidetic imagery do seem to add up to what is usually meant by 'photographic memory'. So perhaps the popular idea has validity, at least where children are concerned? Here we have a closely investigated phenomenon where 'memory' can be invested in a detailed visual image which can be projected at will and over a prolonged period of time. Unfortunately, closer examination reveals one crucial difference between eidetic imagery and 'photographic memory'. And that is that the image is *not* photographic. It is vivid and detailed, but it is not necessarily completely accurate. As would be expected, much depends upon the eidetiker's attitudes and set. If a picture interests him his subsequent image may be very accurate. But if it lacks interest, his accuracy may diminish or he may fail to produce an image at all. Furthermore, the child may enliven or 'complete' his image. If the original picture showed a carriage proceeding along a road or a man turning a corner, the eidetiker may 'see' the action continuing in his image, so that the carriage or the man may disappear from view. Suggestion from the investigator may facilitate or direct such action. Thus one investigator, having presented a picture of a donkey standing at some distance from a manger, suggested that the donkey was hungry. In describing their eidetic images, several of his child subjects reported that the donkey had trotted across to the manger and was busily eating. In other words, eidetic imagery can involve distortion, elaboration and omission. And as Bartlett pointed out, these are related to selective attention in the first instance, to expectancy, to interest and to attitude. Our view of memory as an active, reconstructive process is not impugned by the evidence in this area.

Nevertheless, it is undoubtedly true that eidetic imagery does possess far more detail and higher accuracy than 'ordinary' recall. Why should this be so? The answer may be that the two most significant features of eidetic images—their wealth of detail and their vivid visual character—are themselves evidence of *ineffective schematization*. Firstly, the assimilation of new material to appropriate schemata must involve blurring of detail. And when the original material is recalled, its reconstruction must involve some displacement and further loss of detail, along with the emphasizing of 'significant' detail. For optimal cognitive functioning, the coding and integration

of information implies abstraction and condensation. On this argument, the eidetic image contains so many of the details of the original
material merely because the latter has not been fully 'digested'.
Secondly, it is possible that the very persistence of eidetic imagery in
such an intense visual form is itself an indication that the material
has not been fully processed. For there is increasing experimental
evidence to suggest that, whilst visual input may be held in what
William James called 'primary memory', it is recoded into an auditory form before it passes into long-term 'secondary memory'.

Thus, the ability to project eidetic images, far from being an
enviable talent, may merely reflect immature cognitive development.
This rather unromantic suggestion might explain why, as we have
noted, the ability is relatively common among children, but very rare
among adults. Furthermore, recent studies have reported that the
phenomenon is much more common amongst brain-injured children
and retarded readers than amongst normal children.

5

ANOMALIES OF RECOGNITION

There can be few cognitive phenomena which have proved less amenable to study than the experience called 'recognition'. A major reason for this has been that few experimental psychologists agree as to what the term implies. Some have confused the issue by using quite different but restrictive definitions. Others have evaded the issue by applying the term to an experimental *method* which seems to have very little to do with the experience. Still others have simply blocked the issue by insisting that they are not interested in what recognition is; they are only interested in doing experiments on it. Before looking at the mixed bag of interesting experiences which belong under the heading of anomalies of recognition, it will be as well to try to sort out some of the problems involved in defining the phenomenon.

The verb 'recognize' has several dictionary definitions, but the one which is relevant to our interest is: 'known again, identify as known before'. The essential element here is the *experience of familiarity*. This is recognized by dictionaries of psychology. Harriman's definition is: 'recognition—the feeling of familiarity when a previously encountered situation is present . . .'. 'Recognize' has another meaning when it is used as it was in the last sentence but one. In this sense it means: 'acknowledge the validity or genuineness of . . .'. It can also mean: 'discover or realize the nature of . . .'. But these usages are of only indirect concern here; in psychology and psychiatry the term's technical meaning is limited to that involving the feeling of familiarity. This does not prevent the 'confusion' school of psychologists from using it in one or the other of these ways, nor the 'blocking' school from asserting that any way is as good or as bad as another.

'Recognition' is often used in psychology to imply familiarity, but in such a loose way that the phenomenon in question cannot be differentiated from 'perception'. For example, one excellent book on memory gives as an example of recognition the ability to determine that a figure in a photograph is that of a woman rather than a man. This usage of the word is lexically correct, but at first sight it might seem unlikely to be of help in classifying the experience. The determining of a figure as being that of a woman may be termed identification; it is a conceptual act, such as is involved in all normal perception. It is true that it is accompanied by a generalized feeling of familiarity, but only at the level that all perception involves familiarity. The matter can be pushed a little further by considering whether we could validly term the perception merely of 'a thing' as recognition. This seems unlikely—for instance, somebody who looks through a telescope and reports that he 'can see *something*' would not claim to be experiencing recognition. On the contrary, he is suggesting that he has striven for recognition, but *failed* to experience it. He has merely succeeded in separating an object of some kind from its context. He will only experience recognition when he finally manages to determine what the object is. But this brings us to an intriguing point which psychologists do not seem to have considered. Supposing the object turns out to be a woman? It was just suggested that the perception of an object as a woman does not specifically involve recognition. Yet here is a situation—where the man looks through the telescope and says: 'I don't know—I can see something—don't know what it is—wait a minute—yes! It's a woman!'—where most of us would agree that what he is experiencing can strictly be termed 'recognition'. This apparent paradox will be examined later. Meanwhile, let us return to the original question of whether normal perception can validly be termed recognition.

If we are talking with friends and somebody passes on the other side of the street, we are very unlikely to exclaim: 'I recognize that figure. It is a woman!' We would regard our perceptual feat as so commonplace as not to deserve comment. If we were pressed to make some sort of identificatory statement we would still not talk of recognizing the person. We would probably say (rather impatiently): 'That is a woman', implying: 'I perceive a woman'. When would we use the word 'recognize'? Clearly, when we could say: 'I recognize that woman. It's Molly Brown!' In other words, the level of familiarity involved in recognition is that related to particular individuals, as opposed to the classes or categories to which they belong. This everyday use of 'recognition' is explicitly supported by some psychological authorities. For instance, Woodworth and Schlosberg, in their standard textbook of experimental psychology, state: 'An object is "recognized" as an individual thing or person; it is "perceived" as an object of a certain class.' We do not claim to experience familiarity in reference to the whole human race, but only in reference to individuals we have met before. We never say that we 'recognize' strange individuals. Indeed, if we can recognize them, then they cannot be strangers.

Unfortunately, the question is not quite as simple as that. Firstly, we may recognize an individual whom we neither know nor have met or seen previously. We may recognize a celebrity in the street from photographs. If we are waiting at the station to meet a visitor whom we have never met in the flesh, we can 'recognize' him from descriptions. Secondly, as in the telescope example above, we may experience recognition in the identification of almost any object or class of object, given that the identification has involved some effort or comes after a series of 'guesses'. Thirdly, 'familiarity' is a relative concept. In one sense we feel more familiarity in perceiving any other member of our own species than we would in perceiving, for example, a pterodactyl. And lastly, it is fair to say that we do experience recognition when we identify a completely novel object, *because* we have never seen one before. Given that a pterodactyl lurched out of Loch Ness, many people would excitedly identify it because they had read descriptions of that class of prehistoric monster. And in so doing they would undoubtedly report that they were experiencing recognition. The extreme case of this is that of mythical or literary creations. A well-known example is that, if we happened to run into a horse with a horn in the centre of its forehead, most of us would 'recognize' it as a unicorn, even though we had never before seen such a beast.

These problems can be reduced to some sort of order by accepting that 'recognition' occurs in consequence of perceptual integration and categorization. Categorizations are made at various levels which are hierarchically arranged. Let us consider this in terms of visual perception, and revert to the handy example of looking through a telescope. The lowest level of cognitive categorization is probably that at which we are merely able to discriminate light from dark. The next level might be the perception of tonal characteristics, of hue and saturation. The next might be the abstraction of a figure from the ground, when we merely know that 'something is there'. An advance is made when we succeed in identifying one or more attributes of the 'something', e.g. it is three-dimensional, upright and moving. Next, we may manage to induce the class of the 'something' from its attributes, e.g. it is a primate. After discovering further attributes (e.g. it is relatively hairless, clothed and spectacled) we may be able to allocate it to a more precise category, e.g. it is a human being. And so on, through further refining observations to, for example, it is of stocky build, wearing plus-fours and playing the slide trombone. Finally, it is possible that we can complete the identification by realizing that this particular individual class-member is known to us personally, e.g. 'Good Heavens—it's Auntie Mabel!'

Semantically and in terms of psychological processes, it is quite proper to apply the term 'recognition' to our experience at each of these levels. Probably this is especially so in sudden 'penny-dropping' conditions, when we eventually arrive at the concept only after perceptual effort or the running through and abandoning of various hypotheses. But it seems reasonable to suggest that the *intensity of familiarity* is related to the *level* of integration and conceptualization achieved. The higher the level, the more schemata are employed. So perhaps the degree of familiarity experienced is proportional to the number of schemata applicable to the object. As noted above, we are not strongly aware of the experience of recognition as we achieve a low-level conceptualization, and are unlikely to describe ourselves as 'recognizing' merely a shape, a table, a dog or a person, unless the identification is preceded by perceptual effort. We *are* strongly aware of recognition when we have identified and integrated more cues in a higher-order categorization, so that we realize that the object is a particular one which is known to us.

This leads directly to the zone of the 'evasion' school of investigators. The majority of experimental psychologists use the term 'recognition' with reference to a certain *method* of studying mnemonic processes. A series of items (words, letters, numbers, objects or shapes) is displayed to the experimental subject. Later, the items are presented again, mixed with a number of other items which have not previously been displayed. The subject's task is to indicate which items in this longer array figured in the original presentation. (This method contrasts with the standard 'recall' method, where the subject is required to recall as many of the original items as he can.) Now this sort of task may be said to invoke recognition but only at the level of the ability to identify a figure as being that of a woman. For when, as is usual, all the test items are letters, words, digits, etc., they are *all* familiar to the subject. The task is the same as presenting the subject with a line-up of his closest friends, and requiring him to indicate which ones he has seen during the last week. Would his subsequent responses normally be said to involve recognition?

For the sake of convenience, only examples drawn from the field of visual perception have been considered in the above discussion. It should be noted that exactly the same arguments apply to perceptions in all modalities. We recognize sounds such as voices, birdsong, music, engines and gun-shots, as well as the tastes of foodstuffs and drinks, and the feel of shapes and textures. And traditionally our sense of smell is most capable of reminiscence, bringing back long-forgotten experiences. So that not only do we identify everyday odours, but we recognize smells and their associations after intervals of many years.

Recognition also occurs in association with *inner* signals. Harriman's 'situations' may be cognitive or emotional or somesthetic. We can receive a number of signals from our bodies and suddenly recognize that we are suffering from influenza again. We may process our feelings of discomfort in the context of chest pain and, after abandoning hypotheses such as cancer, cardiac failure and coronary thrombosis, recognize our sensations as those associated with a bout of wind. Finally, we may have a strong sense of familiarity as we remember an idea, the answer to a problem, a melody or some piece of information.

Perhaps the most powerful literary study of recall and recognition is Marcel Proust's *À la recherche du temps perdu*. Proust maintains that what are normally called 'memories' are merely flat and lifeless images which we preserve and evoke by habit. In his view, authentic memories cannot be recalled at will. They are spontaneously re-created from unconscious sources when one experiences some for-tuitious concatenation of features related to the original experience. By comparison with the colourlessness and emotional insignificance of 'automatic' memories, these accidental evocations are rich, vital and poignant. On our present argument this would be because the former reflect simple, rehearsed associations, whereas the latter reflect schematic activation at a high level of organization. This higher-level integration of multiple schemata is more likely to involve what some psychologists term 'redintegration'—the *personalization* of a recollection as opposed to the neutrality of formal memories. For the individual concerned this invests his recall experience with emotion and personal familiarity. Proust extends this to include an almost religious sense of metaphysical significance.

The Proustian theme is best exemplified in the '*petite madeleine*' episode, which occurs in *Du coté de chez Swann* (Volume I of *À la recherche du temps perdu*, and translated as *Swann's way*). The episode is preceded by the narrator's reference to the fact that all memories of his childhood visits to Combray seemed to have been blotted out. He then refers to the Celtic belief that the souls of people we have known are imprisoned in inanimate objects after death. But they can be released *by our recognition*. Having repeated his assertion that true memories cannot be resurrected at will but only as the result of accidental experiences, he then describes how, as an adult, he returns home one cheerless day and is given tea and a *madeleine* (sweet biscuit or cookie) by his mother. As soon as he tastes the crumbs of *madeleine* in a spoonful of tea he is possessed by mystic rapture—'*Un plaisir délicieux*'. He proceeds to analyse in minute detail how the sight, smell and taste of a simple *madeleine* evoked a flood of vivid memories invested with such poignant ecstasy.

'Mais, quand d'un passé ancien rien ne subsiste, après la mort des êtres, après la destruction des choses, seules, plus frêles mais plus vivaces, plus immatérielles, plus persistantes, plus fidèles, l'odeur et la saveur restent longtemps, comme des âmes, à se rappeler, à attendre, à espérer, sur la ruine de tout le reste, à porter sans fléchir, sur leur gouttelette presque impalpable, l'édifice immense du souvenir' (p. 47).

The nosegay of variegated anomalous phenomena to be described below includes several which are not usually discussed in the context of recognition although they are all clearly defined as anomalies thereof. This is probably because they can equally well be discussed in terms of recall, speech or perception. But it may also be due to the sort of confusion that we have tried to sort out, as the phenomena occur at very different 'levels' of conceptualization. They fall into three groups—that at the level of simple object-categorization, that at the level of ideas or concept-formation, and that at the level of total situations.

THE AGNOSIAS

The word 'agnosia' (which was first introduced by Freud) means simply the absence of recognition. The person suffering from agnosia identifies the *properties* of an object, but fails to recognize what the object is. There is no question of him knowing whether he has experienced the particular object in question on a previous occasion. As we have seen, in order to do that it is necessary to succeed at a number of earlier levels of cognitive activity. The agnosia sufferer is unable even to induce the general class concept from its attributes. The disorder is usually classified in textbooks as one of perception or of speech. It is both of these, of course, but as we shall see in some senses perception is unimpaired, whilst the individual has in fact the appropriate verbal labels at his disposal. This can be demonstrated because strangely enough the incapacity usually applies only to one sense modality. Recognition can be achieved normally, using the other modalities, and the appropriate verbal report can then be made. Thus, the subject can describe something placed in his hand as being a long, thin piece of wood, round in section and pointed at one end. But only when he is allowed to *look* at the object does he recognize it as being a pencil.

The various types of agnosia according to the sense modalities involved are considered below.

(1) *Visual agnosia*

In 1881 Munk described the behaviour of a dog after he had removed the lateral parts of its occipital lobes. For some time subsequent to the operation the animal was able to move about freely. Its vision was apparently unimpaired, but it showed no appropriate response to the sight of meat, its master or his whip. Munk termed this *Seelenblindheit*—mind-blindness. This vivid term aptly suggests that, although the eyes are functioning appropriately and signals are being conveyed to the brain, some sort of central processing is absent. Since Munk's time various forms of this condition have been observed in humans.

In *visual object agnosia* some patients fail to recognize small objects, although they may recognize larger ones and other people. Thus, they may be able to describe a coin, but cannot name it or explain what it is for. The functions of common objects such as combs, knives and forks are lost to them; but as soon as they are allowed to handle any of these objects they can name them and explain their use. Such a patient may have to be prevented from putting his hand into a flame, because he can no longer appreciate its significance from visual examination alone.

In some cases of this condition objects may be recognized in their usual context, but not when they are observed in an unfamiliar setting. This parallels a common difficulty which most people experience—that of seeing somebody in an unfamiliar setting, recognizing him, but being unable to 'place' him. But in this case we are 'recognizing' him as a human being, and 'recognizing' him as someone we have met before. It is merely the final stage of recalling his name and the situation in which we have previously met him that is missing. In the case of a patient with agnosia, he cannot 'recognize' where he has previously encountered an object because he cannot 'recognize' what it is in the first place. On the other hand, most such patients do recognize people as being people. But in some cases they may not be able to 'recognize' the faces of their closest friends.

Simultanagnosia is a condition in which patients recognize individual details in a picture, but are unable to recognize the meaning of the whole. Thus, the patient may be able to recognize that one feature of the picture is 'a lady', another is 'a toy' and another is 'a little boy', but is unable to make the further integrative recognition that this is a picture of a lady giving a toy to a little boy. Here there is a problem, because such patients *are* demonstrating the recognition of class concepts from their attributes—they are recognizing the portrayal as a lady, a toy and a boy. The failure relates to a different sort of integration, the symbolic one of appreciating interaction *between* objects.

(2) *Tactile agnosia*

In tactile agnosia the patient is unable to recognize objects by touch. But he has no sensory impairment—his sense of touch is normal, so that he can correctly distinguish size, shape and texture. Equally unaffected are his sense of pain, sensation for vibration, sense of pressure and of passive movement and position. If he is asked to hold objects while his eyes are closed, he can describe a given object as smooth, rounded and with two indentations—but does not recognize that what he has in his hand is an apple. He can describe another object as being a bent piece of wire with a point at one end—but does not recognize it as a safety pin. In one sense, his condition is the converse of that inculcated in themselves by participants in a traditional part of Hallowe'en merry-making. The players—usually well primed with excitement if not with alcohol—sit in a circle in a darkened room. A suitably talented narrator recounts a ghost story, which is often salted with scabrous or bawdy details. Meanwhile, a number of objects are passed from hand to hand. The objects are commonplace but malleable and open to misinterpretation; usually they include peeled grapes, sausages and water-filled rubber gloves. Full enjoyment of the game requires a state of heightened suggestibility during which the player imaginatively projects himself into the narrator's yarn. The patient with tactile agnosia seems unable to set up hypotheses about the objects he touches. The player deliberately allows himself to set up a variety of bizarre hypotheses and enjoys his subsequent 'recognitions'.

(3) *Auditory agnosia*

Here the patient can hear normally, but is unable to recognize the sounds he hears. Thus, familiar sounds such as the rustle of paper, a motor horn, a ringing bell or a running tap have no meaning for him. His condition may prevent him from understanding spoken speech (*word-deafness*) so that his native tongue is either not recognized as communicative or sounds to him like a foreign language. Similarly, he may be unable to recognize musical sounds (*sensory amusia*). This of course is not the same as the 'tone-deafness' to which many healthy people lay claim. Tone-deafness implies a lack of ability in the discrimination of tonal intervals, or merely a failure to appreciate music. The tone-deaf person merely fails to enjoy music; the patient with sensory amusia does not recognize it as being music at all.

The agnosias are all associated with lesions in different parts of the brain. The neurological evidence is classically reviewed in Lord Brain's book, *Speech disorders,* and will not be considered here. What is of primary interest here is their consideration in terms of psychological functioning. At least three implications spring to mind immediately.

Firstly, the handicaps in the agnosic patient's performance lend clinical support to experimental findings which suggest that information received through different sensory modalities is coded separately. Clearly there is interaction and summation; the results of a number of experiments suggest that recognition is facilitated in proportion to the number of sensory channels employed in the initial examination of an object. Generally speaking, the more sensory channels employed, the more information about the object can be received so that subsequent matching can be more precise. But the agnosias demonstrate that the perceptual synthesis and matching required in recognition can be achieved with information in one modality and be ineffective in another.

Secondly, agnosia is in one sense the obverse of *synaesthesia,* where perception in one modality is referred to others. Synaesthesia seems to reflect an abnormal loosening of information processing, which allows undue diffusion or 'seepage' from one input channel to another. Agnosia, on the other hand, seems to reflect a pathological restriction of processing, which *prevents* interaction between the damaged channel and the others, so that the assessment of information received in one channel cannot be augmented by imaging in another.

Thirdly, the effect of the lesions responsible for agnosia seems to be that the *level* of schematic organization of input in the associated modality is diminished. Clearly, *some* matching and schematization takes place. The patient with tactile agnosia can describe the characteristics of the pencil he is holding—it is long, smooth, round in section and pointed at one end. Each of these definitions of the pencil's attributes involves some synthesis and recognition. One cannot, for instance, define the characteristic 'sharpness' without taking into account several subordinate features of texture, angularity and dimensionality. The agnosic patient's failure is not that he is unable to conceptualize information received through the damaged channel, but that he is unable to conceptualize it at a high enough level.

CRYPTOMNESIA

When the author was about ten years of age, he woke up one night with a musical phrase ringing in his head. The phrase developed into a snatch of melody, which he worked at with increasing excitement. Eventually he got out of bed, slipped downstairs, picked the tune out on the piano and transcribed it laboriously in a music manuscript notebook. The next morning before breakfast he expanded and polished his melody, which preoccupied him throughout the morning at school. At lunch-time he rushed home and completed the work, reeling with the heady joy of creation. About an hour later he was racking his brains for a suitable title when he suddenly realized the shattering fact that 'his' melody already had a title. It was the 'Blue Danube Waltz'!

This situation, where a memory is not experienced as such, but is personalized and experienced as an original production, is termed *cryptomnesia*, and is a very common form of recognition failure. Something that has been experienced before is recalled, but without any associated feeling of familiarity. It is therefore experienced as a 'first time' occurrence, which invests some types of content with the glamour of creation or invention. For the most part the 'creator' is not particularly impressed, because most of our ideas are fairly mundane, whether they are original or not. But occasionally, when the phenomenon takes the full-blooded form of unconscious plagiarism, the 'originator' may publicize his apparent achievement, with troublesome or embarrassing consequences. The basic situation is that where a work of art or literature is published without attribution to its real originator. But it may be complicated by questions of dating, of attribution or national pride. The Indian General Chaudhuri has recalled how, as leader of a military mission to Communist China, he was entertained, after a sumptuous meal, to a 'cultural' concert. He was shaken out of his somnolence when the band suddenly struck up 'The British Grenadiers'. The general, who as a young cadet had been trained at Sandhurst, turned to his host in some surprise. 'Ah,' he said, 'I've marched many miles to that tune. I know it so well.' 'Impossible,' came the reply, 'You must have made a mistake, Comrade General. It is a recently composed piece and is the song of our Honan Guerrillas.'

An everyday example of unconscious plagiarism, which does not evoke litigation or professional scandal but can cause strain in personal relationships, is the retailing of anecdotes and jokes in a personal context. For reasons which could doubtless be elucidated by a psychoanalyst, the purveyor of a stolen jest often recounts it at some stage to its originator. As would be expected from our knowledge of serial reproduction, the purveyor always modifies the tale, changing emphases and introducing elaborations and his own stylistic mannerisms. This usually irritates the originator almost as much as the fact that the material itself was filched from him. This is ironic when it is considered that these changes and interpolations are, after all, the plagiarist's personal contribution, so that the originator is complaining both that the story is not original *and* that portions of it are. Such exasperation is more understandable when the original tale was a personal reminiscence, and therefore regarded by its originator as being the vehicle of objectively factual data. Interpolations are then regarded by him as being not only impertinent but immoral. The author once had the delightful experience of hearing a well-meaning cryptomnesic recount the story of a classic cricket match, where he had led his university team to ultimate victory in the face of overwhelming odds. Unfortunately, his audience included the old blue who had been the actual hero of the odyssey in question, and who had told the story in all its tedious detail to the cryptomnesic only a few months before. As the saga proceeded his face assumed an increasingly magenta hue. But with iron self-control he held his peace until the raconteur began to introduce a series of colourful embroideries.

'Damn it man, you might at least get your facts straight!' he burst out at last, spluttering with rage, 'He was the *seventh* man in, not the sixth!' The raconteur frowned in concentration. 'Come to think of it, I do believe you're right,' he replied. 'But fancy you remembering that, old boy. Have I told you this story before?'

Understandably, the failure of recognition involved in cryptomnesia occurs most readily not in reminiscences as in the last example, but where logical memories, ideas and the solutions of problems are concerned. Presumably this is because such material is not embedded in personal associations; it may be said to figure on fewer schemata and so is recalled with fewer identifying clues. It may be noted that recall without recognition of this type does not necessarily involve ideas or solutions derived from others. It is not uncommon for people to think that they have 'just come up with the answer', only to recollect subsequently that the same solution had occurred to them on some previous occasion. The author was once held up in the final stages of an investigation by a small technical problem related to the presentation of some data. One day the obvious solution flashed into his mind, whereupon he happily completed the project. Later, as he was filing away the associated documents, he discovered from his notes that he had thought of this particular solution weeks before—on two separate occasions!

Sometimes cryptomnesic chains can be detected, particularly in the academic world, where references to previous work, problem-solutions and ideas are in constant circulation. One of the author's students rushed in one day to announce exultantly that he had discovered an obscure article of high relevance to his research. The author forebore from pointing out that he had himself unearthed the article, realized its relevance and given the student the necessary reference the previous term. Later, complimenting himself upon his generous self-restraint, he consulted his tutorial notes. He was chagrined to discover that, whilst it was true that he had provided details of the key article, he had himself received them, in another context, from a colleague.

It may be of some consolation when we discover evidence of cryptomnesia in ourselves to realize that it is not confined to persons of limited inventiveness. We share it with great thinkers who have no apparent need to steal ideas from others. In his *Psychopathology of everyday life*, Sigmund Freud sadly describes how he pointed out to a friend that in order to solve neurotic problems it was necessary to postulate an original bisexuality in every individual. The friend replied that he had told Freud exactly the same thing two and a half years before, at which time Freud had refused to consider it. Subsequently Freud recollected the occasion; his friend's claim was quite correct. Freud comments wryly: 'It is truly painful to be thus requested to renounce one's originality.'

What has experimental psychology to tell us about cryptomnesia? The embarrassing answer seems to be: nothing at all. As observed earlier, experimental investigations of recognition have been almost totally concerned with a method, which itself is only tenuously related to the sort of phenomena we have been discussing. But furthermore, the method has restricted investigators' interest to the 'recognition' of external signals. Scarcely any attention has been paid to the recognition of signals from within. A wide range of fascinating questions remains, not only unanswered, but apparently unconsidered. In this section the failure to recognize memories as such has been described. Not only has experimental psychology provided no answers as to why this failure should occur, it has failed to examine how the recognition itself occurs. How do we recognize an idea or the solution to a problem as being old information rather than a new synthesis? When we succeed in recalling a name, a telephone number or some other piece of information, why is it that we recognize it as being what we were searching for? When we are unable to recall a fact, how is it that we know that the facts we run through do *not* include the one for which we are searching? In other words, how can we account for our appropriate *absence* of recognition? And what about TOT and the halfway feeling—when we recognize a piece of information as being *almost* what we have been searching for, but know that it is not quite right? (There is some experimental evidence which suggests that this feeling is valid; subjects who report it in relation to incorrect responses on a recall task may subsequently respond correctly to those items on a recognition task.) Only when answers are available to questions of this type is the problem of cryptomnesia likely to be illuminated.

L'ILLUSION DES SOSIES

Recall our discussion of 'doubles', and in particular the *doppelgänger* experience, where the individual recognizes an hallucinatory apparition as being his own double. Some examples of the *failure* of recognition where memories and ideas are concerned have just been discussed. And in the next section there is a discussion of the *jamais vu* experience, where the individual sees a well-known scene, knows that he knows it, but does not experience an appropriate sense of familiarity. A very rare and bizarre experience which has something in common with all the above is considered here. In *l'illusion des sosies* the individual correctly recognizes all the attributes of another person, but is unable to recognize the person as such. He becomes convinced that he is dealing with an impostor or double, and no amount of argument or evidence can persuade him to think otherwise. He becomes preoccupied with the situation, perplexed as to how and why the 'substitution' has taken place, and is often worried as to what fate can have overtaken the 'real' person.

In the discussion of doubles, it was noted that many eminent writers have been preoccupied with, or have directly experienced, *doppelgänger*. At least one famous poet, Cowper, is reported to have experienced *l'illusion des sosies* in relation to his intimate friend, the Reverend Newton. For several years after a depressive illness Cowper was never convinced that Newton was the *real* Newton. The cases described in the psychiatric literature have usually been diagnosed as suffering from paranoid psychotic illnesses. But when *l'illusion des sosies* occurs it dominates other symptoms and preoccupies the patient, so that French psychiatrists (who have shown most interest in the phenomenon) have tended to view it as a syndrome or illness in its own right. In a case described by Enoch *et al.* (1967) a quiet, fifty-year-old man was admitted to hospital with hallucinations and delusions that he was being persecuted by the police. Later, he began to believe that 'something had happened' to his wife, and that the person who visited him in hospital, although identical in every respect to his wife, 'is not my wife, but a double'. 'I love my wife very much,' he asserted, 'but not the woman double.'

The French word *sosie*, meaning an exact image or double, derives from classical mythology, where the god Mercury assumes the appearance of Amphitryon's servant, Sosie. The term '*l'illusion des sosies*' thus means 'the illusion of doubles'. Clearly, this is not a completely apt title, because the phenomenon just described would not conventionally be classified as an illusion. As noted earlier, Warren's definition of an illusion is: 'a misinterpretation of certain elements in a given experience, such that the experience does not represent the objective situation, present or recalled'. In the present instance the 'elements' are all perceived and interpreted appropriately. Descriptions in the literature stress that the experience is not related to inattention, intellectual deterioration or organic confusion. But in any case the sufferers not only describe all the attributes of the 'double' appropriately, but concede that they are identical to those of the 'original'. To use the terminology employed in discussing illusions, the subject receives all the attributes, sets up appropriate criteria and passes appropriate levels of match. But he is unable to accept the overall outcome. Thus the problem is not so much one of misinterpretation as of misidentification. But its major characteristic is the failure of recognition—the absence of the experience of familiarity. Why should this be? The main clue probably lies in the fact that the experience always relates, at least initially, to just one other person. The sufferer has no difficulty in identifying and recognizing his surroundings and all the objects therein. Nor do the other people around him seem anything but what they are. His problem relates specifically to one person. And that person is his spouse, lover, close relative or intimate friend. In other words, the person in question is always someone very important to the sufferer, a key person in his emotional life. Now in most of the cases reported, some prior grounds for doubt or hostility towards the key person have been elicited. And very often the patient, just prior to his illness, had evinced towards the key person an upsurge of affection or sexual yearning which had been repulsed. Thus the root of the problem seems to lie in an *ambivalence of attitude* towards the other person—an unresolved love-hate conflict.

It seems plausible that *l'illusion des sosies* can be explained along the lines of the previous arguments. If recognition is thought of as involving synthesis at various levels, the subject may identify and recognize every feature of the other person right up to the final level of schematic integration. But there the conflict area is reached. Suppose that the subject is a man and the unrecognized person is his wife. (In fact, the opposite is somewhat more common.) His 'my wife' schema may include all sorts of attributes and sub-schemata such as 'five foot two', 'eyes of blue', 'turned-up nose', 'turned-down hose' and 'never had no other beaus'. So far, so good. Each match is acceptable, and integration proceeds appropriately. But then further hierarchic matching is required, along the lines of 'could she love, could she coo?' And, suddenly, overall acceptance is blocked. For the overriding characteristics attributed by the subject to his wife may be 'she loves me, and I love her'. Whereas, unconsciously, he has come to detest her, and thinks he has some evidence that she is not too fond of him either. This is a not uncommon dilemma, and people find different ways of dealing with it. The obvious rational way, particularly when the conflict is consciously realized, is to modify the schema by cancelling such criteria as 'lovable', 'loves me' and so on. But one way is to say: 'Yes, this person is of exactly the right height and eye colour as my wife. Indeed, *all* her physical features are identical. But my "my wife" schema includes "loves me". I suspect that this person doesn't love me. So this person *can't* be my wife. She must be a double.' This position allows the subject to retain his 'my wife' schema intact, and at the same time justifies the conscious expression of his hostility, because this can now be directed at the villainous double.

This sort of approach will be developed, both in the remainder of this chapter and in the rest of the book. For not only is *l'illusion des sosies* a problem of recognition which reflects back to the discussions of illusions and *doppelgänger*, but it has direct implications for the study of such phenomena as derealization. And because it involves a false, preoccupying and unshakeable belief it is also directly connected with what will be said about delusions.

DÉJÀ VU

In the 'believe it or not' section of repertoires of personal anecdotes there is often one like this:

'I was about fifteen at the time. We'd gone on a school excursion to York [or Canterbury, Zürich or Wigtwistle-on-Sea]. I came around a corner from the High Street into one of those little eighteenth-century side streets. And suddenly *I knew I'd been there before*—I recognized the butcher's shop and the old inn sign—everything. The joke is that there's no doubt whatsoever that I'd never been near the place before in my life . . . I know it sounds rather mysterious. . . .'

The raconteur then shrugs modestly and sits back while his (or her) audience earnestly discuss possible explanations of the mystery.

Modestly, because the explanations usually imply that the raconteur possesses 'unusual powers'. (The skilled raconteur will often gently laugh off such suggestions, but follow up rapidly with that story about how he foretold all the First Division football results one week in 1967 but forgot to post his Pools coupon. Or that one about how he dreamed about Uncle Herbert's nasty accident with a combine harvester sixteen weeks before it actually occurred. . . .)

The 'unusual powers' suggestion is advanced because it is central to the three most common explanations of the 'been there before' phenomenon:

(1) The subject *had* been there before—*but in a previous life*. His 'unusual power' is that of being able to experience vestigial fragments of an earlier existence; he is walking evidence for reincarnation.

(2) The subject had not been there before in person. He had, however, experienced the situation vicariously through somebody else's mind. His 'unusual power' is that of telepathy. Or, if the other person lived long ago, he must be capable of mediumship.

(3) The subject had not been there before, therefore his previous experience of the scene was prophetic. His 'unusual power' is that of soothsaying, prophecy, the Sixth Sense or the transcending of time boundaries.

All such explanations may give the raconteur interest or status in the eyes of his audience; they certainly lend colour and interest to the social gathering by providing a talking point. They do not, however, find favour in the eyes of experimental psychologists, who tend to be sadly mundane in their approach to strange experiences and decidedly sceptical about 'unusual powers'. But it is not necessary to suggest that the raconteur is guilty of fabrication or even false recall. What he has described is not at all uncommon. It is an example of the experience known as *déjà vu* or *fausse reconnaissance*—the feeling of recognition accompanying perception of a scene or event which in fact has not been experienced previously. This is often reported by epileptics and psychiatric patients, but normal, healthy people may experience it occasionally. McKellar (1957) found that of 182 Aberdeen University students almost 70 per cent had had *déjà vu* experiences.

The converse of *déjà vu* is the *jamais vu* experience, where the individual reports that a situation or scene which he has experienced before does not have the quality of familiarity—'I knew it was my room, but I felt as though I'd never set eyes on it before.' *Jamais vu* is less common than *déjà vu* and it is possible that it is attributable to quite different mechanisms. But in phenomenological terms, the two

experiences are obviously comparable. Both are anomalies of recognition—one because the feeling of familiarity is inappropriately
intense, the other because it is inappropriately weak.

A related phenomenon is the *pseudo-presentiment*, where the person
witnessing an event feels, not that he has actually witnessed it before,
but that he has previously *foretold* it. The question is not one of
whether he did in fact prophesy it earlier. There is never any indication that he actually made any such prophecy prior to the event, nor
does he generally claim to have done so. The feeling is a pseudo-
presentiment, because it only grips him at the moment he is watching
the event unfold. There is a dream-like quality about the experience
of pseudo-presentiment, as there usually is about *déjà vu* and *jamais
vu*, and this may suggest to the individual that the presentiment
itself was revealed to him in a dream. This, he may subsequently
argue, is why he did not consciously recall it prior to the actual
event.

Déjà vu and its related phenomena have been described and discussed extensively in the psychiatric literature as disturbances of
memory or *paramnesias of temporal reference*. Janet, however, argued
that *déjà vu* should be regarded as an anomaly of perception. He
pointed out that the experience is a denial of the contemporary
presence of an event rather than a conviction of its pastness. It is to
do with how an individual *perceives* a situation, rather than how he
remembers anything. And it is true that the question is not primarily
one of whether or not an event has occurred before and is therefore
being remembered appropriately or not. It is certainly misleading to
place emphasis upon the event itself. The lay 'unusual powers'
approach, it will be noted, is based on the presumption that the witnessing of the event is in fact the *second* experience and focusses
attention on the hypothesized 'original' or *first* experience. But the
psychological problem involved is not the event itself but its accompanying flavour of 'I've seen all this before'-ness. In short, the issue
is not one of recall, although the subject may describe his experience
in terms of memory. It is not that he has remembered something
incorrectly, or failed to remember something, but that *he feels as
though he has*.

It seems most reasonable to classify these experiences, as done here,
as anomalies of recognition. *Déjà vu* could be termed an example of
false positive recognition, as opposed to *jamais vu*, which could be
termed a case of false negative recognition. But categorization of this
type does not of itself explain the phenomena, any more than the
unusual powers hypothesis. A major difficulty is that, as in many
other areas of unusual experience, the phenomena are not readily
amenable to experimental examination. People cannot experience

them to order. On the other hand, can one point to experimentally controlled situations in which subjects report similarly anomalous feelings of familiarity?

Clearly, emotions or 'feelings' are often inextricably associated with cognitive activity of which we are not aware. In the case of *déjà vu* it seems reasonable to suppose that the feeling of familiarity springs from recall activity which is not accessible to voluntary consideration. Bannister and Zangwill (1941) tested this experimentally by showing hypnotized subjects a series of pictures, and then inducing post-hypnotic amnesia. A few days later the subjects were again shown the pictures. Many of the subjects, whilst not recalling that they had seen the pictures before, reported a strong feeling of familiarity which they were unable to explain. Zangwill has pointed out that the findings suggest that there is a relationship between *déjà vu* and the memory of a psychologically associated event which is inaccessible to voluntary recall. The experiment was also a useful illustration of the production of 'feeling' in an experimental situation. On the other hand, it would be incautious to suggest that such findings 'explain' *déjà. vu*. These subjects might well be expected to experience a sense of familiarity as they looked at the pictures. After all, they had in fact seen them before. *Déjà vu* is usually experienced, or at least noticed, in circumstances which could not have been experienced by the individual before. He may, for instance, be on holiday abroad for the first time. There may be clear proof that he could not possibly have witnessed the event or scene in question previously.

Furthermore, the 'unavailability' approach cannot account for *jamais vu*. *Jamais vu* is rarer than *déjà vu* and no reports have been published of its occurrence in normal people. As we have noted, the two phenomena may not be associated. But phenomenologically the central feature of each is that of anomalous feelings of familiarity. Clearly, any hypothesis as to the psychological mechanisms involved will gain in plausibility if it can encompass both experiences. Unfortunately, as was implied earlier, the traditional 'recognition' experiments are unlikely to offer us any help here. But there are two types of experiments which seem to have something in common with the *jamais vu* experience. The first is the well-known 'loss of meaning of words' (LMW) phenomenon. If the reader cares to select a word and focus his attention upon it, staring at it for about a minute, he will find that it loses its significance. The word will no longer suggest any meaning to him, and may in fact no longer seem like a word. This effect, which may be a humble parallel to one of the techniques used to induce a state of mystical contemplation in oriental religions, is usually ascribed to cortical inhibition.

The second type of possibly relevant experiment is concerned with the effects of recall upon recognition. Bartlett's 'reconstruction' view of memory would suggest that attempts to recall a stimulus or event will involve modifications such as condensation, an emphasis on dominant details and interpolation. Each time the scene is recalled further modifications will be introduced. The subject's reconstruction may depart so much from the original that it is possible that if the original is reintroduced he will fail to recognize it, because in many ways it will no longer match the reconstruction. Belbin (1950) left her subjects in a waiting room for two minutes; on the wall facing them was a safety-first poster. The experimental group was then asked to recall as much as they could about the poster, prompted by standardized questions. The control group spent an equivalent time engaged in an unrelated task. They were then shown the original poster and asked if it was the one they had seen. Only four of the sixteen experimental subjects identified it correctly, whereas fourteen of the sixteen control subjects did so. Further experiments showed the same trend. As suggested above, recognition seemed to be related not so much to the number of items correctly recalled, but to the number of items erroneously imported during recall in an attempt to fill gaps. Bartlett had said that dominant details 'set the stage for remembering'. Belbin noted that, whilst setting the stage for remembering, after recall they upset the stage for recognition as though the 'scene-shifters had worked too hard'.

Perhaps in discussions of recognition too much stress has been put on the stimulus itself. Perception, as has been seen, is not a matter of passive reception or even of non-dynamic matching; it involves active structuring and synthesis. It is possible that, in experiencing a sense of familiarity, what we recognize is not the features of the stimulus itself, but that we have carried out the same perceptual and conceptual *structuring* before. Furthermore, our perceptual activity does not merely organize discrete, static stimulus items, but their patterning and interrelationships, both spatial and temporal. Thus when we recognize a friend after twenty years, many features of his earlier appearance will have changed. Some items may in fact have disappeared, whilst new ones will have been added. He may have lost his spots and much of his hair in the interval, but gained spectacles, wrinkles and a paunch. In practice then, we do not recognize him merely on a photographic or Identikit basis with allowances for age. It is more likely that we respond to dynamic patterning, such as mannerisms, posture or the way he smiles, i.e. not discrete visual items as such, but their temporal interrelationships. This might explain why we often fail to identify faces in school and college photographs. The photograph presents our classmates' features as we knew them. But it allows only a restricted range of spatial relationships to be restructured. (When we do experience vivid familiarity in examining such a memento, it is usually because we have fondly examined it at intervals over the years. In that case our sense of familiarity may be associated not with recognition of the people themselves, but with our previous study of this or similar photographs.) The process may work in the opposite direction in the case of people whom we have not seen in the flesh. It is often easier to recognize a celebrity from a picture or photograph than in person. This may be because the identifying features available to us are conveniently coded in a static manner in the photograph. They are submerged when we see the man himself by a wealth of dynamic relationships. So that it is possible that the very spatio-temporal dynamics which enable us to recognize people we know well will confuse those who only know them from photographs, and vice versa.

Again, we neither register nor recall separate items in any given situation with equal clarity. Some details dominate the others, because of our set and available schemata in conjunction with the associations or intrinsic interest of the details. If I try to visualize the view from my study window, I have a general 'feel' of the whole and can reproduce the overall scenic pattern. But the only individual item that I can image in detail is the chapel tower at the far right. It is a celebrated and very unusual architectural feature, and one which affords me considerable aesthetic satisfaction. Not only am I unable to image the row of houses in the left background; I have in the past failed to recognize a photograph of them. Out of context they gave me no sense of familiarity. So it is not surprising that we sometimes fail to recognize a person on second meeting. We probably failed to study his appearance with any care on the first occasion, or noted only some dominant feature. And this feature may not be in evidence when we see him next. We may have been introduced to the man on the street and vaguely registered his general stance and the fact that he was wearing a trilby hat. The next time we meet may be at a party, where he is seated and hatless. The most common source of embarrassment in this connection is attributable to changes in contextual relationships. We recognize somebody, but cannot 'place' him, simply because we associate him with a different situation. The perplexed sense of recognition without recall that we often feel in such a situation is very close to the *déjà vu* experience. This suggests that the mysterious *déjà vu* phenomenon may be not so much a question of anomalously present recognition as of a failure to recall features of a situation which have appropriately evoked the sense of familiarity.

The above suggestion has much in common with that proposed by

Zangwill, and at first sight they both seem to ignore the crucial feature of *déjà vu*—that the subject has in fact never experienced the situation before. But this is to emphasize again the objective stimulus features of the situation. It must be repeated that a situation to which we react with a *déjà vu* feeling may well have involved us in *perceptual organizing activity* sufficiently similar to what we have done previously to impart the sense of familiarity. This might well be the case even though no particular item in the field is identical to any we have previously encountered.

In practice, of course, no situation can be so novel as to contain nothing we have experienced before in some form. Indeed, a nice philosophical question of the 'how many angels . . .?' variety is posed by consideration of how we would respond to a display which was completely novel. As observed before, perception is in a sense a problem-solving, hypothesis-testing activity. Given that all the features of the display were novel to us, we should possess no categories to which we could assign it or any of its parts. In that case the question of recognition could not arise, because we should be unable to perceive anything in the first place. It may be noted that the medium or seer possessed of 'unusual powers' may now leap in to assert that this would explain why most of us are unable to perceive the spirits of the dead who coexist with us. Those with no experience of spirits, she might argue, have no categories to which to assign their attributes and are thus 'perceptually blind' to that class of phenomena. The answer to her claim would be the enquiry how, in that case, could she herself see them? To which she might well tartly reply that that was where her 'unusual powers' come in. . . . Similarly, it might be argued that the *absence* of familiarity in response to a known situation occurs when the perceptual structuring demanded is novel, despite previous experience of elements of the situation. But here, it must be admitted, we are on shakier ground.

On the other hand, if this is the answer, why is it that *déjà vu* is not more common than it is? It could be argued that during any individual's life-span he must do similar perceptual 'work' repeatedly. The answer here is that perhaps we *do* experience *déjà vu* more than we think, but discount the experience or fail to pay attention to it. Possibly what we should be trying to explain is, not why we sometimes experience an 'inappropriate' sense of familiarity, but why we are not aware of it more often.

6

ANOMALIES IN THE EXPERIENCE OF SELF

Experimental psychologists have shown an understandable reluctance to examine one topic which is central to psychology—*one's awareness of oneself*. Philosophers and psychiatrists, on the other hand, have devoted considerable attention to the subject, because the experience of self is fundamental to the whole of the individual's psychic life. It underlies, determines and colours all other experiences. Like other critical aspects of mind, we take it for granted and are only aware of it when it is disturbed in some way. It is almost impossible for a person in normal health to imagine what it would feel like *not* to be experiencing oneself as oneself. This is doubtless because imagining, like all other mental activities, normally occurs in the context of self-experience.

Clearly the experience of self is inextricably involved in all other cognitive activities and states because it underlies them and acts as a selector, integrator and synthesizer. In a sense all the experiences we care to discuss affect, or are affected by, this central experience. So it would be possible to discuss it partially in terms of, for example, attention, registration, memory, thinking or emotion. Being oneself determines how we attend and to what we pay attention. It is a product of all our stored experiences, and it determines our emotional responses. At the same time, the idea 'me' is a concept, the development and range of which can be considered like other concepts. However, so long as we bear in mind that the contents of this chapter will overlap considerably with those of the others, we can draw together a number of aspects of self-experience in which anomalies and disorders occur. It will be convenient to classify these separately, · but again it must be borne in mind that there is considerable overlap between these aspects also. The person who suffers a serious disorder in one type of self-experience may well suffer disorder in others. This is particularly the case in schizophrenia, which may involve disintegration of personality at a number of levels.

There are many ways in which we feel 'selfness'. Jaspers has presented an elaborate and rather confusing categorical system, but a simpler grouping will be employed here. We can consider the types of experience under four headings, disorders or anomalies of which can be arranged in order of decreasing severity or levels of disintegration:

(1) *Anomalies in the experience of the self as distinct from the outside world.* This represents disturbance at the most primary level of self-experience—the capacity to discriminate oneself from the environment. Disorder of this capacity implies that the person loses his awareness of himself as an individual.

(2) *Anomalies in the experience of the self as recognized in personal performance.* The individual may appreciate that he is a discrete entity, and yet not recognize ideas and activities as being his own. In this case, he may attribute some of his thoughts, imagery, actions, etc. to agencies outside himself.

(3) *Anomalies in the experience of the unity of self.* The individual may be aware of himself as an individual and recognize the personal origin of his activities, but yet experience a detachment or split in the unity of his self. He may feel as though he is standing apart from himself.

(4) *Anomalies in the experience of reality of oneself and the environment.* The individual may be fully aware of himself and his actions, experience himself as a unity, but yet experience a lack of conviction of the reality of himself and/or the environment. He feels an uneasy sense of change and strangeness.

THE BLURRING OF EGO BOUNDARIES

Patients suffering from certain illnesses often describe experiences which suggest that they have lost the capacity to distinguish between themselves and their environment. Such a patient may report, for instance, that objects and people around him are *inside* him or that he is a part of them. For example, one patient referred to other people in the ward as: 'All moving, rushing inside my head. . . . They're swinging round, pushing the head out.' He may experience occurrences related to other people or to inanimate objects as though they were happening to him. Another patient complained that he was being pushed when he saw a trolley being trundled down the hospital corridor. A woman patient hearing nails being knocked into a wall could feel them penetrating *her*. A man seeing a carpet being beaten asked why *he* was being beaten. The patient may feel as though he has become abstract, or as though he exists only as an attribute of things in the environment. 'Just a spot . . . a dot . . . a point like in geometry. No shape. . . .' Interestingly enough, the reports given by patients often betray some confusion in the use of personal pronouns and possessive adjectives, as in the first example. One patient, when asked how he was feeling, replied: 'It doesn't feel. He is existing among everything. . . . Their head is sort of swimming. . . .'

All these experiences suggest a failure to maintain a distinction between 'me'-ness and 'out there'-ness; they imply that the *self-concept* has become diffuse or faulty. The subject has lost subjective awareness of his autonomy, and can no longer appreciate that he is an individual entity separate from the environment. This is referred to as the *blurring of ego boundaries*. It can occur in a number of illnesses, but when it persists in a patient whose consciousness is clear (i.e. who is not delirious, drowsy or semi-conscious) it is regarded by most psychiatrists as being a primary symptom of schizophrenia. Indeed, authorities such as Federn (1952) maintain that the blurring of ego boundaries is not merely a symptom of that illness, but the process responsible for it. Can it occur in normal people? Clearly, a man who takes a walk in the garden and reports that he is grass, or that he is being mowed, or that he is a cabbage or the space between the cabbages, would in our culture immediately forfeit his right to be regarded as unequivocally normal. And the examples given above are similarly bizarre and not consonant with what we would usually accept as normal experiences. However, the oddity of all these cases resides in their *content*. If the *form* of the experience is considered it is certainly unusual but can be detected in experiences which would not be regarded as pathological.

One example of an experience which possesses the same form as the schizophrenic experience, but a content which is not only accepted but respected is *nirvana*. In the original Sanskrit, nirvana means 'blowing out' or extinction. The term is used to refer to the extinction of individuality and *absorption into the supreme spirit*. In Buddhism and certain other religions nirvana is the attainment of perfect beatitude, an experience to be striven for as the high-point of existence by the devout. Similarly, several of the classical phenomena associated with mysticism in our own culture as well as many others present the same formal characteristics. The experiences described as 'oneness', 'unity', 'oblivion' and 'expansion of consciousness' all involve the merging of the individual's self with the outside world, although this is described in different ways and with metaphysical connotations. Far from being regarded as pathological symptoms, such experiences are regarded by society with a certain awe, as bearing witness to the spirituality, virtue and self-discipline of those who experience them. The subjects themselves are not only undisturbed by the experiences, but welcome them and actively search for their attainment. As William James observed: 'The overcoming of the usual barriers between the individual and the Absolute is the great mystic achievement. . . .' This emphasizes the nice point that in certain contexts ego boundaries may be viewed not as desirable cognitive structures, but as undesirable barriers. Far from maintaining them, the devout person should aim towards their dissolution.

It may be suggested then, with some caution and in the face of most psychiatric opinion, that the phenomenological form of ego-boundary blurring is not pathological *per se*. The subjective experience of this phenomenon, like so many others described in this book, is determined by *cognitive labelling*. When it is experienced in association with delirium, toxic states or epilepsy it is regarded by the individual as strange or frightening. Similarly, when it is experienced by a person who is suffering from a psychotic illness he reacts to it with perplexity and disturbance, because he is already perplexed and disturbed. But when the experience occurs in a mystical or religious setting it may be welcomed as the transcendental ultimate in spiritual bliss.

So far, we have discussed the blurring of ego boundaries in terms of its extreme manifestations as though these were discrete phenomena. But it is at least possible that the schizophrenic symptom, as well as nirvana, unity and so on, merely refer to the extremes of a continuum. In fact, there are two continua to be considered. Any given individual on a given occasion may have the experience with more or less intensity. The mystic may induce more or less blurring of boundaries, but only report himself as having experienced unity on the occasions when he induces more; the symptom may only be recognized in the schizophrenic when it is extreme. But apart from these differences *within* individuals, there are clearly differences *between* individuals. And this will apply not only to the extreme manifestations, but to the milder ones. In other words, the degree to which individuals' ego boundaries vary from clear to blurred may constitute a *personality variable*. Some experimental work which may be of high relevance to this suggestion will be considered below.

In normal health we sustain a flexibility and balance in our transactions with the world around us. As discussed earlier, our attention to the environment varies appropriately, we sample in-coming signals, order them according to the demands of the moment, organize them and store them. In operation, the strategy requires selection among signals, which presupposes discrimination and analysis of the field so that relatively irrelevant elements can be filtered out. At the same time, significant signals are being assimilated into appropriate schemata. A busy, adaptive state is thus maintained. But this can be disturbed by extremities of intensity or unexpectedness in the input on the one hand, or by impairment of the cognitive processes themselves.

Here again, the work of the Witkin group is of direct relevance. One way of interpreting the behaviour of the extremely field-dependent person is that his relative failure in differentiation applies to his awareness of his own body in relation to its surroundings. It may be suggested that he is insufficiently conscious of *himself* as a separate entity. He finds difficulty in determining the boundaries between his ego and the environment. This applies not only to his body in relation to his physical environment, but to his inner life (somatic signals, cognitions, etc.) in relation to outside events. There is an interesting parallel here with the findings of developmental psychologists, several of whom have noted that at first the infant is unable to differentiate himself as an entity. Piaget, in *The language and thought of the child*, refers to this as 'adualism'. The child has to learn to differentiate between its own processes (perception, thinking, motor activity) and between the inputs from its different sense modalities. But first it has to distinguish between its own sensations and external correlates, between internal and external events. (This is very similar to Freud's views regarding object relationship; he maintained that the child's first object relationships were merged with itself. The development of the concept of self as a separate identity, Freud termed 'primary identification'.) It was noted earlier that patients who experience the blurring of ego boundaries often show confusion in their use of personal pronouns. There have been several studies of children's use of pronouns which indicate that at first they refer to themselves in the third person, e.g. 'Timmy poorly!' Later, they refer to themselves as 'me', e.g. 'Me want bicky!' Finally they develop the concept and usage of 'I'.

Freud's view that the development of the 'self' concept involves the internalization of objects of social interaction has been paralleled by socially-orientated writers, who stress the individual's assimilation of the characteristics and attitudes of people who play a significant part in his upbringing. And Fisher and Cleveland (1958) maintain that the degree of definition of ego boundaries is a direct reflection of the degree of structuring of these early social relations. If they were well defined in childhood, the individual will attain a clearly articulated 'role' and his ego boundaries will be precise. If they were vague or inconsistent, then his ego boundaries will be similarly diffuse.

The field-dependent person, therefore, might be regarded either as being retarded in certain aspects of development, or the product of inconsistent socialization. He is either relatively immature or relatively poorly reared where primary identification is concerned. And similarly it could be argued that the schizophrenic is grossly retarded in this respect (or, more plausibly, has regressed to an infantile level) or has suffered an upbringing of remarkable fluidity and contradiction. Equally, it could be that the retardation is itself due to inconsistent socialization.

So far, a *cognitive style* or personality characteristic has been discussed which is presumed to be continuously distributed in the population, with ego-boundary blurring at one extreme of the distribution. It is postulated that there are differences between individuals in terms of this characteristic which is generally consistent *within* the individual. But as shown, not only do we each have our individual level of ego-boundary strength, but it can be modified. Boundary blurring can occur as a result of physical changes; or we can induce it—either by deliberately arranging the physical changes, or by psychological techniques. One relatively common example is that of getting drunk. William James noted that in the 'maudlin' stage of drunkenness: 'The centre and periphery of things seem to come together. The ego and its objects, the *meum* and the *tuum*, are one.' (This James described as the 'immense emotional sense of *reconciliation*' characterizing the 'maudlin' stage which, he claimed: 'seems silly to the lookers-on, but the subjective rapture of which probably constitutes a chief part of the temptation to the vice . . .'.) The same experience is characteristic of the effects of psychedelic drugs taken at fairly high dosages. Thus Downing (1969) reports that at dosages of two micrograms of LSD per pound of body weight: 'ego integration is lost and consciousness of individual personality, the "I", disappears like a drop of water merging with the ocean'. However, strictly speaking, these experiences are not identical with the schizophrenic one, because during intoxication with alcohol or psychedelic drugs the individual's consciousness is not clear. But this objection does not apply to mystic experiences which are voluntarily induced, usually after stringent training, meditation and self-discipline.

For many centuries the most common way of inducing mystic states has been by the practice of 'contemplative meditation'. In recent years this has become popularly associated with Zen Buddhism, an off-shoot of Mahāyāna Buddhism. Zen was originally formulated in China, but has been a central feature of Japanese religion and culture for some seven hundred years. However, contemplative meditation has figured among the devotional activities of many other religions, including Taoism, Hinduism (yoga is the Hindu ascetic practice of meditation) and Christianity. The content of meditation exercises differs, of course, from religion to religion. But the basic form of the practice is surprisingly similar, although different features are emphasized in the various teachings. Firstly, the subject learns how to relax physically without falling asleep; this may involve series of breathing exercises and the assumption of appropriate body postures, such as the cross-legged 'lotus' position. Then he practises concentrating upon a single thought, a name or, more usually, an object such as a flower, a cross, a bowl or his navel. Eventually he acquires the capacity to concentrate upon this to the exclusion of all other stimuli, whether external or internal. Environmental distractions are completely ignored and active cognitive activities are inhibited. The subject becomes intensely aware but passively receptive of a spontaneous stream of experience. (This deliberate inculcation of a passive, receptive attitude probably accounts for the decline of mysticism in Western cultures, which have stressed for several centuries the desirability of active, competitive and reality-orientated attitudes.) The experience is clearly similar to that of a subject in a hypnotic trance; the main difference is in the content element and the subsequent emotional attributions. The mystic's experience is in a spiritual setting, and so he invests it with feelings of ineffable bliss or tranquillity. The hypnotic subject's experience is usually in a neutral setting so that he has no particular emotional response, nor any feeling that he has attained a state loaded with special significance.

The psychological state of contemplative meditation described above can be induced experimentally, although of course without any mystic content. Deikman (1963) has reported a study of four subjects who were encouraged to meditate during twelve short (about fifteen minutes) sessions over a three-week period. They sat comfortably in a small, quiet room, being instructed to concentrate on a blue vase. Subsequently they reported many of the phenomena classically associated with mystic states, including perceptual changes, changes of consciousness and visual dedifferentiation. One subject reported that she had begun to feel 'almost as though the blue and I were perhaps merging, or that vase and I were. . . .' Again, the blurring of ego boundaries has been reported by subjects in sensory-deprivation experiments of the kind described in Chapter 2. These subjects were not instructed to concentrate on anything. But characteristically, sensory-deprivation subjects become passive and receptive; and whilst they are not encouraged to shut out distracting stimuli, such experimental situations are deliberately devised to eliminate as many stimuli as possible.

The central feature of the mystic experience and its experimental analogues seems to be the *redeployment of attention*. Attention is focussed upon one feature to the exclusion of all others, whilst active, on-going cognitive activity is suspended. It could be said that by intensive, narrow focussing the feature is divorced from its schematic setting. In effect, a temporary de-synthesis of schematic relations is thus effected. Few individuals are motivated to try to achieve this situation. But in any case, it may be presumed that there are great individual differences in the capacity to achieve it. Mystics and drug-takers, it must be assumed, are people who are prepared to reject the hard-headed criteria of reality-orientation which are normal in our culture. For various reasons they are motivated to loosen their normal conceptual bounds and cognitive organizations. At the same time, their motivation itself may well be associated with their normal cognitive style. Perhaps we can summarize this by saying that the individual who can readily experience the blurring of ego boundaries is probably a Witkin-type 'global' perceiver employing a Gardner-type 'focussing' strategy.

THE LOSS OF PERSONAL ATTRIBUTION

Psychotic patients often complain that their thoughts are not in fact their own, but are derived from some external source. They may believe that their actions or impulses are influenced by an outside agency, or that their thoughts and impulses are shared by others. Many such experiences may be regarded as representing the breakdown of ego boundaries described in the last section. But conventionally they are considered separately, in terms of a feature they all have in common—the *loss of personal attribution*. The experience of one's own activities as being reflective of, or due to, some force outside oneself necessarily implies the absence of awareness of the personal quality of those activities. Normally, it is practically impossible to divorce our activities, mental and physical, from their flavour of 'mine'-ness; indeed, in a sense, our thoughts, feelings and actions *are us*. So that, whilst it is easy to think of analogies to the situation, it is very difficult to imagine what it would feel like. One analogy would be the subject in a hypnotic trance, but a closer parallel is that of some inanimate object which is directly manipulated by its controller, such as a marionette. The idea of a living person being at the same time a marionette has eery and disturbing connotations. It has chilled men from time immemorial and figures in many myths, superstitions and primitive religious beliefs. Perhaps the best-known example still in circulation is the zombie, which originated in a West Indian superstititon that dead bodies could be revitalized by witchcraft. Thenceforward the corpse acted as a projection of the witch, putting into effect her evil desires. The horrifying feature of the zombie is, of course, that it has no desires of its own, no will, thoughts or personality. It is a human body without a mind. The normal person can imagine how a zombie might behave, but not how it feels. But similar experiences are characteristic of schizophrenic illnesses, and indeed are regarded by many psychiatrists as being among the most important diagnostic indicators (Schneider's 'first rank symptoms') of those illnesses. Several types of this experience have been differentiated.

Alienation of thought is the term applied to the patient's experience that his thoughts are controlled, influenced or participated in by others. At the simplest level of this, as of the other related experiences, the patient does not attribute control to any specific agency. He is merely uneasily aware that his thoughts are not really his own. But many patients try to 'explain' their experience by attributing it to some outside power or influence. They may blame mysterious forces or agencies such as the police, secret agents, members of political groups or religious sects, personal enemies or even the doctors who are treating them. These agencies are imagined to exert their influence by a variety of means such as hypnosis, telepathy, X-rays, radio or television transmitters.

In *thought insertion* the patient believes that his thoughts are drained away by some outside power. This is quite beyond his own control, being done despite his efforts. He may complain that at one moment his mind is occupied with a stream of thoughts; at the next, somebody has siphoned them all off. (This may be the subjective experience of the phenomenon known as *thought blocking*, when the patient is presumed to stop thinking because he may be observed to cease responding, attending, speaking, etc. This is reported to be outside the patient's control; if he is aware that it has happened, he may subsequently say that his train of thought just stopped. This may leave a vacuum, or replacement by a completely different set of thoughts.)

In *thought broadcasting*, as the term implies, the patient believes that everybody is able to 'tune in' to his thinking. He may feel that the 'listeners' are merely an interested, but usually critical audience. They may, however, share or participate in his thoughts. Or they may think in unison with him.

If the patient attributes any of the above symptoms to an outside force, but does not specify its nature, they are referred to as *passivity experiences*. If he provides delusional 'explanations' as to the agency responsible for the exertion of influence, then his experiences are termed *delusions of passivity*. So far passivity has been considered only in relation to thinking, but it is also experienced in relation to motor activities, impulses and feelings. Thus, the patient may believe that his limbs are being manipulated as he moves about; this would be termed *motor passivity*. Or he may believe that his emotional responses are imposed upon him, which can be termed *emotional passivity*.

Passivity experiences are characteristic of schizophrenic illnesses, and it is generally accepted that they occur rarely, if ever, in normal, healthy people. They are usually reported by patients who are suffering from other psychiatric symptoms, and the more bizarre manifestations of delusions of passivity are described by patients whose personalities have become seriously disorganized. But the bizarrerie relates to the *content* of the experience. The basic feature of the *form* of passivity is that thoughts, actions, feelings or impulses are experienced as lacking personal quality. Normal people frequently have experiences which are at least similar to this. The main differences are that these 'normal' experiences (1) occur in unusual circumstances, usually involving some sort of stress, and (2) they are of short duration, usually lasting only as long as the precipitating situation. Passivity experiences, on the other hand, are not related to particular situations, unless the patient's illness be regarded as a 'situation'. They become part—very often a dominating or preoccupying part—of the patient's everyday mode of thinking. They last as long as his illness; indeed, some psychiatrists might say that the disturbance which they represent *is* his illness. In a chronic schizophrenic they may remain with him all his life. In short, the crucial difference is one of duration. There would appear to be no qualitative differences which would cast doubt on the drawing of parallels or comparisons between the cognitive processes underlying the pathological and the common experiences as far as form is concerned. This will be attempted at the end of this chapter.

But what of delusions of passivity, where the patient attributes his experience to something, and thus introduces content? Strangely enough, it is easier to find parallels among normal people's experience in this respect. Three phenomena immediately spring to mind—ESP, mediumship and revelation. The telepathic percipient believes that he has the power to receive the thoughts of others. Whilst actually indulging that power, therefore, it follows that he must believe that certain of his cognitions are not his own. And he is committed to making the attribution that they belong to other people, notably his 'agent'. Given that he sincerely believes this, then, in the terms we have been employing, he is suffering from delusions of passivity.

Similarly, the medium claims that during her trance she is merely the agent or channel for the thoughts and communications of other people or, more usually, their spirits. Indeed, the content of her attributions may be more bizarre than that of many schizophrenics. The schizophrenic's influencers are usually his contemporaries or extant organizations; the medium's 'controls' have usually been dead for a very long time. Furthermore, the schizophrenic's policemen, scientists and secret agents pale into insignificance beside the medium's Red Indian chiefs, Chinese mandarins and ancient Egyptians.

In the case of revelation the subject experiences a vivid and sudden insight which he attributes to divine intervention. Not all revelations are attributed in this way; sometimes the subject may simply feel that he has been granted the ability to perceive the truth. But in many cases the percipient believes that his revelation was put into his mind by the Almighty. The reason why he was selected to be the recipient of wisdom in this way may not be communicated to him. It may be taken to be part of a divine plan which is not amenable to mortal understanding. But he may believe himself to have justified his selection by the strength of his faith or his unswerving devotion to the right path. Again, strictly speaking, if he sincerely believes all this he is suffering from highly systematized delusions of passivity. And to those who do not share his faith, these beliefs will appear to be about as bizarre as can be.

Why is it then that none of the above experiences is generally categorized as pathological? Simply because each possesses considerable (though diminishing) consensual validity. They are not deviant in terms of the norms of belief prevalent in our culture. A large number of people accept the validity of ESP and mediumship, and many more accept the validity of certain types of religious faith. Each set of beliefs presupposes the desirability, if not the necessity, of suspending objective standards of determination. And each not only allows for, but requires that experiences of the sort described should occur. To those who believe, such experiences are not only accepted, they are *expected* to occur. To the person who believes in ESP the telepathic percipient who possesses thoughts which are not his own is not out of the ordinary; on the contrary, it is the telepathist who possesses only his own thoughts who is abnormal. Whilst to the adherents of many religious creeds, the maintenance of their faith depends upon certain of their number occasionally receiving thoughts from outside themselves. Here we have an example of the way in which societies gauge the individual's experiences in terms of cultural norms which vary with time and between societies. According to the prevailing norms, the setting in which it occurs and the individual's personal response to it, an experience may be deemed highly desirable on the one hand or dangerously pathological on the other. In the present instance, however, passivity usually occurs in a setting of wider disturbance. It is unwelcome or distressing for the individual, and he does not manage to adjust to it, or interpret it in a manner which solaces him or is acceptable to society. The very similar experiences involved in telepathy and revelation occur in people of intact personality who welcome and even strive for their occurrence and who place them in a cognitive setting which is gratifying to them and highly acceptable to society.

IMPAIRMENT OF THE UNITY OF SELF

Both of the changed self-experiences described above—the blurring of ego boundaries, and passivity feelings—are, in their characteristically severe forms, associated with serious mental illness. The phenomena to be described in the remaining two sections are often reported by psychiatric patients, but are also quite common amongst normal people under certain conditions. Although they are usually described as separate phenomena and may be discriminated in terms of their phenomenology, they are closely related and are probably manifestations of the same sort of disturbance in psychological functioning. For this reason they will be considered together in the discussion at the end of this chapter.

It was seen how in emergency situations our attention becomes limited and segmentalized. The effects of emergency situations on mnemonic processes were subsequently noted. Just as certain features of threatening situations demand attention at the expense of others, so we recall certain pieces of relevant information, but not all their interrelationships or their appropriate temporal ordering. In both cases there seems to be a fragmentation of component elements, a loosening of global synthesis. Now exactly the same sort of de-synthesization may be observed at other levels of cognitive organization under conditions of stress. And disturbance may occur not only in situations involving actual danger, but in the face of almost any intolerable threat. What constitutes an intolerable threat varies from individual to individual, both as regards the degree of stress involved and the nature of that stress. A skilled mountaineer may be quite composed as he negotiates the hazards of a 1000-foot rock face. He may suffer the agonies of the damned if called upon to play postman's knock at a party. The actress may thrill to the challenge of manipulating an audience of hundreds, but go to any lengths to avoid what is to her the intolerable strain of coping with the ardent advances of one admirer in the back seat of a taxi. The writer has known several jolly extroverts, well known for their skill as raconteurs, who have dissolved into states of near-collapse when called upon to make a short after-dinner speech. Some people cannot face the prospect of face-to-face conflict, however just their cause; others flee from social gatherings if they include an unexpectedly high proportion of strange faces. All these examples relate to social situations, but there are many other areas of conflict where the figure of threat is the man within. Furthermore, inner turmoil may result more from the *prospect* of an event than from the event itself. The dentist's waiting room sees more anguish than his chair. Again, every individual's life has its quota of failures, disappointments and tragedies. Each of us faces his own struggles for adjustment to these blows; and the battles are usually fought out in privacy. So, although we shall continue to refer to 'stress', 'danger' and 'emergency', it should be remembered that these terms have reference to many situations besides those which involve physical danger and objectively determinable threat.

Extreme danger often seems to evoke a peculiar sense of detachment. It is as though the threatened person walls off his reactions, so that he is no longer aware of emotion. This is termed *dissociation of affect*. It may be seen as a biological defence which prevents the individual from being swamped by excessive emotions. It is adaptive, inasmuch as it allows him to endure the situation and continue to function for the time being. Later on, of course, he may suffer a reaction as emotional awareness floods back. Thus combat troops and aircrew may break down after prolonged action. But, during the stress of action itself, it is common for them to experience a sort of 'emotional tunnel-vision'. This prevents them from responding to all the terrifying implications of the situation, to its abhorrent aspects or to those which would induce an excess of pity. Instead, they experience an unnatural, blunted calm. The experience has been described as 'feeling drugged' or 'machine-like'. 'After the first few hours it wasn't me in that slit trench,' recalled one young soldier, 'it was a zombie with a machine gun.' Fish quotes as an example David Livingstone's description of how he felt as he was being savaged by a lion: 'It caused a sense of dreaminess in which there was no sense of pain nor feeling of terror, though I was quite conscious of all that was happening.'

As indicated above, the milder threats of everyday life also evoke dissociative defences at various levels. Perhaps they are most commonly experienced, as suggested, in socially stressful situations, particularly where evaluation of the subject is implied. Thus, many examination candidates and interviewees who are very anxious before the ordeal commences, report that they feel unnaturally calm during the situation itself. But they may observe that their bodies betray them—however 'tranquil' they may feel, their hands sweat, their throats are dry and their knees knock. Meanwhile, their performance in the examination or interview is not necessarily improved by their unusual sense of calm. Some athletes complain that their psychological defences are too efficient just before important races, and they may deliberately allow themselves to feel 'worked up' just prior to the start in order to 'put an edge' on their performance. Similarly public speakers, actors and entertainers who suffer from stage fright may experience dissociation of affect as soon as they are actually on the stage. But this may impede their attempts to give a convincing or emotionally-toned performance. They have to try to strike a balance between the disintegration of performance associated with panic and the preternatural detachment associated with dissociation. Unfortunately, dissociation is not amenable to voluntary control; the performer can only try to modify his state of mind by psychological preparation before the event.

Another form of dissociative reaction to stress is *ego-splitting*. Here, instead of, or as well as, feeling unnaturally calm, the subject experiences an even more explicit type of detachment—he feels as though he is actually *outside himself*. The sensation is of being suspended outside one's body, at some vantage point from whence one can calmly observe and hear oneself in the third person. Ego-splitting appears to be fairly common among young university teachers delivering their first lecture to a large class. 'There was a Madame Tussaud's figure propped up against the lectern. I was floating about six feet above its head, watching it.' 'I could hear this voice drooling on. Suddenly I realized it must be mine!'

One experience which may initially be emotionally overwhelming is that of bereavement. Dissociation of affect or ego-splitting are common defensive reactions to the loss of a loved one, as witness the comment: 'She didn't seem as upset as you'd expect. The news hasn't sunk in yet.' This implies that when the news does eventually 'sink in' the bereaved person will display the catastrophic emotional reaction which is at first absent. The apparent callousness which bereaved relatives sometimes attribute to each other is often due to dissociative defences in individuals who might otherwise have suffered disintegration. 'I couldn't cry. I didn't really feel anything. Everything seemed unreal, including me. It was as though I was seeing it happen to somebody else.' These words of a young widow describe the experiences of both dissociation of affect and ego-splitting. The reference to unreality suggests that she was also depersonalized, an experience which will be discussed in the next section.

THE LOSS OF THE EXPERIENCE OF REALITY

For most of us, most of our waking life, we experience ourselves and our surroundings as 'real'. This is a normal state of affairs which we generally take for granted; so much is this so that few people ever entertain the possibility that things could be otherwise. Only very introspective individuals, mystics and those with a philosophical turn of mind give much consideration to the matter. The majority of us are unaware of the fact that we feel real until something happens to make us feel less so. Such occurrences are not so rare as might be thought, but the nature of the experience escapes our attention for two reasons. Firstly, at the time we are usually in no condition to engage in introspective analysis, and secondly the experience usually occurs in circumstances that we subsequently prefer to forget. For instance, it must be experienced in thousands of homes on the First of January each year as the result of over-enthusiastic Hogmanay celebrations. The sufferer from a severe hangover generally pays for his revelry with queasiness and a variety of aches and pains. But he often also has the strange experience that, whilst the things around him are the same as ever though viewed through a haze, he is not himself. It is not merely that his head is aching and his stomach bubbling; his total self is different or unfamiliar. He may describe this in different ways—he feels 'as though I'm not here', or 'this isn't me'. Sometimes in the midst of his discomfort he feels an odd tranquillity, as though the quivering carcass clutching its ice-pack is not *really* going through all this at all.

This experience is called *depersonalization*. Its basic form is that the individual, whilst retaining his awareness of personal identity, feels himself to be *altered* in some way. In itself, the subjective awareness of change is not unusual; we say that we 'feel a new man' after a bath or a hearty meal, or that we 'are twice the man we were' after fulfilling an ambition or otherwise being cheered up. Conventionally, the term depersonalization is not applied to such normal, happy feelings of change. Indeed, some authorities have claimed that clinical depersonalization is always accompanied by a 'flattening of affect', inasmuch as the patient complains that he feels incapable of warm emotional response. But this may merely represent the introduction of an intervening variable. The patients observed may have been anxious or depressed in the first place. Their affective state is not necessarily associated with depersonalization as such but with the disturbance which induced them to present themselves as patients. Cheerful depersonalized people are unlikely to feel the need for psychiatric help. But the depersonalization experience also involves a sense of *unreality* or strangeness related to that of change, and this may well be disturbing. Again, however, most of us have experienced a sense of unreality at some time without regarding it as unpleasant. People who have just fallen in love or won a fortune on the Pools often say that they cannot believe that they are awake, that nothing seems real any longer, and so on. But they are seldom heard to complain about it. Many people engage in religious rites or mystic rituals with the express purpose of transcending the bounds of mundane reality. Similarly, drugs such as alcohol, hashish and opium all blur or diminish awareness of reality in some way. Many such conditions may correctly be termed depersonalization, although, conventionally, this is presumed to be an unwelcome and unpleasant experience.

Finally, most authorities also claim that the depersonalization is accompanied by *insight*. Not only does the subject remain aware of his personal identity but he appreciates that his sense of change and unreality is subjective and does not represent any *real* change. In the schizophrenic experiences we discussed earlier, the patient is unaware of the subjective nature of his experience and is thus the victim of delusion. It is asserted that in depersonalization patients recognize the 'as if' quality of their experience. They neither believe that any objective change or reality shift has occurred, nor do they elaborate or systematize the experience in a delusional manner. But this claim seems to lose sight of the fact that a psychotic patient may well suffer from depersonalization, in which case he may well interpret the experience delusionally. As Ackner (1954) has pointed out, different aspects of the depersonalization experience have been emphasized by different writers; at the same time, it coexists with many mental states and disorders and may be due to many different causes. Psychiatrists searching for a neat syndrome have thus found it difficult to establish acceptable criteria, and Ackner decided that it was probably impossible to give a precise definition of the experience. But the central features seem clear enough. It is generally agreed that depersonalization refers to an experience where the subject, whilst retaining awareness of his personal identity, feels himself to be changed and has an uncanny sense of unreality. It seems probable that most of the terminological and diagnostic confusion has been due to failures to distinguish between (1) depersonalization itself and concomitant experiences related to primary mental disorders, and (2) depersonalization and the other disturbances of self-experience which we have described above. Thus, on the one hand, a psychiatric patient may combine his depersonalization experiences with, or express them in terms of, hallucinations or delusions. On the other, his description of passivity or the weakening of ego boundaries may be labelled as depersonalization by the psychiatrist.

Depersonalization is experienced occasionally by many normal people. In one survey of college students, almost half gave questionnaire responses which suggested that they had experienced dissociative depersonalization at some time. The experience seems to be most commonly associated with stress situations, especially those involving social embarrassment. In the example at the beginning of this section, that of hangover, it is caused by the toxic effects of alcohol, but it can also occur as the result of other physical conditions such as fatigue, or in association with the languor of convalescence from illness. As might be expected, depersonalization is a common feature in psychiatric cases. Occasionally it may be the only discernible symptom, when the patient is diagnosed as suffering from a 'depersonalization syndrome'. Usually, however, it is reported in the setting of some more general disorder. It can occur in any mental illness, but seems to be most common in obsessional disorders and in depressive states. In clinical practice the phenomenon is reported with most distress by young female patients, in some of whom it may persist continuously for years. In other cases it may be transient, but nevertheless cause considerable distress. Patients suffering from depressive psychoses are wont to interpret their depersonalization experiences as indications that they have been 'cut off from God's grace'. When dissociation of affect is also present they may add to the self-approach which is characteristic of their illness by interpreting their condition as a sign that they have lost the capacity to love their families. Such conviction of isolation and unworthiness often triggers off thoughts of suicide.

The feeling of unreality or change may have reference to the person as a whole or to some part of him. This may give rise to some very bizarre ideas. Thus, in middle-aged depressives, severe depersonalization can lead to delusions that their bowels have rotted away, or that they themselves have ceased to exist (nihilistic ideas or *délire de négation*). Or they may believe that their bodies have swollen to a fantastic size (*délire d'énormité*). One outcome of the latter delusion is that some patients are afraid to urinate in case they flood the world. Such a case was described by Soranus the Elder in the second century A.D. Somewhat more recently, André du Laurens, physician to Henry IV of France, gave an amusing account of how a similar problem was cured by an early form of behaviour therapy:

The pleasantest dotage that ever I read, was one Sienois, a Gentleman, who had resolved with himselfe not to pisse, but to dye rather, and that because he imagined that when he first pissed, all his towne would be drowned. The Physitions shewing him, that all his bodie, and ten thousand more such as his, were not able to containe so much as might drowne the least house in the towne, could not change his minde from this foolish imagination. In the end they seeing his obstinacie, and in what danger he put his life, found out a pleasant invention. They caused the next house to be set on fire, & all the bells in the town to ring, they perswaded diverse servants to crie, to the fire, to the fire, and therewithall send of those of the best account in the town, to crave helpe, and shew the Gentleman that there is but one way to save the towne, and that it was, that he should pisse quickelie and quench the fire. Then this sillie melancholike man which abstained from pissing for feare of loosing his towne, taking it for graunted, that it was now in great hazard, pissed and emptied his bladder of all that was in it, and was himselfe by that means preserved.

Other depersonalization content appears to be culture bound. 'Koro', for instance, is a type of depersonalization syndrome which is associated with the southern Chinese. It has been reported in South China, Hong Kong and among Chinese communities in Malaysia and Indonesia, but is apparently unknown in Japan, Korea, South Asia, the Philippines and the Near East. Only very few cases have been reported in Europe (by Kraepelin, among others). Koro is a state of acute anxiety and partial depersonalization in which the sufferer is convinced that his/her genitalia are shrivelling into non-existence. It is reported that male patients rush to their doctors in extreme panic, complaining that their penises are disappearing. Such a patient may be accompanied by his wife or a friend whom he has induced to hang on to his penis to prevent it shrinking out of sight. Or he may have anchored it by lashing it to a heavy object, a jeweller's weight-box being a popular anchor.

Associated with depersonalization is *derealization*. Here the individual feels, not so much that *he* is changed or unreal, but that his *surroundings* have lost reality. The things around him seem to be flat and lacking in significance. One young woman described the experience as follows: 'Everything seemed muzzy, as though it wasn't really there. I couldn't understand it—it was like walking through a dream. Everything was ordinary, but nothing was real any longer....' It should be noticed that the experience does not imply any failure in perception. It is not a question of input lacking intensity, vividness or discriminability, and judgment is not impaired. What the individual is noticing is that the *quality* of perception is different. He no longer feels convinced of the *reality* of what he is perceiving. The same point applies to depersonalization—the individual is quite aware of his identity, and quite capable of distinguishing between himself and his environment. But he no longer feels himself to be real by comparison with his environment. Depersonalization and derealization may well be experienced simultaneously, in which case everything seems unreal to the individual, including himself.

How can dissociation of affect, ego-splitting, depersonalization and derealization be considered in terms of cognitive psychology? It has been shown that these terms refer to conditions in which we are aware of our identities as individuals and can discriminate between ourselves and the outside world. But we may experience personal attributes as split, we may feel detached from ourselves, or we may experience a sense of change in ourselves or in parts of ourselves. Or we may experience a lack of conviction of the reality of ourselves or our surroundings. Normally, our experience of self is a global one which subsumes the various features of self and has reference to our context; the conviction of the reality of oneself and one's surroundings is implicit in this general experience. Its component experiences are organized hierarchically, and function in a balanced and interactive synthesis. For this reason we are not consciously aware of them, any more than we are usually aware of the component motor activities involved in, for example, running or jumping. We become aware of them only when their function becomes disturbed, just as in running we become aware of the movements of our knees or the soles of our feet only if we sprain a joint, strain a muscle or develop blisters. In the phenomena under discussion here, we become aware of aspects of ourselves and of our environment which previously were so integrated as to be taken for granted. In other words, a key feature of these phenomena is the redeployment of attention, a concept we used in our discussion of ego-boundary blurring. In the mystic experience, attention is focussed upon one feature to the exclusion of all others; in the present phenomena the problem seems to be one of *anomalous emphasis*. Features which do not normally receive attention now assume prominence, so that an imbalance of relationships ensues. This novel refocussing of attention may be termed a *breakdown of automatization*. It can be readily observed when coordinated physical activity is disturbed, and has been experimentally examined in studies of the performance of skilled tasks under stress.

A key technique in *The basic lost game play*, according to Stephen Potter, is to ask your winning opponent what muscles he is using, and from what part of the body the 'sequence of muscular response' begins. If he replies that he is not aware of using particular muscles, Potter suggests that he should be shown a diagram which is reproduced in the book. This is an illustration of a golfer, anatomically dissected to display his musculature. The quite valid point of this joke is that if we consciously try to consider the elementary components of a complex, skilled activity, we disturb their organization and thus our actual performance. As Bryan and Harter (1897) pointed out in their classical study of telegraphy, we develop a skilled activity hierarchically, proceeding to a new level of organization only when the previous one is established. The sub-levels do not necessarily become automatic in the sense of being stereotyped, but they are automatized in the sense that we perfect them to the point where we no longer need to pay explicit attention to them. If we do start paying explicit attention to component sub-levels the serial higher-order organization suffers. Thus the golfer's drive involves complex sequential organization. It is impaired if he breaks it down by trying to 'hold in his mind' each of its separate elements. Having once learned the appropriate stance, grip, back swing, shoulder and head posture, etc., he must aim for the higher-level serial organization of all these features. If he concentrates upon each discrete feature separately the serial organization is disordered and its synthesis—his overall performance—disintegrates.

Again, when the performer of a skilled activity is put under stress, he tends to become aware of the discrete and formerly automatized elements of his activity, which then deteriorates. This is particularly so in the case of performers who have not yet mastered the skill in question. Indeed, one criterion of the expert or 'pro' sportsman is that his performance is less likely to deteriorate under stress than that of the beginner or even the good amateur. The latter may be capable of matching the professional on occasion, but his performance is less consistent and more liable to be affected by the stress of, for example, competition play or public appearance. De-automatization is particularly evident when the stress takes the form of danger or conflict. Thus, in an emergency, matters may be made worse for the car-driver if he suddenly starts to be aware of elements of his driving which are usually habitual.

What is being suggested here is that what applies to motor skills and activities may also apply to purely cognitive skills and activities. That is to say, the disturbance of cognitive organizations brings into conscious awareness aspects of experience which are normally 'automatized' like the components of a motor skill. What the sufferer from depersonalization is complaining about is the strange sensation caused by breakdown of his normal integrated experience. The breakdown itself is attributable to attentional re-emphases related to shifts in hierarchical organization. We are left with the problem of why such shifts should occur. It is possible for them to be voluntarily induced, as in contemplative meditation, by deliberate concentration. But as we have seen, dissociative experiences are most commonly reported as responses to some disturbing situation. How can we explain such experiences as resulting from stress?

One possible approach is suggested by a closer consideration of Bartlett's concept of the schema. Bartlett argues that the components and organization of schemata are determined by 'appetite, instinct, interest and ideals'. The order of predominance of these 'active, organizing sources' of schemata in any given individual is exactly what we mean by 'personality'. Or, as Barlett puts it:

This order of predominance of tendencies, in so far as it is innate, is precisely what the psychologist means by 'temperament'; in so far as it is developed during the course of life subsequent to birth, it is what he means by 'character'. (Bartlett, 1932, pp. 212–13)

Bartlett goes on to suggest that this is what gives memory a characteristically 'personal' flavour. For remembering demands the utilization of schemata which themselves have been organized in accord with the individual's personality and which are now employed in a hierarchical organization which also reflects his personality. So that, if the order of predominance of the appetites, etc., which direct the schemata is disturbed, the individual's experience of his memories will be altered. Their personal attributes will be absent, so that he will not recognize the memories as being his own, even though he is aware that in fact they are. This may be extended to cover all cognitive activities, including thoughts, perceptions and body schema. And this lack of personal attribution might well explain the strange feeling of unreality or changedness with which we are concerned here. It also suggests that the cognitive processes which underlie depersonalization and its associated phenomena might be the same as those discussed in reference to anomalies of recognition.

It is still left to consider exactly what is meant by a disturbance in 'the order of predominance' of appetites, instincts, interests and ideals. But perhaps this is not so mysterious (or question-begging) as it seems at first sight. Given that each individual develops a particular pattern of prepotency among his drives (activators, motivators, etc.), then it may be presumed that this pattern can be changed so that the prepotency of certain drives is altered in relation to the others. There are a number of conditions which might cause or facilitate such a change. For instance, any attempt to cope with an emergency situation might well demand a transient re-ordering of motivational factors. Prolonged preoccupation or deliberate self-training might have longer-term effects. Take a crudely over-simplified example. A high-living hedonist may have developed the following hierarchical ordering of schemata-determiners: (1) sexual conquest, (2) social prestige, (3) physical comfort ... (n) submissiveness. One dark night his flat is invaded by a hate-crazed mob of muscular, wronged husbands, brothers and fathers, who are clearly intent on tearing him limb from limb. . . . The only way to escape with his skin intact is to prostrate himself, offer a series of tearfully abject apologies and promise faithfully to change his ways. Given that he is not both exceedingly tough and a consummate actor, such a change of role will demand a complete reversal of his hierarchy. In this situation it would not be surprising if our hero experienced some sort of depersonalization feeling. Indeed, emergency, threatening or severely socially embarrassing situations are very common precipitants of dissociation or depersonalization. Now look at the converse of our Lotharian hero—a saintly and ascetic hermit. His hierarchical ordering might be just the opposite, i.e. (1) submissiveness, (2) self-denial . . . (n) sexual conquest. One dark night his cave is invaded by a nubile sex-crazed nymphette. Again, reversal and consequent depersonalization cannot be discounted. Both these examples would be predicted to involve only transient depersonalization experiences, because it is likely that in each case the original patterning would be rapidly re-established after the episode was over. In cases of long-term reversals, it may be presumed that as the individual adjusts to his new patterning a revised hierarchy of schemata will be established. And with this re-synthesis, his experience of depersonalization should decrease. On the other hand, mystic states induced by long training in contemplative exercises include a pronounced element of depersonalization of some kind. Perhaps what the mystic is achieving is the deliberate splitting off or isolation of certain of his schema 'sources'. In such cases, schematic re-ordering may be effected by the withdrawal of elements of the patterning.

What has been suggested is that dissociative experiences, like other anomalous self-experiences, may be considered in cognitive terms. They may be regarded as the outcome of shifts in the hierarchical ordering of schemata which gives each individual's cognitive activity its 'personal' quality. The new ordering or repatterning may in turn reflect temporary changes in the hierarchy of schematic 'sources' caused by stress or by the deliberate redeployment of attention.

7

ANOMALIES OF JUDGMENT AND BELIEF

This chapter considers unusual beliefs. The main concern will be to examine *delusions*, and these are not sufficiently defined by the term 'unusual beliefs'. But this serves very well as a description of the various phenomena to be discussed, for in order to examine the problem of primary delusional experience one must distinguish between the latter and some similar experiences which are often confused with it.

Many unusual experiences can be coloured by or related to delusions, so that these are of high theoretical interest. Furthermore, delusions are regarded as crucial symptoms in the diagnosis of psychotic illness. And finally, in the eyes of the layman they represent the phenomenon most classically associated with mental disorder. The man who thinks that he is Napoleon is the stereotype lunatic in countless jokes and apocryphal anecdotes. It is surprising, therefore, that little is known about the causation of delusions, or about the psychological mechanisms involved in their development. This may be partly because psychologists, particularly socially-orientated psychologists, have generally failed to make certain phenomenological distinctions. In the vast majority of cases even standard textbooks of abnormal psychology have used a loose definition of delusional experiences which stress their content rather than their form. This has allowed the inclusion under the heading of 'delusion' of quite different experiences, so that in many circles a 'delusion' has become synonymous with a 'funny idea'. The difficulty is the not unusual one of there being posed about a class a problem which does not in fact relate to certain members of that class. The admittance of these members to the class has confused the issue, because it is based on some surface characteristic which, though shared by all the members, is not itself central to the problem. This can be backed up by taking the analogy of an intelligent but isolated tribe, the scientific members of which are puzzled by the question of how beasts manage to breathe under water. Suppose that their study of physiology has developed much more rapidly than that of zoology, so that they fail to distinguish between mammals, reptiles and fish. They include in their considerations all those creatures which they have observed to be able to propel themselves under water, e.g. porpoises, crocodiles, and salmon. In other words they have confused beasts which can dive under water for short periods with those which must come to the surface at intervals with those which remain permanently under water. The wise men of the tribe will now fall into two groups: (1) those who point out that they are well aware how crocodiles and porpoises breathe, so that no problem exists, and (2) those who point out that nobody knows how salmon can breathe, so that the problem is insoluble.

Now, if we include in our class of delusions anything which savours of a false belief or a funny idea, we can explain things in terms of normal psychology, just as the wise tribesmen could explain the respiration of crocodiles and porpoises. But in so doing we are including too much and explaining too little. For most of us have ideas and beliefs which are funny in the eyes of other people. And in any case, funny ideas are developed in the same way as any other ideas. If this approach were correct, there would be no problem about delusions, so long as the salmon in the case were ignored. However, there *is* a problem. We are unlikely to come up with a satisfactory solution here. But we can weed out one of the relatively innocuous experiences which are often lumped in with delusions and which can be explained in terms of normal psychology. We can then make a distinction between two types of delusion which is usually overlooked by psychologists, despite the emphasis placed upon it by phenomenologists.

First, we shall consider '*over-valued ideas*'; this is a category which is well known to psychiatrists, but which does not seem to be used by psychologists who generally lump over-valued ideas in with delusions.

Then we shall take a fairly close look at delusions in general. Finally we shall consider *primary* and *secondary* delusions. In the author's view (although admittedly he may be expressing an over-valued idea) this distinction contains the key to the problem of delusions. Secondary delusions can be regarded as our porpoises, because it can be argued that they are just as explicable as the crocodiles of over-valued ideas. They can be discussed in cognitive terms without recourse to the postulation of any pathological mechanism. It is in the area of *primary* delusions that it is difficult to apply explanations drawn from normal psychology.

OVER-VALUED IDEAS

Over-valued ideas share some of the characteristics of delusions, but should not be confused with the latter, which have much more serious diagnostic implications. Delusions are associated with psychotic illnesses, as we have noted, whereas over-valued ideas, although often reported by psychiatric patients, are at least as common in the general population. Over-valued ideas are beliefs of varying degrees of plausibility which are affectively loaded and tend to preoccupy the individual and to dominate his personality. They differ from true delusions primarily in the fact that they are *psychologically comprehensible* in terms of the individual's personality and life experience. They differ from obsessional ideas and preoccupations because, far from regarding them as unwanted intrusions to be struggled with, the individual regards them as highly desirable and important. They may be regarded as the products of normal learning processes, though the experiences determining their development may have been unusual. For instance, an individual may be consumed by an ambition to ensure that parents sleep in the same bedrooms as their offspring. The idea is unusual, but may be the understandable outcome of a miserable, lonely childhood and the memory of night terrors. A man may have the over-valued idea that formal education is a social evil. But his belief may be traced back to a series of real or imagined injustices related to his lack of educational qualifications.

A further difference between over-valued ideas and delusions is that the former may have some 'consensual validation', inasmuch as they are often shared with other people. Thus the shared-bedroom believer may find considerable support from other people whose upbringing resembled his own. On the other hand, over-valued ideas, like delusions, are usually held with noticeable zeal; their possessors are often prepared to suffer or even die for their beliefs. They are also not usually content merely to believe; they generally engage in vigorous defence of their beliefs, coupled with active attempts at proselytization.

The expression 'over-valued' raises the mischievous but quite valid question: '*Over* what?' That is, what are to be regarded as the criterial norms of value and who is to determine them? This merely points up the fact that, like many other anomalous and 'abnormal' phenomena, judgments are relative and assume some cultural norm. Norms are seldom objectively determined, or indeed amenable to objective determination without a vast research programme. And this would probably be not only unjustifiable but misleading, because cultural norms are continually subject to change. So in practice the implied 'norms' are intuitive, and thus reflect the assessor's width of experience and perspicacity as well as his own attitudes and degrees of conviction. A clinician who is himself eccentric is clearly capable of making some very unusual assessments of what is to be regarded as deviating from normality. If he shares his patient's abnormalities, he is likely either not to regard them as abnormal or to over-react by regarding them with far more criticism than would his more conventional colleagues. This fact can afford considerable amusement to any clinical worker who has the opportunity to compare his colleagues' different assessments of the same person. The author once gleefully observed the different pictures of a patient drawn by two clinicians of high intelligence and professional competence. One had written: 'Rigid, intolerant, authoritarian type. Over-valued ideas related to fascist ideology. Paranoid.' The other: 'Intelligent man of considerable character. Articulate and rational. High moral standards. Over conscientious.' The two descriptions are not at all irreconcilable in general or clinical terms. But they suggest considerable differences in emphasis which reflect the different attitudes of the clinicians.

Nevertheless, despite the personal biasses of observers, extremes of belief are generally recognizable, not in terms of the content or nature of the idea itself, but in terms of its *dominance*. If the subject is wrapped up in his belief—if, as it were, his psychic economy is out of balance—then most observers would regard his valuation of that idea as unnecessarily high. Similarly, if he holds an idea with pronounced intensity and his considerations of it clearly spring from heightened emotion, the observer will have doubts as to whether his evaluation is based on rational analysis.

Over-valued ideas may be personal, such as the conviction that one's talents have not been sufficiently appreciated, or that some episode in one's life possessed a particularly symbolic significance. More usually, such ideas are related to political, religious, humanitarian or social issues. People with over-valued ideas are prominent in political movements and religious cults, as well as in crank organizations and extreme minority groups. They are presumably well represented at Speakers' Corner in Hyde Park, at political demonstrations and amongst the contributors to newspaper correspondence columns. In all these areas of activity, it is not so much the content of the belief that is significant but its preoccupying power, and the degree to which the believer finds it necessary to force his ideas upon others. But it may be noted that this last characteristic is directly associated with minority or unpopular beliefs. A person may have preoccupying beliefs of a kind which are shared by a large proportion of people in his culture. He may, for instance, believe that democracy is a good thing or that Jesus Christ died to save mankind. Because these beliefs are (or have been) highly acceptable in our culture he is unlikely to be described as holding over-valued ideas. But this is not only because his ideas are culturally 'normal' and may well be shared by the assessor. It is also because people who hold majority views do not usually find it necessary to proselytize. Let such a person start parading down Oxford Street, bearing sandwich boards and button-holing passers-by, and the assessor's opinion will shift radically. And if it further transpires that the believer devotes much of his time to the consideration and expression of his idea, then almost certainly the assessor will argue that, whilst that sort of behaviour is appropriate for politicians, monks and other full-timers, a normal layman should be balancing his psychic economy rather differently.

In cognitive terms, it could be said that the person holding over-valued ideas over-schematizes his experience by elaborating only a few of the schemata available to him. New ideas and experiences are, to use Piaget's words, *assimilated* but in a biassed manner, whilst the schemata involved do not *accommodate* sufficiently. Thus the hierarchic ordering of schemata is disturbed, because the restricted range of schemata maintains dominance. The development of new schemata and the modification of those already available are limited.

This state of affairs may be attributable to excessive affective loading which results in over-weighting and consequent imbalance in the ordering of Bartlett's 'schematic sources'. But what accounts for the preoccupation and the proselytizing activities of the holders of over-valued ideas? Both can be neatly explained in terms of 'cognitive dissonance', the well-known theory which was developed by Festinger (1957). It is postulated that we tend to maintain harmony between 'cognitive elements' (e.g. our knowledge of our own and other people's attitudes, feelings and behaviour). When some of our cognitive elements are incompatible with each other we experience psychological tension. The theory of cognitive dissonance is concerned with how such incompatibility or dissonance arises, and the ways in which we strive to reduce the tension by decreasing the dissonance. For instance, we may continue to smoke cigarettes, despite our knowledge that this is a health hazard and the arguments of our friends who have broken the habit. We can reduce our subsequent dissonance by convincing ourselves that the medical evidence associating cigarette smoking with lung cancer is invalid, and that our friends are guilty of weak-mindedness and unnecessary timidity. On their part, the same friends may well suffer dissonance between their knowledge of the fact that they enjoyed smoking and the fact that they have given it up whilst we have not. They may reduce their dissonance by emphasizing the validity of the evidence whilst regarding us as weak-minded victims of habit. But there are other ways in which dissonance can be reduced. For instance, we could stop smoking, or our friends could start again. Or we could all withdraw from the conflict area by smoking herbal mixture instead of tobacco.

One common mechanism for the reduction of dissonance is that of seeking social support. Our virtuous, non-smoking friends would feel less tension if everybody in our circle could be persuaded to stop smoking. But we smokers would feel much easier if everybody else smoked too, especially if we could prevail upon them to chain-smoke. This reduction strategy is particularly likely in situations where some limited social support is already available for a belief to which the individual is totally committed but which is refuted by incontrovertible evidence. This is very much the position in which many holders of over-valued ideas may find themselves. In *When Prophecy Fails*, Festinger and his associates reported a fascinating 'field test' of this hypothesis. They had joined a group of 'believers' which had formed round a suburban housewife, Mrs Marian Keech. She had announced that she was in contact with beings from outer space who sent regular messages in 'automatic writing' (i.e. writing by the subject, but which she claims to be beyond her voluntary control). The space contacts had selected her as their representative to warn people on earth that on 21 December the North American continent would be submerged by a deluge. A group of followers, led by a doctor from a nearby college town, took Mrs Keech's assertions seriously. Almost all of them made public profession of their belief, many gave away their belongings and some gave up their jobs in preparation for the cataclysm. On 20 December Mrs Keech received a message warning her and her followers to be ready for evacuation at midnight, when a visitor from outer space would come to escort them to a waiting flying saucer, which would fly them to safety. The group solemnly assembled in Mrs Keech's house to await salvation. But midnight came and went, and no astral visitor arrived.

The situation outlined above offered Festinger's group a real-life test of their hypothesis. Here was a group of people who were committed to their belief in a culturally unacceptable idea and who were now faced with incontrovertible disproof of its validity. How would they reduce their consequent dissonance? The answer is that, far from deserting the belief, they immediately engaged in enthusiastic

proselytization; the clear disconfirmation of Mrs Keech's predictions resulted in their redoubling their efforts to win converts. For
Mrs Keech received a message to say that God had spared the world
because of their demonstration of faith. The group energetically
strove to publicize this miraculous intervention, interpreting it as a
sign of the validity of Mrs Keech's communications. However, other
believers reacted quite differently. They were members of an affi-
liated group in the nearby town, who had not assembled at Mrs
Keech's house. Most of them, in fact, were students who had gone
home for the Christmas vacation. They thus received no social
support from fellow-believers when events disproved Mrs Keech's
predictions. They achieved reduction of dissonance by giving up
their belief.

Observations such as the above, as well as several findings from
experimental studies, suggest that the vigour with which over-valued
ideas are held may be explained in terms of cognitive dissonance. The
holder of such ideas may strive to reduce dissonance by invoking
social support. If he is successful, group membership will then result
not only in his *not* abandoning the ideas should they be subsequently
disconfirmed, but in his renewed endeavour to convert others. In
other words, the sillier the idea the more intense the crusading.

DELUSIONS 1—INTRODUCTION

Delusions are usually defined simply as 'false beliefs', but this definition requires amplification. Firstly, the word 'false' is relative; it
applies only in relation to what is culturally acceptable as 'true' or
'factual'. And this in turn is dependent upon the information available to one's society, its presumptions, attitudes, religious beliefs and
so on. These vary widely between societies and with time. In certain
primitive tribes today it is taken to be manifestly true that rocks,
woods and other natural features contain their own spirits. In our
society it is presumed that human life is sacred. Neither of these
beliefs is open to direct verification, and both would be unacceptable
to many other cultures. Both propositions are 'true' only in the sense
that they follow naturally from principles and convictions which are
culture-bound. Similarly, in our own society, in relatively recent
times, it was known that witches engaged in commerce with the Devil
and that it was impossible for men to set foot on the Moon. The first
of these was believed to have been verified, whilst the second did not
require verification because its converse—that men *could* land on the
Moon—was absurd. Changes in attitude on the one hand, and scientific and technological advances on the other, have reversed the status
of these beliefs. Both are accepted as being patently false, the first

because it is absurd and the second because it has been disproved.

So a given belief can only be regarded as 'false' if it is unshared by other members of the culture in question. This poses problems for the psychiatrist called upon to examine foreign patients, or even patients of his own nationality but from a different sub-culture. Care has to be exercised by the English psychiatrist in assessing, for instance, a Pakistani patient, and by the Pakistani psychiatrist with an English patient. But to a lesser extent the same applies to the interaction between a Cockney and a Dalesman. Each sub-culture has its own presumptions, beliefs and superstititions which may appear irrational to others. Furthermore, there are class and educational differences which cut across these regional variations.

Secondly, the word 'belief' in the definition above suggests merely 'acceptance' or 'opinion' in its current usage. With reference to delusions the words 'faith' or 'conviction' would be more appropriate. For a delusional belief is held with intensity and is taken to be incontrovertible, in much the same way that a very devout person regards the basic tenets of his creed. Typically, deluded patients continually seek out signs supportive of their delusions. But this does not imply that they feel the need for such 'evidence' to prove the validity of their convictions. On the contrary, they regard these as being so self-evident as not to require verification. The 'evidence' is taken to be merely supportive and confirmatory. (This raises the interesting point, to be discussed later, as to why they continue to look for further evidence. The devout person, for instance, recognizes the work of God all around him. If he has complete faith he does not find it necessary to go about looking for it. An associated point which also invites consideration later is that many deluded patients do not behave in a way consistent with their delusions.)

Thus, our original definition might be appropriately amplified to read:

'A delusion is a belief which is demonstrably false by the standards of the individual's socio-cultural background, but which is held with complete conviction.'

It may be noted that neither of these characteristics—falsity or conviction—is of itself sufficient to indicate delusion. Our society shows a notable tolerance towards people with odd ideas and for the non-conforming individual. The eccentric is regarded with amused indifference or, in some cases, cherished as bringing colour to the social scene. For instance, flat-earthers are not seriously considered to be suffering from a delusion; they are generally thought to be merely whimsical. This of course may be due to the fact that most of us cannot really believe that *they* really believe what they say. Similarly, those who profess to believe in the powers of witchcraft are not stamped as deluded; they are regarded as morbid thrill-seekers. Social tolerance of this kind is presumably related to our emancipation from the more extreme types of theological and political dogma. In the past, the person who did *not* accept that the earth was flat was regarded as a dangerous free-thinker, whilst the person who denied the supernatural powers of witches laid himself open to severe punishment for heresy. Furthermore, tolerance of others' opinions is not only condoned by our society but formally inculcated. One of the most explicit tenets of western civilization is that within fairly broad limits, individuals are allowed freedom of thought and the right to express their beliefs. The toleration of minority viewpoints is a hallowed cornerstone of democratic outlook, which has led recently to considerable heart-searching along the lines of whether society should tolerate minorities who are not prepared to tolerate society. Unusual views are generally not muffled or discouraged because they are false, irrational or absurd, but because their accept-ance would prove inconvenient or costly to the discouragers. The latter may be well able to envisage themselves holding similar views if the situation were different. The holder of unpopular views is not regarded as deluded but as representing a threat to others' values, comfort or habitual way of life.

Flat-earthers and witches hold beliefs which are unusual but are shared by small groups of individuals. As will be shown later, even minimal 'consensual validation' of this kind is not typical of delu-sions, which are quite idiosyncratic. But the above considerations do apply to the individual eccentric. A man may be known to believe that a local pond is bottomless, that his garden-shed is haunted or that his neighbours are doomed to eternal damnation. Most readers must know people who believe in garden spirits, who credit them-selves with second sight or who know that they are sexually irresist-ible. We do not label such people as deluded. We say that they are superstitious, suggestible or faulty logicians. Or that their evidence is flimsy, that we personally will retain open minds and that they may conceivably be right. . . .

Before this question of falsity of content is left, it may well be noted that idiosyncratic exaggeration of a view which is culturally tolerated does not of itself qualify as a delusion if its proponent's extreme attitude is psychologically comprehensible to others. For instance, most non-Germans who remember the events leading up to World War II and the domestic activities of the Hitler regime tend to regard Naziism as a wicked, ruthless and dangerous creed. But few would have any urge to weed out and punish every ex-member of the Nazi party. However, if an erstwhile victim of the Gestapo or a concentration camp victim believes that this should be done, he is not regarded as deluded. His belief is comprehensible, however extreme, in the light of what he has suffered. We may remark that if we were in his shoes we would probably feel the same.

As regards the degree of conviction with which somebody holds an opinion, this also does not of itself imply delusion. How do we react to a friend who believes deeply that all men are innately virtuous? We probably tend to think that his knowledge of child psychology is limited and that he must have a happy knack of ignoring everyday evidence. We do not brand him as deluded, but as bravely idealistic if somewhat naive.

Clearly neither falsity of belief nor extreme conviction can be taken singly to constitute delusion. Indeed, there are certain areas of belief where the existence of *both* features in our amplified definition still fails to demonstrate it. The most obvious area is that of religion. In our society, a person may hold religious beliefs of a kind which are quite alien to the vast majority of his fellows, and may hold them with the deepest conviction. But few psychiatrists would dare to substitute the term 'delusion' for 'devout religious faith'. Again, a mother's fervent assertion that her son is 'a good boy, really' in the face of extensive evidence to the contrary, or a husband's profound confidence that his plain wife is the most beautiful woman in the world, are regarded as touching, but admirable. It may well be, of course, that in our culture we respect the individual's religious faith and family love so much that we tacitly abandon cold analysis in these areas because invidious comparison is taboo.

There are in practice features other than those mentioned in our definition which must characterize a belief before it is conventionally classified as a delusion. These may be termed incorrigibility, ego-involvement and preoccupying propensity.

Incorrigibility

Delusions are notoriously unshakeable. Whatever counter-evidence is presented, however much experience denies it, the delusion remains firm. No amount of persuasion, argument and demonstration can serve to convince a deluded patient of the falsity or irrationality of his belief. Normal beliefs, however cherished, can be changed or modified by education, persuasion, coercion or the cumulative effect of contradictory evidence. A simple example is provided by the campaign to publicize the effects of cigarette smoking on health. This has succeeded in modifying the attitudes of many intelligent and well-informed people who for years were convinced that there was insufficient evidence to support the view that a relation exists between smoking and lung cancer, or that any association was merely a statistical artefact. Even when a belief is quite rational, in accord with facts or at least culturally acceptable, it can be reversed by deliberate indoctrination. One well-known example in recent history was the so-called brain-washing or political re-indoctrination which was successfully used during the Korean War by the Chinese to convert American prisoners to Communism after rejecting their original attitudes and beliefs. Even more dramatic were the series of public trials in eastern Europe during the Stalinist era, when the accused were not only conditioned to renounce their life-long beliefs, but to make fervent public confessions that they were traitors whose ideas had corrupted others and that they fully deserved extreme punishment.

None of this seems to apply to psychotic delusions. It is clear that many victims of medieval witch-hunts were deluded, but savage torture often merely elicited further claims that they were in league with the powers of darkness, that they did have the evil eye and so on. The brutal treatment meted out to psychotic patients under bygone medical regimes likewise failed to reduce delusional convictions.

Ego-involvement

Another characteristic of delusions which has been stressed by psychiatric authorities is that they are highly personalized. That is to say, their content is crucially related to the individual's personal fears, needs or security. But it may be that this aspect has been unduly emphasized; for common sense suggests that it could scarcely be otherwise where *any* belief is concerned. The intensity of normal beliefs increases in proportion to the degree of ego-involvement. The more we are personally concerned in an opinion or attitude the less likely we are to abandon it. Likewise, the longer we have held a belief and the greater the conviction with which we have held it, the more inextricably does it become a feature of our personality and the more determining a role does it play among our cognitive structures.

Preoccupying propensity

Normal beliefs, however strongly they are held, do not generally preoccupy us. Indeed, the more established the belief the less likely it is to be continually in the forefront of consciousness. Our most fundamental beliefs become assimilated to the point where we are scarcely aware that we hold them. Only when they are attacked do we consciously formulate and discuss them. Otherwise the beliefs that we hold up for examination are usually peripheral or incompletely established. Deluded patients, on the other hand, ruminate continually about their delusions, and spend much of their time restating them and noting new 'evidence'. Patients with delusions of persecution gear their lives to defensive or vengeful measures.

Delusions of jealousy drive their possessors to make the most radical changes in their workaday routines. As against this, many of the observations about the preoccupying power of delusions have been made about hospitalized patients who really have very little else to do but brood about their problems. Furthermore, the ethos of a traditional mental hospital is often highly conducive to the focussing of awareness upon one's symptoms and to associated ruminations. Again, the person who is not preoccupied by his delusions and whose life is not radically affected by them is unlikely to be brought to the attention of a psychiatrist in the first place. So it is possible that this feature is not so much a characteristic of delusions as of deluded people who receive psychiatric treatment, particularly as in-patients.

DELUSIONS 2—THE CONTENT OF DELUSIONS

Clearly, the content of delusions, like that of all other psychic phenomena, is derived from the individual's store of experiences and information. And equally clearly, this is largely determined by his cultural background. Primary experiences, such as love, jealousy and hate, are shared by most members of mankind, so it may be predicted that some content areas will be common to deluded individuals in many different cultures. And it is true that delusions of persecution, for example, seem to appear throughout the world. On the other hand, the details and elaborations which are developed within such content areas may be predicted to vary from culture to culture. They will be determined by the socio-economic structure of the individual's society (e.g. its degree of emphasis on hierarchic status or material possessions), to beliefs and information which are informally propagated (e.g. folklore, myth and superstitition) and by formally prescribed information (e.g. the contents of educational curricula, technical skills and technological/scientific knowledge).

So, two men from very different cultures may each suffer from delusions of persecution. One may believe that his enemies are attempting to bisect him with a laser beam. But if the other man has never heard of lasers, the ways in which he is threatened cannot include that particular device. On the other hand, if he happens to be a member of some remote tribe of South American Indians, he may be convinced that his enemies employ poison from the zeruc berry, a mechanism which is unlikely to occur to the first man.

There exists a considerable literature on cross-cultural differences in psychopathology. Much of this, however, must be assessed with caution, because few anthropologists have had psychiatric training or skill in phenomenological method. However, there is an increase of comparative studies by psychiatrists among which is some relevant evidence. This tends to confirm that the *form* of mental disorders is the same across cultures, but that *content* varies in the manner suggested above. For instance, Tooth's (1950) studies of mental illness on the Gold Coast (now Ghana) include an account of the differences in content of the delusions held by schizophrenics brought up in different parts of the country. In the north and amongst bush people, content was related to primitive religious beliefs and the fetish system. Mental illness was believed to be the result of offending the nature spirits or one's ancestral hierarchy. So local schizophrenics believed that they were plagued by spirits in the guise of dwarfs and demons, or by the ghosts of their forbears. The southern area of the country was more sophisticated, and formal education was prevalent. There, delusional contents were similar to those common in Europe and North America. Instead of supernatural forces, persecutors were believed to be other persons or organizations, usually associated with the government. Their *modus operandi* included the use of electricity, wireless and television.

As might be expected, very similar variations in delusional content can be traced over time in our own culture. The hypothesized persecutors have changed from evil spirits to wicked foreigners to the members of contemporary organizations. Their weapons have similarly changed—from sorcery to poisons to gas to electricity to atomic radiation.

Within any given culture at any given time, however, delusions seem to have belonged to recognizable 'primary' groups. Those which have been most common are conventionally classified under the headings of delusions of persecution, jealousy, love, grandeur, poverty, ill-health and guilt. (The term *paranoid* is often used to subsume the first two or more of these, but strictly speaking this is incorrect. Paranoia is one of the many technical terms which has acquired a slightly different meaning in lay usage. Non-technically, 'paranoid' has come to mean 'suspicious', 'brooding', 'jealous' and 'hostile'. It has acquired moralistic overtones and we commonly use it as a term of approbrium or abuse. But Hippocrates used it to mean 'mental disorder', whilst its current definition is a condition characterized by systematic delusions, i.e. it has a wider connotation than its lay meaning, having reference to *any* systematized delusion.)

(1) Delusions of persecution
The person with persecutory delusions is convinced that he (and perhaps his loved ones) is the target of malevolence and threat. This may be attributed to a particular person, but is more usually believed to be part of a plot by some organization. The organization is nomi-

nated according to the individual's predisposition and current attitudes, but almost any organization, club or creed may be selected by
different individuals. Thus the Jews, Catholics, Methodists, Free-
masons, Communists, Capitalists, Trade Unions, Army, Police and
national and local governments are all popular choices. Among the
more esoteric attributions reported to the author was that of a group
of Irish hypnotists. Sometimes the organization is more personalized,
the persecution being seen as the work of a group of conspirators
among the victim's friends or neighbours. Thus another patient
claimed to have narrowly escaped from a series of homicidal attempts
perpetrated by the members of a church choir.

Some patients believe that they are being infected, poisoned or
robbed of their virility. Often such beliefs are associated with hallucinations of taste, touch or smell. In the face of such imagined perils,
people with delusions may take active counter-measures. Or they
may change their jobs or homes, only to realize that they have been
traced and further agents recruited to continue their persecution.
More commonly, the delusional threat is less specific, but equally
ominous. The sufferer may not be sure of the precise goal of his tor-
mentors. It may be the prevention of some deserved achievement, the
sabotaging of his career or the engineering of his social downfall.
One patient believed that her doctor was in league with the chemist
and the local hospital to degrade and cheat her. The chemist fed her
with aphrodisiacs and will-reducing drugs, whilst her doctor employed a concealed X-ray machine both to weaken her and to discover whether she was to receive an inheritance.

Associated with persecutory delusions are *ideas and delusions of
reference*. The patient sees hidden meanings in the behaviour of
everybody he meets; their voices, gestures, expressions are all interpreted as having sinister connotations which bear reference to him.
A complete stranger coughs in the theatre queue; the patient realizes
that this is a signal to others that she is unsuitable for admission to
the orchestra stalls. The radio announcer pauses; another patient
knows that this is intended as a warning to *him*. The most innocuous
activity can be interpreted by the deluded patient as an indication
that people are denigrating, slandering or threatening him. One young
patient found that the plot against him involved messages in secret
code which were cunningly circulated by insertions in jazz magazines.
'Bassist needs gigs' or 'Dankworth Big Band Scores Hit' conveyed
information about him. He *knew* this without being able to fathom
what the code could be or how the insertions could be effected.
Depressed patients believe that others are publicizing their sins or
arranging for their punishment. Some have concomitant delusions of
guilt of such severity that they feel they deserve the imprisonment or

lynching which is being organized. Others attribute their depression
to the constant humiliations they suffer. A road-sweeper may blow
on his hands on a frosty morning; the patient knows that the neigh-
bourhood is being informed of her sexual malpractices. A lift-
attendant stabs a button; word is being spread that another patient
is mentally defective and cannot count.

(2) *Delusions of jealousy*

This term is applied to the morbid conviction, without supportive
evidence, that one's spouse is unfaithful. (The term is thus inept; the
individual does not have delusions that he is jealous. He *is* jealous.
His delusions concern his partner's behaviour.) Morbid jealousy is
common, and it acquires delusional intensity in all sorts of conditions,
ranging from organic states to personality disorders in which it may
be the only presenting symptom. The sufferer seizes upon the most
innocuous and trivial events as 'evidence' for his delusion. His wife's
face may be flushed as she stands over the oven—her agile lover must
have just made his exit by the kitchen window. She has just glanced
out of the bedroom window—a signal to that passing policeman to
return later. Her hair is out of place, her skirt creased—evidence that
she has just left her lover's embrace. Her hair is *not* out of place and
her skirt has been freshly pressed—evidence that she has had to
spruce up after some orgiastic excess. A deluded female may accuse
her husband of inattention—he is preoccupied with his extra-marital
affair. Or he *is* attentive—a clear sign of guilty feelings. One woman
haunted the office block where her husband worked, until in despair
he managed to transfer to another firm. His wife took this as proof
positive of his infidelity; what other reason could he have for
changing his job other than that he wished to be nearer to his
mistress?

An ironical aspect of this sort of situation is that in some cases the
patient's spouse may actually be engaging in a clandestine love
affair. In fact, the patient's incessant accusations can themselves pre-
cipitate this. The prolonged strain of life with a paranoiac may
understandably drive the partner to seek solace elsewhere, so that the
patient's delusions can be self-verifying. But so long as no inkling of
the real infidelity reaches the patient his suspicions are still delusional, because they are based on false evidence. Indeed, cases have
been known where the patient has come across indications of actual
infidelity, but discounted them. He may even regard them as attempts
to divert him from the real 'facts'. Thus, one man had developed delusions of jealousy shortly after his marriage, and rapidly became convinced that his wife was grossly promiscuous. From then on he made
increasingly violent accusations that she was having sexual inter-

course with practically every man they knew. After about six years of unhappiness, his wife, who had until then led a blameless life, formed an association with a family friend. One day she was horrified when her husband intercepted a passionate letter from her lover. But far from reacting to this as proof of his suspicions, he berated her for attempting to draw a red herring across his investigations with what he asserted was a crude forgery!

On the other hand, self-verification of jealousy delusions may have tragic consequences. The spouse, after years of strain, continual accusations and merciless bullying, may 'confess' to the accusations, inventing an identity for the 'lover' or invoking the name of an old flame. The deluded partner may then erupt into uncontrollable rage which not uncommonly culminates in murder.

(3) *Delusions of love*

Delusions of love, or *'erotomania'*, are manifested by individuals who, without any evidence of any kind, are convinced that some other person is madly in love with them. Thus these delusions may be regarded as the obverse of both persecutory and jealousy delusions. Very often the object of such a belief is some person whom the individual has never met and who is not even aware of his or her existence. Persons of eminence or public note such as politicians, film stars of pop idols are often selected. But the victim may be the local doctor or clergyman, or some inoffensive person who happens to work in the same building or catch the same bus.

As with the other delusional areas, the most trivial actions may be taken as proof—in this case, of undying affection. The absence of more explicit protestations is explained in terms of the 'admirer's' bashfulness or the need for discretion. The deluded person is often won over by these imagined overtures, and decides to reciprocate. The victim may then find himself bombarded with messages, tokens and telephone calls. His embarrassed denials or silence are taken either as further evidence of shyness or as an indication that some malicious person is hindering true love by intercepting the messages or malignly influencing the beloved. Eventually the subject may react with depression or with a campaign of vengeance against the faithless admirer who may now find himself exposed to slander, personal assault or litigation.

(4) *Delusions of grandeur*

This term is applied to the belief that one's abilities, achievements, social status or all of these are wildly superior to what they are in fact. The direction and degree of bizarrerie of such delusions tends to vary with types of illness. Manic patients merely take it that they are in general more successful, popular, healthy and lucky than other people. Some psychotics may develop highly systematized delusions that they are the Pope, the Virgin Mary, a king or head of state. Their beliefs may be reinforced by hallucinatory experiences such as confirmatory voices.

(5) *Delusions of poverty*
This type of delusion used to be commonly associated with depressive illnesses. Presumably this reflected a very real fear which preoccupied large sections of the community before the introduction of improvements in social security provisions. Briefly, the patient believes that he and his family are poverty-stricken and faced with total destitution.

(6) *Delusions of ill-health*
Patients with depressive illnesses quite commonly become convinced that they are suffering from an incurable condition such as cancer, leukaemia, arteriosclerosis or brain tumour. Sometimes they interpret their mental illness as a form of degenerative insanity. They may believe that they have infected their families or that their children have inherited their 'diseases'. Among schizophrenic patients such delusions may start during a depressive phase and be supported by somatic hallucinations. As would be expected, the precise nature of the delusional illness is determined by the patient's level of sophistication and medical knowledge. Less educated patients will describe the most improbable illnesses and betray primitive or distorted ideas about the insides of their bodies. One woman thought that 'the tube between my heart and my stomach is knotted'. An elderly man believed that his bowels were so completely blocked that his stomach had also become jammed with faeces. Ideas of the organs rotting, the flesh decaying and the bones crumbling are not uncommon.

   A cardinal feature of depressive patients with delusions of ill-health is the fact that they view their 'illnesses' as incurable. The ordinary hypochondriac is constantly demanding medical attention and the most up-to-date treatments. The depressive views his end as inevitable—his condition is beyond hope.

(7) *Delusions of guilt*
Depressive illness is characterized by self-reproach which may develop into the conviction that the patient is worthless and destined for eternal punishment. The sins which he may claim to have committed range from trivia such as possessing a 'sneering expression' up to crimes of unmentionable enormity. Perhaps most commonly reported are sexual misdemeanours, masturbation and adultery. The sins may

have been isolated and committed years before, or may have been habitual for years. Some may well have been perpetrated; others are manifestly impossible, in which case the patient is exhibiting a delusional memory as well as delusions of guilt.

Patients with delusions of guilt are convinced that they fully deserve the most severe retribution, and fear that the same punishment will be meted out to their innocent families. Some agitated depressives may believe that they are already dead, perhaps as a form of divine retribution, and that their minds and bodies no longer exist. These delusions are termed '*nihilistic*'. They often extend to the belief that those around the patient are also dead and that the whole world has stopped.

DELUSIONS 3—SECONDARY AND PRIMARY DELUSIONS

So far, delusions in general have been discussed with descriptions of their characteristic features and range of content. We have examined some problems concerned with what is to be regarded as 'false', and some differences between the ways in which delusional beliefs are held as compared with normal beliefs. But it may be noted that, by comparison with over-valued ideas, these differences are largely ones of degree. Furthermore, the types of content which have attracted attention in the study of delusions are really not surprising, although their details and elaborations may strike the observer as grossly distorted or irrational. In short, these features can be explained in terms of learning, emotional stress, cognitive dissonance and so on. So that although these are the topics conventionally discussed under the heading of 'delusions' in most textbooks of abnormal psychology, one must go a little further to see exactly why delusions are generally regarded as pathological. To get to the nub of the delusional experience one must distinguish between two types or levels of delusion.

Secondary delusions

'*Secondary delusions*' are also referred to as *delusion-like ideas* or *delusional ideas* (although this usage varies from author to author). They differ from primary delusions inasmuch as they are due to other abnormal experiences or morbid affective moods. For instance, in attempting to interpret his experience of depersonalization, the patient may develop an explanation which is clearly faulty, and may come to hold this explanation with great conviction. But his 'explanation' is odd because the experience itself is odd; it is not amenable to logical, everyday explanation because it itself is neither logical nor everyday.

Thus the secondary delusion, like the over-valued idea, may be objectively irrational but it is *psychologically comprehensible*. Given the necessary information, the observer can empathize with the subject; if he himself were to have such an unusual experience he would express beliefs about it which would be just as unusual as those of the subject.

Secondary delusions are conventionally associated with schizophrenia, endogenous depression and psychogenic (neurotic) reactions. But this merely suggests that they can occur in anybody who experiences disturbing phenomena, whilst retaining the ability to think clearly enough to devise explanations of those phenomena. The fact that they are expressed by neurotics as well as psychotics indicates that they could just as easily occur to people who are not psychiatric patients at all. But the original experience which prompts the secondary disturbance may have already brought the subject to the attention of a psychiatrist.

It may be presumed that not all people suffering from unusual experiences will formulate verbal explanations of them. After all, there are wide individual differences among normal people in their modes of solving problems or resolving conflicts. It seems likely that the mode of choice is related to other cognitive characteristics and personality traits. Indeed, Witkin (1968) has claimed that when global/passive (field-dependent) people break down they are more likely to experience hallucinations than differentiated/analytic (field-independent) people, who tend to express delusions. Differentiated individuals have strong ego boundaries and a rigid detachment from their environment. So it is possible that when they suffer disturbance they strive to maintain their identity by developing idiosyncratic ideas in the face of environmental denial.

The suggestion that the development of secondary delusions may be related to the individual's cognitive style is also reconcilable with their consideration in terms of cognitive dissonance. The person suffering from a disturbing experience is usually aware that it is incompatible with objective reality. The world may appear grey and flat to him, whilst at the same time he knows that this is not actually so. The associated tension and perplexity may be regarded as the result of cognitive dissonance, and it would be predicted that the sufferer will attempt to reduce this. As we noted in the previous section there are a number of ways in which reduction may be achieved. One individual might deny the experience, another might abandon objective standards. But a less extreme strategy might be to try to evolve an explanation which would reconcile the two incompatible conditions—in other words, produce a secondary delusion. And it seems reasonable to suggest that the individual who selects this strategy is likely to be one who has employed it previously as his method of choice for handling other types of dissonance.

A feature stressed by phenomenologists is that among the disturbing experiences which can give rise to secondary delusions is that of *primary delusion* itself. This may be difficult to grasp at first, because most of us tend to think in terms of *content* rather than *form*. The point is that secondary delusion consists of the attribution of an explanation, and this is expressed through content. For instance, the patient suffering from depressive mood or depersonalization may attribute his experience to the use of hypnotism by wicked physicians. The layman (as well as many non-phenomenologically orientated clinicians) would classify this reference to the imaginary activities of malignant physicians as constituting the *delusion*. But this is only the *content* assumed by a secondary delusion. Its *form* is the fact of faulty attribution and the manner in which it is held, not the nature of the attribution. Now *primary delusion*, as will be seen, is a content-less feeling or experience. As soon as the patient engages in the cognitive activities of attribution, explanation or description, he may start to introduce content in an attempt to make the experience meaningful. The beliefs which he now develops and maintains can be validly classified as *secondary* to his *primary delusional experience*.

Primary delusions

Primary delusions are also referred to as *true delusions, delusions proper* or *apophany*. The experience is basically the uneasy awareness of a *change in significance*. Everything seems to be different, changed and disordered. Patients suffering from this primary delusional experience naturally find it difficult to describe. They feel a sense of frightening uncertainty, an awareness of a sinister 'atmosphere', an apprehension of disintegration. As might be expected, they strive to structure this diffuse experience by giving it content. In later stages of schizophrenia the primary experience is submerged by content attributions. In other words, patients begin to express secondary delusions.

Phenomenological psychiatrists have differentiated between three aspects of the primary experience:

(1) *Delusional perceptions.* The patient perceives objects and events appropriately but either feels that their significance is vague or ascribes *new meanings* to them. They may seem uncanny, mystifying and indescribable: 'Everything was the same and yet it seemed strange.' 'The people all looked unnatural somehow.' 'I noticed the cat particularly. It was stretching in an eery sort of way, as though it was on remote control. Or he may experience them with immediacy

and clarity, but incorrectly. Often their new 'meaning' has reference to himself. People in the street are criticizing him, gestures have hidden significance, casual remarks convey secret intimations and so on. 'She asked if I wanted them by Saturday. She meant I was a tart.' 'Somebody must have sent him to get me. He never looked at me.'

(2) *Delusional ideas or memories.* The patient may suddenly think that he realizes the significance of a memory. For instance, he may recall seeing the Prime Minister at a public meeting. Suddenly he realizes that the ministerial wave must have been directed at him personally, as an indication that he was to be the next Leader of the Opposition. Or he remembers a woman in a shop, whose eyes were shining. Now he realizes that she must have been responsible for his present condition.

(3) *Delusional awareness.* Patients may become aware of universal or cataclysmic events. Such awareness may be unsupported by perceptions or any clear idea about the 'event'. For instance, the patient may suddenly know that the end of the world has come, or that the earth is being taken over by 'something'.

The crux of the primary delusion is that it involves, as Jaspers puts it, an 'experience of reality in which the environment offers a *world of new meanings*'. Jaspers goes on to say that all thinking is a thinking about meanings, and all perception is at the same time a perception of meaning. His view accords very well with those of modern psychology, which stress, as seen in earlier chapters, the hypothesis-testing, problem-solving nature of cognitive activities. We perceive, image, recognize, recall, and think about a person or a plate because we have developed concepts of persons and plates. We organize input and operate upon ideational material schematically. The experience of primary delusion involves the immediate, intrusive awareness of meanings, as does normal cognitive activity—*but the meanings have been transformed.* In other words, some information is received appropriately at the input stage and is then coded correctly. (To use a computer analogy, data are coded, taped and fed into the machine quite efficiently. But gross errors have crept into some of the programmes, which now include inappropriate sub-routines.) 'Seeing new meanings' suggests not, as has often been implied, that information is inappropriately schematized *but that the schemata themselves have shifted their interrelationships.* It is this shift in inter-schematic organization which constitutes the experience of primary delusion. The patient's subsequent attempts to reconcile this shift lead to his development of 'explanatory' secondary delusions. His explanations are peculiar, as we observed before, because the task is impossible.

He may be forced to develop a complex, interlocking argument, which is termed *delusional systematization*. The more perplexing his experiences the more complex and idiosyncratic his systematization must become in order to accommodate them.

Perhaps the above argument can be clarified by taking an absurdly over-simplified example. Suppose that we see a box on the table. We perceive the physical attributes of this innocuous object correctly and classify it appropriately. Our 'box' schema has such characteristics as 'container', 'receptacle of rigid material', 'I once had a tin box', 'usually has a lid', 'Aunt Agatha's jewel box' and so on. Unfortunately, this schema has slipped out of mesh with our other schemata. Instead of being organized hierarchically in relation to, for example, 'things of use to man', 'objects which can be put in containers' and so on, it is now either quite out of gear or is associated with inappropriate schemata, for example, 'things which may hurt me'. If the latter is the case, we may try to solve this perturbing enigma by developing an 'explanation'. Why and how can this box hurt us? Because an enemy aims to destroy us. He has planted this box on the table, having constructed it of, or filled it with, some destructive compound—high explosive, perhaps, or radio-active fibres. Or perhaps the box is merely his *symbol* of evil intent? The explanations we propound are the outcome of ordinary reasoning and guesswork. They are secondary to the primary experience, which could be termed '*schematic slippage*'. The problem of primary delusion is how such slippage can occur.

It will be noted, then, that the experience of primary delusion is *not* simply a question of faulty reasoning or peculiar belief, which is what is suggested by many textbooks. These imply that cognitive structures are unimpaired but that cognitive processes are faulty, inasmuch as false postulates are erected and that subsequent checks are biassed in the direction of false positive results. The present argument would be that cognitive *processes* are not necessarily impaired, but that there has been a shift in cognitive *structures*. The false postulates are erected only as a result of this shift, and the content is explicable as merely part of the attempt to find a new fit for the experienced new meanings. In short, it is not so much *what* the deluded person believes which is of importance, but *how* he believes it.

The present approach goes some way towards explaining why deluded patients often behave in a way which, to the observer, is not in accord with the delusions they hold with such conviction. A man may believe that he is Adolf Hitler and can determine the fate of Europe. Yet he spends his days happily making paper chains in the occupational therapy department. This discrepancy is very puzzling if it is presumed that his cognitive structures are unimpaired. It is less puzzling on the present view; his 'Hitler' schema may now be meshed with some very unexpected ideas, which may even include the notion that Europe's fate can best be decided by making paper chains. Again, the fact that deluded people continue to amass 'evidence' although holding their views with unshakable conviction poses a problem for the conventional, content-orientated view. For this places the central emphasis on the false postulate—the 'belief'; and normal people with strong beliefs do not usually continue to search for evidence. If they believe fully, this implies that their minds are made up, so that no further evidence is required. The present view, as has been seen, de-emphasizes the content of the delusion; the 'belief' is itself only an attempt to structure the diffuse primary experience. The normal person with faith does not suffer from cognitive dissonance, and thus has no need to strive for reduction of tension by amassing evidence. The deluded person may be presumed to experience not only dissonance between his views and those of others, but primary dissonance due to his cognitive slippage.

Can any experimental evidence be cited in support of the 'schematic slippage' approach proposed here? There has been relatively little experimental study of delusions as such; but there is a wealth of evidence regarding the general area of schizophrenic *'thought disorder'*. This term is applied to the various peculiarities which characterize schizophrenic thinking where its *form* is concerned—'thought blocking', 'poverty of thought', 'pressure of thought' and so on. Several theories have been proposed to account for these abnormalities, but during the last decade two approaches in particular have stimulated energetic psychological research. The first of these was originated by Norman Cameron (1946), who proposed that schizophrenics are unable to preserve their conceptual boundaries. For instance, if required to sort or classify an array of objects, the severely thought-disordered patient may include the top of the desk, other furniture in the room, the window or even the experimenter himself. Cameron suggested that, in a similar way, ideas of only tenuous relevance become incorporated into the schizophrenic's concepts. These become more diffuse and less consistent; and as they lose precision they become more abstract. This loosening of categorical limits Cameron termed *over-inclusion*. His suggestion has been intensively studied, notably by Payne (1961) and his associates, using object- and card-sorting tasks. The performance of *some* schizophrenics (typically those with delusions or in the acute stage of illness) has proved to differ significantly from that of other groups.

Now it will be noted that 'over-inclusion' refers to the breadth of concepts—in other words, to anomalies *within* schemata. The 'slippage' view proposed here has reference to disorganization *between* schemata. Neither view rules out the other, of course—it would be not at all surprising if it transpired that both types of disorder coexist. But the evidence for over-inclusion cannot be taken as support for the slippage approach. However, the interpretations of that evidence have subsequently come under attack. Recent work suggests that the tests used by Payne and his associates are not measuring the same thing. And there is now considerable doubt as to whether the way in which they are performed by schizophrenics is to be regarded as due to 'over-inclusion' at all. It is now argued that some schizophrenics perform as they do because they are free-associating, and their associations themselves are peculiar. This would suggest that they have not been shown to be unusual in the breadth of their categories, but in their manner of drawing upon those categories.

At the same time as doubts have been increasingly expressed about the validity of over-inclusion studies, another theoretical approach and methodology has found favour among psychologists. This is due to the work of Bannister (e.g. 1962) which springs from Kelly's (1955) Personal Construct Theory, and uses modifications of Repertory Grid technique. Kelly's theory is based on the assumption that each individual is a 'scientist', in the sense that he is continually engaged in attempting to predict and control his world. To do this he construes or conceptualizes people, things and events, developing a personal hierarchical system of interrelated constructs. These constructs not only structure the individual's world; they are also used as predictive instruments. They enable the person to organize his experience, determine the way in which he anticipates the course of events and help him to decide the responses appropriate to given situations and relationships. In fact, to all intents and purposes, Kelly's 'constructs' seem to be similar to the dynamic structures to which we have referred throughout as 'schemata'. Kelly's own definition of a 'construct' was 'a way in which two things are alike and by the same token different from a third'. Repertory Grid testing is a way of identifying verbal constructs. Subjects may be required, for instance, to nominate a series of people known to them, and to categorize each one as, for example, kind – unkind, trustworthy – untrustworthy, honest – dishonest. Or they may be asked to sort photographs of strangers according to similar categories. Sorting and cross-sorting allows comparisons between conceptual categories to be measured statistically. It will be immediately evident that the technique is of high relevance to the present 'slippage' hypothesis. For it is intended not to examine the range of separate conceptual categories, but the *relationships between them*.

Bannister's own basic hypothesis is that schizophrenic thought disorder is attributable to the '*serial invalidation*' of constructs. He argues that the schizophrenic is somebody whose experiences have continually denied the expectations generated by his constructs. For instance, if one's mother is construed as being kind and sincere, the construct is invalidated if she behaves in a cruel or insincere manner. A different construct must now be developed; but this may in its turn be invalidated if she subsequently reverts to being kind or sincere. The more inconsistency the individual experiences in his interpersonal relationships the weaker the relationships between his constructs will become. Their inter-correlations will become lower than those of normal, integrated personalities, because the individual will become less consistent in his linkage of associated constructs, or will apply them loosely. This will lead to failures in his predictions about the world, and subsequent breakdown in his responses to the environment.

Using various types of Repertory Grid techniques, Bannister has been successful in differentiating thought-disordered schizophrenics from other psychiatric patients and normal people. We need not be concerned here with the assumptions underlying Bannister's position. The important point is that his series of studies provides evidence which is reconcilable with the present argument. Delusional experience is the outcome of a loosening of the normal organization of cognitive structures—a shift in the relationships *between* schemata, as opposed to anomalies in the contents of the schemata themselves.

8

ANOMALIES OF CONSCIOUSNESS

We began this book by considering varieties of attention. We shall close with two chapters discussing the closely related topic of consciousness—a core experiential state, without which we could not be said to function as thinking creatures, but one which has so far baffled psychologists.

What is meant by 'consciousness'? What is its nature? The short answer is that nobody knows. Numerous theories, models, and analogies have been proposed in regard to the concept, but little agreement has been reached. Indeed—and this, perhaps, lies at the root of much of the controversy—the very definition of the word is still in doubt. So the diversity of theoretical approaches should not be surprising; there have been almost as many theories advanced in this much-debated topic as there have been debaters. At one extreme of the wide range of philosophical accounts, there is that which doubts that there is any such animal as consciousness. Such concepts, it is argued, simply reflect our use of words. At the other extreme is the assumption that consciousness is a primary experience, totally elemental and therefore not amenable to analysis. Many intermediate views derive from different positions on the classical mind–body controversy, including various forms of dualism and monism. The classical dualistic position of Descartes is that consciousness is of different substance from, but co-exists with, the corporeal being. Some monists have thought of it as a thing—a mechanism or device. Earlier thinkers seemed to conceive of this 'thing' as being located in its own 'seat' in the body, rather like the soul was once held to abide in the chamber of the pineal gland.

When psychology first established itself as a separate discipline, the study of consciousness was seen as one of its primary functions. Indeed, psychology was often defined as the 'science of consciousness'. And as the new discipline had emerged from that of philosophy, it was natural that nineteenth-century psychological studies should be in line with those of the parent field. William James, whose discussions in his *Principles* still rank as the most distinguished of psychological contributions to the topic, was primarily a philosopher. Ironically, so was John B. Watson, the father of Behaviourism. In 1913, Watson published the call to arms of his new movement, a polemical paper that has been called the 'Behaviourist Manifesto'. There he asserted flatly that: 'The time has come when psychology must discard all reference to consciousness'. The Behaviourists' objections to the study of consciousness were basically methodological; moderates like Tolman did not attack the validity of the concept itself, but simply doubted whether it was a suitable topic for psychological investigation. Nevertheless, Watson's paper heralded a dramatic change of approach in psychology, which involved the virtual abandonment of its study. For almost half a century, the discussion of consciousness, along with other "mentalistic" concepts such as will, was discouraged, if not *verboten,* among psychologists. Even today, Skinner, perhaps the most influential modern thinker in the discipline, regards consciousness as simply an epiphenomenon of little significance.

However, the *zeitgeist* of the discipline has changed radically in recent years. With the return to grace of cognition, consciousness has also emerged from the shadows, and there has been a tidal wave of relevant publications. Much of this renewed enthusiasm has derived from two sources, one reflecting societal interests of the 1960s, the other precipitated by a dramatic surgical technique. The first of these was the parallel spread of recreational (and other) drug use and a fashionable interest in meditation, derived from such Oriental belief systems as Zen Buddhism and Sufism. The other source was 'split-brain' surgery, with its evidence regarding hemispheral specialization and the implications of dual functioning. As might be expected, because of these two origins, many recent examinations of consciousness have not in fact been to do with the nature of consciousness itself, but with its altered or alternative states, or with speculations (often verging on the metaphysical) as to whether we possess multiple consciousnesses. The most plausible theoretical models have been derived not from the two 'fashionable interest' sources, but from the less colourful domain of information-processing. Oddly enough, most of the modern tough-minded approaches echo the philosophical ideas propounded by William James. From his distinction between primary, as opposed to secondary, memory has been derived a currently influential view of consciousness as the mnemonic short-term store, a view that has stimulated a great deal of productive research. Again, according to James, consciousness is a 'selective agency', which enables us to choose among stimuli and thus to adapt to changing conditions. One important contemporary approach is to equate consciousness with selective attention, and this has led to its conceptualization as an information selector or input regulator. Even more active and complex functions are implied in sophisticated models that see consciousness as an internal programmer, a computer-operating system or an executive supervisor that sets goals and activates appropriate behaviour systems.

At this point, let us pause for reflection. Despite the lack of consensus as to the nature of consciousness or even its precise definition, several of its characteristics have been generally accepted. These may be summarized as follows:

> Consciousness is a personal state, characteristic at least of humans, which involves selective awareness of both external and internal events, which exemplifies knowing, allows insight, evidences memory and is to a large extent subservient to the will.

Now it would seem reasonable to assert (although very few, if any, writers seem to have done so) that as an existential state or condition, consciousness cannot be an active agent. Most of the modern theoretical models just mentioned allocate to it executive or control functions. They suggest that consciousness determines, activates, initiates, or regulates the flow of input, thoughts, and images. But surely, consciousness itself does not do anything at all. It is not a mental engine or a source of energy; it is not a control mechanism or an active processor. It does not cause, power, or drive events. Our mental lives involve many functions and activities—we select, initiate, regulate, augment, inhibit, make decisions and implement them. We are conscious of many of these activities. But that does not mean that consciousness is the cause or author of them. Rather, it is a filtering screen that allows inspection, observation, and verification. In other words, consciousness is not analogous, as has been suggested, to a programmer or operating system, but rather to the video monitor that allows the operator to see some of what is going on in the computer. Computer and cybernetics analogies, incidentally, can be particularly valuable in the present context because they serve to remind us that consciousness can be conceptualized in terms of systems and programmes. These de-emphasize or avoid the necessity of postulating energizers and drives.

At the same time, Tart (1975) and Luria (1978) have argued convincingly that consciousness consists of many components or subsystems. Perhaps part of the problem for many discussants has been the assumption that consciousness is an entity, an assumption that probably descends directly from the older idea that it was a 'thing'. Much of the semantic and conceptual confusion that has characterized psychological discussions of consciousness might have been avoided if we had restricted ourselves to the adjectival form of the word, and agreed to a general moratorium on the use of the noun. Admittedly, we should have been left with some tricky definitional questions. But by proscribing the word 'consciousness' we might have avoided the trap of thinking of its referent as an intact device or mechanism. There is nothing innovative or radical in this wistful suggestion. Indeed, it has not only respectable but classical antecedents. As noted above,

William James's meticulous discussion of the topic in his *Principles* has served as a source for many subsequent studies. What are less often cited are his subsequent pronouncements, in particular an article published originally in 1904 (nine years before Watson's famous attack) entitled 'Does Consciousness Exist?': 'For twenty years past I have mistrusted "consciousness" as an entity. . . . It seems to me that the hour is ripe for it to be openly and universally discarded.'

To summarize, we have as yet failed to reach a consensus as to the nature of consciousness, or even an agreed definition of any precision. What has become clear is that not only may it be said to function at various levels, but that it is composed of many subsystems. Furthermore, it seems probable that these are arranged hierarchically, as are our physical systems. Perhaps we should concern ourselves, as James in fact suggested, not with an assumed totality nor with separate components, but with their interrelationships.

A wide variety of anomalies of consciousness have been described, ranging from those associated with the everyday, health-maintaining condition of sleepiness through to those such as coma, which are symptoms of serious, pathological disorders. Some are the direct results of central nervous system (CNS) malfunction, toxicity or brain injury. Others have been described from a purely phenomenological viewpoint, without reference to any underlying biological problem. In line with the general approach of this book, we will not emphasize etiology here, confining ourselves to descriptive outlines of some of the better known anomalous states. We will group them under four headings: (1) anomalies in the intensity and clarity of awareness, (2) anomalies in the range or focus of awareness, (3) anomalies in the consistency of consciousness, and (4) anomalies in the integrity of consciousness. It should be emphasized that these groupings have been derived simply for expository convenience, and probably have little, if any, theoretical import.

ANOMALIES IN THE INTENSITY AND CLARITY OF AWARENESS

The classical example of a condition that by definition involves diminution of the intensity and clarity of awareness is sleep. But this is not a simple ON/OFF condition. There are at least five levels of sleep, which have been studied intensively, especially in terms of brain activity using the electroencephalogram (EEG). At first thought, it might be assumed that at least deep sleep involves the total absence of awareness. But a little reflection suggests that this is not the case. Even when there is ambient noise at a significant level, an unexpected or sinister sound will often wake the soundest of sleepers, a fact that can be vouched for by countless sleep-deprived parents.

Again, we seem to be able to monitor our sleep, an ability that is at odds with the idea that slumber automatically dispels awareness. Most people can estimate the passage of time during sleep, and wake themselves at a predetermined hour, often with uncanny accuracy. Many people wake each morning just *before* the alarm clock sounds, and few of us can not have experienced spontaneous waking when an unusually early start to the day is required. A special self-preservation skill is displayed by those who can sleep soundly throughout after-dinner speeches, yet awaken just in time to join in the applause as the speaker thanks them for their attention. Generations of students, of course, have brought this time-monitoring technique to high levels of efficiency. Unhappily, the technique does not seem to include the storage of events external to the sleeper, *pace* the much-advertized 'sleep-learning' courses. As a young soldier, the writer was once a less than enthusiastic auditor of a 'Current Affairs' lecture given to the whole battalion by a distinguished civilian authority. Wearied by several days of route-marching and battle training, he made himself comfortable in an inconspicuous position near the rear of the mess hall, and fell into a deep and refreshing sleep. An hour later, he awoke promptly, as the visitor was drawing his peroration to a close, and was the first to leap to his feet when the commanding officer asked for questions. 'What would you say, sir', he inquired brightly, 'are the chances of a Second Front in Europe?' There was a prolonged and terrible silence, during which he was horrified to notice a number of persons in authority rising to their feet to identity the miscreant. Afterwards, he was subject to furious abuse from both his platoon sergeant and the company sergeant major, in regard to what the latter termed 'Your impossibly bloody stupid question!' In response to his querulous request for enlightenment, the sergeant major pointed a quivering finger at a poster, advertizing the evening's educational event. The subject of this important lecture, the rude soldiery had been informed, was to be: 'Will there be a Second Front in Europe?'

Sleep represents only a diminution or interruption of consciousness. A state which seems to involve the total absence of consciousness, and which is decidedly anomalous, is *coma,* which results from brain damage or disease, often associated with circulatory or toxic disorders. In the comatose state even reflex functioning disappears, and the victim is reduced to an almost vegetative level. Unlike sleep, it is not possible to waken the sufferer. If he recovers, he will have total amnesia about the whole episode. A less extreme condition is *torpor,* a pathological drowsiness where the sufferer is in continual danger of slipping away into a profound and dreamless sleep. During this drowsiness, any focussed attention or thought is almost impossible, perception is difficult and fragmentary, no interest or motivation is felt, and affect is flattened. *Sopor* is also marked by extreme drowsiness, but intentional reactions can be elicited by strong stimuli.

Delirium is characteristic of a variety of acute organic states, particularly toxic poisoning. It is usually described as a dreamlike change in consciousness, in which attentional processes are grossly diminished and conceptual thinking is fragmented. Perception of the external world is drastically disturbed, and often confused with memory images. Illusions, pseudo-hallucinations, hallucinations, and delusions are common in severe cases. A well-documented type is delirium tremens, to which we referred in Chapter 3. The 'D.T.s' are usually accompanied by negative affect, ranging from anxiety to terror. Pleasant affect is reported to accompany opium and hashish deliria, which are characterized by grandiose and sexual hallucinations.

Similar in many ways to delirium are the *oneroid states*. The word 'oneroid' means dreamlike, and it is the dreamlike quality of the experience that is its central characteristic. However, the 'dream', unlike the disconnectedness and confusion of delirium, is on-going, vivid, and coherent. Its hallucinatory contents are consistent; they may have a narrative quality and are often scenic in nature. They occupy the individual's whole attention and interest. Oneroid states may persist for weeks. Like delirium, they appear in toxic illnesses, but also in the early, acute phases of schizophrenia.

Perhaps the classical example of diminution in intensity and clarity of awareness is *clouding of consciousness*, which is symptomatic of many traumatic and degenerative physical disorders, including cardiac arrest, brain injury, and senile dementia. It may be transient, resulting from trauma, or it may develop as the predominant feature of a full-blown organic 'confusional state'. Clouding (or obfuscation) of consciousness refers basically to the dulling of mental abilities, a feeling of confusion and an increasing lack of contact with the world. The term applies, of course, to people who are delirious. But the converse is not necessarily so, for the clouded state does not at first involve the florid hallucinatory features of delirium. The first sign of clouding in confusional states is often that the individual begins to show temporal disorientation—he is not sure of the time, day of the week, or date. He begins to be aware that he is not thinking clearly, and is unable to concentrate. This may be followed by disorientation in place; he begins to lose his way, particularly in unfamiliar locations, and even familiar landmarks become hazy. The next stage of disorientation is that the sufferer becomes unsure of the identities of acquaintances and even friends and relatives. Memory disturbances increase, particularly for recent events, as in the mnestic syndrome we discussed in Chapter 4. At the same time, the capacity for abstract thought and reasoning deteriorates significantly. This applies also to the sufferer's social awareness, so that he may begin to show embarrassing or ludicrous behaviours in public. He may squeal piercingly while scattering his food across adjoining tables in the restaurant, or undress and curl up on the floor of the concert hall. During this deteriorating progression, after some initial worry and irritation, the individual may become quite indifferent to his condition, and even deny his increasing inadequacy. In the later stages of the disorder, he drifts into the completely dreamlike world of profound delirium, responding only to a jumble of visual, auditory, tactile, and olfactory hallucinations. And from there, he descends into coma.

ANOMALIES IN THE RANGE OR FOCUS OF AWARENESS

In Chapter 1 we used the analogy of a searchlight in discussing individual differences in the narrowness or diffusion of attention. Many of us must be personally familar with the 'tunnel vision' resulting from intoxication, anxiety, fear, fatigue, or shock. Whether the causes are physiological or psychogenic, the range of awareness becomes unduly limited. In perception, one feature of the environment is focussed upon, and the remainder excluded. Psychiatrists refer to this as the 'narrowing of object-awareness'. The writer was once smitten by extreme alarm upon observing the approach of a creeping artillery barrage. Nearby was a field enclosed by a single strand of wire, and in the middle of the field were several craters. With what he subsequently assured himself was laudable prudence, he vaulted nimbly over the wire and dived into the nearest crater. When the barrage had receded, he emerged from his funk hole and returned to the track. Only then did he register an improvised sign suspended from the wire at the very point where he had jumped across. It bore the pithy warning: 'DANGER! MINEFIELD!'

In the same way, one idea or fear may dominate consciousness at the expense even of those which may be more salient. The anticipation of some forthcoming ordeal may preoccupy us to the point where we are unable to assess the question objectively. Thus we fail to plan appropriate strategies that might alleviate or even avoid the ordeal in question. A young candidate for a research position experienced considerable apprehension as to whether he possessed sufficient technical expertise to cope satisfactorily with advanced statistical analyses. These seemed to him to be the crucial requirements of the job in question, and an aspect with which he was far from comfortable. As the day of the interview approached, he became totally preoccupied by this assumption, and devoted himself to the rehearsal of appropriate answers to the sorts of questions he would face. As it happened, such technical matters were of little concern to the selection committee. After some preliminary courtesies, they got right down to business by asking how, if called upon, he would approach the public relations task of explaining the work of the unit to lay groups, including school children. The candidate reflected briefly and then solemnly replied: 'My preferred technique would be multiple regression analysis!' Such tunnel thinking is not restricted to apprehension or terror, but may result from any heightened emotion, including tenderness and anger. The lover is notoriously incapable of recognizing in the loved one any of the blemishes that are so obvious to others. And almost by definition, the angry person is incapable of seeing both sides of the situation. It is not coincidental that we describe people as being 'blinded by love' or 'blind with fury'.

At its clinical extreme, this inappropriate restriction of awareness is termed a *Twilight State*, not a particularly well-chosen term, but one sanctified by long psychiatric usage. Among several others of less importance, there are two types of experience to which the term is applied. The first, or 'affective' type is an extension of the examples offered above. It is an extreme emotional reaction to some powerful psychological trauma, which involves a restricted comprehension of the situation and thus a distorted assessment. The sufferer may then behave in an irrational or ill-conceived way, often displaying an absence of social restraint, and sometimes with unpredictable violence. Such a twilight state may develop into an amnesic fugue. In some cases, drivers who go on their way after being involved in serious accidents could be regarded as being in twilight states. Objectively, their flight achieves nothing: there may have been several witnesses who can identify them, and damage to their vehicles may provide incontrovertible proof of their involvement. Again, after messy accidents, it is not unusual for people to wander about, thinking of other problems, even when they have not been injured.

The second group of twilight states includes those of organic origin, such as temporal lobe epilepsy and punch-drunkenness. During an attack, the epileptic may continue to engage in some activity, only to 'wake up' as the attack recedes, with total amnesia regarding what has happened. Punch-drunk boxers have been reported to be engaged in their craft quite normally, weaving and punching with controlled skill, only to break off to embrace the referee and parade around the ring with him. In organic twilight states, unlike the affective or psychogenic variety, there may also be considerable clouding of consciousness. But the main feature is that the field of consciousness is restricted to a few ideas, often accompanied by hallucinations or delusions. The patient's behaviour may not seem unusual to the observer, but he may feel confused and disoriented.

ANOMALIES IN THE CONSISTENCY OF CONSCIOUSNESS

To underline a point made in the introduction to this chapter, in some cases there exists a noticeable discrepancy between the various components or subsystems of consciousness. A good example of this is *déjà vu*, which we discussed in Chapter 5 as an anomaly of recognition. In *déjà vu* and the much rarer *jamais vu*, the individual has the disturbing awareness of a discrepancy between his on-going perception of a scene and his conscious memory (or absence thereof) of what he is seeing. In Chapter 6, we described several examples of the breakdown of consistency, including depersonalization, where the individual knows who he is, but feels strangely unreal. In everyday life, inconsistencies of consciousness are not uncommon. For instance, episodes of diminished mental acuity may be accompanied by heightened affective colouring, which encourages us to feel as though we are operating at a high level of cognitive efficiency. Our normal self-monitoring is grievously divorced from our actual performance. The reason people who are objectively incapable of carrying out skilled tasks insist upon driving home after drunken parties is that they believe that their powers of coordination, anticipation, and judgement have never been so good. Characteristically, our sense of well-being and heightened enjoyment is usually accompanied by this lowering of self-criticism. Indeed, there seems to be a direct relationship between the two, perhaps of a causal nature, although it would be difficult to determine which is the cause and which the effect. It is possible that the second half of the twentieth century is among the most hedonistic in human history (at least in the Western world), so it is not surprising that it has been marked by enthusiasic searches for 'highs', for 'psychedelic experiences', and for 'consciousness-broadening'. Such pursuits of bliss include positive affective changes, accompanying either excitation or tranquillity. All involve a diffusion of ego individuality, and therefore a reduction in self-judgement, accompanied by relief from responsibility.

Perhaps the most widely practised exercise for the induction of such gratifying states of consciousness is immersion in intensified rhythmic input. The effects are heightened by social support, so that group indulgence is the norm. The rock music movement, spearheaded by the Beatles concerts of the early 1960s, offers the contemporary paradigm of this sort of experience. The crucial auditory element of rock is the heavy, implacable, metrical beat. During public performances, this is presented at levels of amplification that, in the work place, would provide grounds for mass compensation suits. Modern rock concerts and discotheques reinforce this auditory basis with the integrated visual input of dazzling strobe 'light shows'. The changes of consciousness induced by such patterned sensory bombardment have an immediate biological source. It has been shown in the laboratory that intense rhythmical input has a 'driving' effect on the brain. The frequencies of the brain's electrical patterns become coincident with those of the input—a very pretty example of the individual's cognitive activity being brought under direct external control. Ironically, while the rock enthusiast's subjective experience and motor activity are those of euphoric excitement, EEG recordings reveal that cognitively he is asleep. The same mechanisms operate in many communal contexts around the world. In primitive societies, tribal war dances are characterized by rhythmic drumming, shield-beating, and stamping. At revivalist meetings, the congregation accompanies highly rhythmical hymn-singing by clapping and stamping. Excited subservience is whipped up at political rallies by the incessant chanting of rhythmical jingles or the names of political leaders. Indeed, the deliberate intensification of rhythmical input, and the resultant changes in consciousness seem to have accompanied religious celebrations and preparations for battle as well as merry-making throughout history. The technical resources of modern times merely enable us to augment the sensory input required.

Similar effects can be achieved by the ingestion of a variety of 'hypnotic' drugs, such as the barbiturates and meprobamate, and euphoriants like cocaine and hashish. But a more innocuous method of inducing 'altered states of consciousness' is engagement in meditation. As we saw in Chapter 6, this was once common among devout Christians in Western cultures, but now usually implies application to exercises derived from Oriental religions.

Unlike the sensory overstimulation described above, meditation techniques depend upon the reduction of sensory input and the deliberate exclusion of external and internal distractions. As we have seen, the individual aims for physical relaxation, and focusses his consciousness upon some nonstimulating object, such as a flower, a bowl, or a mandala pattern. He may whisper or chant a particular (often meaningless) word—his *mantra*. The goal is to retain clear consciousness while emptying the mind of all contents except the subject of contemplation. In the original religious context, this would be some mystical abstraction, such as the nature of Divine Truth or the Ultimate Being. Such exercises were intended to help the devout person to attain nirvana, which we discussed in relation to anomalies in the experience of self (see Chapter 6). Their adoption in the West has more usually been for secular purposes, including rest and relaxation, psychotherapy, or simple curiosity. However different in form from participation in rock concerts or protest rallies, all these activities have something in common. They all involve a reduced consistency of consciousness, inasmuch as they induce a gratificatory state where cognitive efficacy is reduced while self-criticism is loosened. A conviction of mental acuity and heightened sensitivity is established, accompanied by a sense of worth or virtue, in the face of impaired cognitive functioning.

The most colourful examples of consciousness inconsistency are probably those associated with the hypnotic trance and, even more dramatically, responses to post-hypnotic suggestion. The rock music fan abdicates personal control to the external stimulus of the auditory beat; the meditator also hands over responsibility, but in his case the recipient is the product of his preparatory set. In the hypnotic state, the subject is under the control of the hypnotist's voice. His or her awareness is more or less subjugated, according to the depth of hypnosis induced. Under deep hypnosis, at least, the subject's consciousness is no longer ego-bound, and could be said to be whatever the hypnotist determines. When he is brought out of the hypnotic state, the subject reverts to his normal level of consciousness and sense of self. But subsequently he may find himself engaging bemusedly in absurd or atypical acts in conformity with predetermined suggestions. He is now himself again, fully conscious of the world around him and his place in it. Yet he finds himself engaging in certain actions as though they were controlled by some other self, one which is not available to conscious examination.

Let us think of the individual's 'normal' state of full consciousness as involving a balance between external input and an on-going sampling of stored material—schemata, floating images and fantasies, reasoning, and so on. Both hypnotic states and other altered states of consciousness (ASC) derive from disturbances of this baseline pattern. Of course, this is also exactly what is happening as we fall asleep. But as we noted above, natural sleepiness results from a reduction of cortical activity, with an ensuing blurring or clouding of consciousness. ASCs involve at least one other variable—the previous inculcation of a set to remain awake at some level. This set is established either by the individual's own intention or by the hypnotist's instructions. In other words, the individual remains aware of one or more classes of input, while ceasing to process others. In this regard, an ASC has much in common with the restricted awareness we discussed in the previous section.

ANOMALIES IN INTEGRITY OF CONSCIOUSNESS

In the introduction to this chapter, it was emphasized that consciousness is not an intact, indivisible entity, a popular view derived from our use of the singular noun and the idea of consciousness as a unitary 'thing' or substance. In earlier chapters, the selectivity of attention and other cognitive processes was stressed. We have seen how perceptions may be regarded in terms of hypotheses and best guesses, and how memories are subject to dynamic revisions, elaborations, and abbreviations. We have also considered some of the ways in which our sense of identity can falter or split. In varying degrees, all these normal processes and their associated anomalies are of necessity reflected in consciousness, and all offer support for the view that consciousness is an interactive multiplicity of systems. In the present chapter, we have seen how the so-called twilight states are those in which certain percepts or ideas appear in consciousness while others are blotted out. We shall conclude by looking at some cases in which the integrity of consciousness as a whole is broken, where the individual's normal pattern of consciousness is, at least for a time, replaced by another.

In other words, our interest will go beyond restrictions or distortions of the content of consciousness to changes in the form of consciousness itself.

In the Introduction to this book, the reader was warned that many of the topics to be covered could equally well be discussed in the terms suggested by several chapter titles. Already we have reconsidered anomalies that figured in earlier chapters. Many of these topics may be drawn upon to illustrate this final section.

Perhaps the most widely experienced of everyday phenomena that may be taken as examples of divided consciousness is the 'time-gap', which we explained in Chapter 1 in terms of automatization. Here, certainly, seems to be one sort of breakdown of unified conscious experience, for it involves carrying out a skilled task for a protracted period without, apparently, being aware that we are doing so. Yet, when the situation demands it, the required integration of consciousness returns as the normal input/storage balance is restored. An extreme extension of this situation is where an individual's total identity is replaced temporarily by another, complete with different life-style and personal attributes. The individual is apparently unaware that the metamorphosis has taken place or that he has an alternate persona. The classical example of this is the fugue state, discussed in Chapter 4 as an anomaly of recall, because hysterical amnesia characterizes such cases. Fugues are among the 'dual' or 'mutiple personalities' which have always excited popular as well as medical interest, and provided material for such fictional classics as Robert Louis Stevenson's *Dr. Jekyll and Mr. Hyde*. Dr. Jekyll is a gentle physician, who is acutely aware of the mix of good and bad in his nature, and intrigued by the implications of separating these two skeins. He discovers a drug that enables him to absorb all his evil attributes into an individual personality—the appalling Mr. Hyde. The two personalities alternate, but then Hyde begins to take over, as the drug loses its power to restore the original Jekyll. It may well be that the lasting appeal of the Jekyll and Hyde story is that it carries a deep-rooted, mythic symbolism. The 'dual personality' is popularly taken to be the good and the bad sides of the individual struggling with each other by manifesting themselves as separate personas. There is a long tradition behind this view, of which the concept of 'possession' is but one component. The struggle between virtue and evil can be seen as one facet of the external war between God and Satan for the souls of mankind. 'Possession' means the invasion and inhabitation of human beings by evil spirits, an idea that dates back to antiquity and has appeared in most parts of the world, usually in association with religious beliefs. The victim of such possession can only be freed from demonic control, and thus restored to grace and normalcy, by expelling the invader. This has usually been attempted by special rites and ceremonies of exorcism. In the case of witches, it was deemed most expedient to burn the demon out of his host, which, of course, involved burning the host as well. A more rational approach, coupled with better understanding of mental disorders, has led to the abandonment of such practices in the Western world and their replacement by less inhuman techniques. But exorcism is still practised in primitive cultures and, although it is rarely invoked, the Catholic church still recognizes a special ritual for exorcism.

Another explanation of a 'possession' type is that of the spiritualistic medium, who believes that during her trance her body is used, not by a demon, but the spirit of a dead person. The latter is the 'control' who, as an inhabitant of the after life, can act as a channel of communication with other spirits.

Such explanations of 'dual personality' make the assumption that the condition indicates (a) the existence of two different persons or Beings, who (b) share the same physical body. The more scientific view is that only one person is involved, and that the two (or more) others reported are simply facets or components of the individual. The fact that one of the other facets can be projected without awareness of the other(s) is evidence that the individual's consciousness can be fragmented, and the parts exist independently. This is the extreme version of the dissociation of affect that we discussed in Chapter 6. Dissociation phenomena excited keen interest in the medical community towards the end of the last century, being examined most authoritatively by Pierre Janet. 'Multiple Personalities' was a hot research topic of the time in scientific circles as well as in the newly-established area of parapsychology, which had attracted many leading thinkers. The interest has reemerged in recent years, and the whole question of divided consciousness has received a modern fillip from an unexpected quarter.

Cerebral commissurotomy involves the surgical severance of the corpus callosum, the mass of fibres that joins the two cerebral hemispheres. Thus, it has become known popularly as the 'split brain operation', a term that is not entirely accurate, for connections still exist deeper in the brain. The psychological effects of the procedure were first reported by Sperry, Gazzaniga, Bogen, and their associates in the early 1960s. Their findings had an immediate and dramatic impact because they demonstrated that each hemisphere has a specialized function. In brief, the left hemisphere is superior in the processing of linguistic, abstract, and logical tasks, using an analytic and objective approach. The right hemisphere is superior in the processing of spatial relationships and music, using a holistic and intuitive approach. These reported differences, which have been well summarized by many authorities (e.g., Sperry, 1973) precipitated a flood of research and speculation, which still continues. But several notes of caution must be sounded. First, the original, hard evidence was derived from a very small pool of subjects. Only about a score of patients had been subjected to the total commissurotomy operation, and this number is unlikely to increase, because the treatment has been superseded. Second, these subjects, of course, were not normal, healthy people; on the contrary, the surgery was only employed to alleviate intractable epilepsy. Not only was the neurological status of the patients in doubt, but they were receiving massive doses of anticonvulsant drugs. Third, the patients did not constitute a homogeneous group, and the findings (often anecdotal, and open to various interpretations) were often unjustifiably overgeneralized. An admirably detached review of the relevant evidence has been provided by Beaumont (1981).

Of more importance for our present topic than the details of the 'split-brain' research is the stream of theoretical speculation regarding consciousness, which has constituted a major spin-off from the original studies. Sperry himself introduced such discussions soon after the first experimental reports appeared, and has subsequently written extensively on the issue. It proved to be a short step from the identification of different, specialized functions in the two hemispheres to the suggestion that they therefore represent two minds. It was an even shorter step to equate 'minds' with 'consciousnesses'. This was stated explicitly by Sperry (1964):

> Everything we have seen so far indicates that the surgery has left each of these people with two separate minds, that is, with two separate spheres of consciousness.

Variations have been proposed, but several of these share some basic assumptions with the original position, which may be summarized as follows:

a) Consciousness is identical with, or is located within, an anatomical structure.
b) That structure is the brain or, to be more precise, the brain's two cerebral hemispheres.
c) Each hemisphere has now been shown to have its own specialized functions.
d) *Therefore,* the individual possesses two consciousnesses.

Briefly, it may be pointed out that the first of the above assumptions involves acceptance of the 'identity' hypothesis, which, at least in this extreme form, has been firmly rejected by philosophers, psychologists, and neuroscientists. As we noted earlier, consciousness has been regarded as a state, a system, a function, a process, or merely an epiphenomenon. Nowadays it would not normally be regarded as a *thing.* But, to continue to the second assumption, if we were to accept the identity hypothesis, why should the hemispheres be the organs of consciousness? There are other structures within our skulls with equally valid claims to be accepted in this role. In fact, the most plausible contender in these metaphysical stakes would surely be the entire central nervous system.

The problem with (c) above has nothing to do with the statement itself, for which there is ample evidence. What are dubious are the shaky implications that have been drawn from it. The experimental work with normal subjects has of necessity been limited to artificial activities within very restricted situations. Despite this, it seems reasonable to accept that the two hemispheres have different functional specialities. After all, why shouldn't they? But that is not tantamount to saying that they operate independently. On the contrary, even in split-brain patients, some inter-hemispherical communications exist, while in normals the two hemispheres are complementary. And they are not simply co-workers yoked together to work in parallel; they are fully integrated, synchronized components of a single system.

The crux of the split-brain/dual-consciousness argument is contained in (d) above, about which it may fairly be suggested that (d) simply does not follow from the preceding postulates. To do so would mean a redefinition of consciousness, equating it with differing hemispherical functions. And if this were valid, then the present argument would suggest that each of us rejoices in two consciousnesses which are not only separate but different in kind.

The split-brain studies reflected a significant technical achievement and produced a number of very valuable findings. They were dramatic in their implications, exciting and stimulating. Indeed, they spawned a fashionable academic industry in psychology, wherein practically everything that moves is to be explained in terms of hemispherical specialization. But the very drama of their nature encouraged a wealth of speculation, much of it imaginative but coupled with shaky assumptions and dubious leaps of logic.

What are we to make of all this, as far as the study of consciousness is concerned? We are forced back to the questions posed at the beginning of this chapter. The strength of the cerebral hemisphere evidence will be determined by one's conception of consciousness.

ANOMALIES IN THE RATE
OF FLOW OF CONSCIOUSNESS

In this chapter, we shall retreat from the general field of consciousness to focus our attention upon one small segment—the rate at which cognitions present themselves in consciousness. (Use of the word 'cognitions', rather than 'thoughts', emphasizes that our interest covers all sorts of conscious mental activity—thoughts, arguments, fears, doubts, hopes, plans, memories, images, and so on.) Unhappily, limiting our attack in this way does not simplify the conceptual problems. Perhaps for this reason, even our narrowly circumscribed topic has not been satisfactorily analyzed at the theoretical level. Indeed, in the vast literature having to do with consciousness, cognition, and associated areas, any convincing examination or even description is noticeable by its absence. What follows here can be no more than tentative toe-dipping in uncharted seas.

Obviously, any hypothesis as to the rate of change of conscious cognitions will depend upon what is accepted as a model of consciousness itself. And as we saw in the last chapter, that question is still an open one. If you happen to conceive of consciousness as a mechanism or engine, then the rate of through-put is readily explained in terms of the mechanism's speed of operation. We have already attacked the idea that consciousness is a mechanism. But there is another reason to suggest that the 'engine speed' analogy is inappropriate. In the present context 'rate' is marked by 'change'. In the 'engine' analogy, the rate in question is one of function—the engine's revolutions, which can increase or decrease. The function or operation does not change in kind. The pistons simply move more or less rapidly. The functions that contribute to consciousness may also change their speeds of operation. But what we experience consciously are not the operations themselves, but the changing flow of contents. We recognize a change in rate of our cognitions by the number of shifts of content that we experience during a period of time.

The same criticism, among others, applies to another variety of mechanistic analogy, where the emphasis is placed not on the engine, but upon its product. For instance, consciousness may be conceived of as the toothpaste squeezed from an endless tube, or the plastic piping spewed out by an industrial extrusion process. Analogies of this kind have an advantage over the 'engine' kind; they differentiate between the machine and its output, and offer content equivalents. But they cannot get us very far. They rely upon some odd assumptions, are simply (and faultily) descriptive and, more importantly, do not allow for the ever-changing nature of consciousness.

The recognition that the rate of passage of conscious cognitions is marked by content shifts leads us once again to the seminal work of William James. In his discussion of the 'stream of consciousness', James was concerned to emphasize the continuing, unbroken nature of consciousness. His metaphor of a flowing stream or river is a classical one, with its roots in antiquity. It is a vivid and intuitively acceptable model, but by its very nature it can be misleading. The individual is pictured as sitting on the river bank, watching the water flow by. The flow is continual but, of course, the stretch of water under observation is ever-changing. This image allowed James to emphasize that one can never think the same thought twice, any more than a particular water molecule can flow past the observer a second time. In one sense, this is a very good point. Our minds are not rag-bags of discrete thoughts, which can be produced repeatedly for display. Contemporary psychology would argue that cognitions are assimilated into dynamic, ever-changing cognitive structures—the *schemata* that we have discussed in previous chapters. So it is surely correct to assert that, once it has been thought, a particular cognition does not remain discrete and available for conscious re-examination in its original form. But James's argument may be misunderstood. It may be taken to state that a thought can never reappear in consciousness at all. And this, of course, is simply not so. We can, and regularly do, consciously recall thoughts, facts, arguments, affronts, images, and the like. For some of us, as we shall see, this may go too far and become a disturbing or even handicapping propensity. But, as was discussed in Chapter 4, it should be borne in mind that what we are recalling are not original data points but the schemata into which these were incorporated. In other words, cognitions certainly reappear (that is what memory is) but not in their earlier forms. And this at once suggests a crucial weakness in the 'stream' metaphor. It does not allow for the dynamic, integrative, feedback aspects of consciousness. Far from being a stream, each drop of which, once past the observation point, is gone forever, consciousness is more like a continuously re-circulating system. But unlike the standard central heating system, in this one the fluid is continuously replenished, enriched, and mixed.

How is the above relevant to our basic theme, the *rate* of flow of cognitions in consciousness? Well, at the very least, it serves to remind us to distinguish between 'raw' items and schemata. An un-assimilated item may have few association links. A schema, by definition, is itself a dynamic network of associations. The size and complexity of the network is a function of the amount of processing to which it has been subjected, and the connotative range of its contributory segments. These factors produce the *quality* of an experience. And the term 'level of consciousness' refers to this qualitative aspect—to the clarity and richness of conscious apprehension. To what extent is the level of consciousness related to the speed of cognitive operations? This is yet another tricky question, and one that may well not be amenable to solution in this form. Schematic quality and operational speed can scarcely be regarded as directly correlated. The rapidity with which thoughts and images present themselves in consciousness cannot be said to reflect richness in their apprehension or acuity in their processing. Equally, slowness may reflect productive contemplation on the one hand, or on the other, sterile preoccupation or simple sluggishness. However, the rate at which ideas succeed each other in consciousness is in one sense a function of the availability of schemata, and the richness and range of the activated associative nets. Obviously, the richer the nets, the wider the range of associations, and therefore the more options there are for associative shifts.

The speed of our conscious thought and, to a lesser extent, its quality are often under our own control. We may deliberately speed up the making of a decision, turn from one line of reasoning to another, cease to struggle consciously with a problem, or persist in wrestling with it. We may allow ourselves to indulge in daydreams or apply our energies to pragmatic issues, conjure up some bittersweet memory or refuse to contemplate it. But although these sorts of choices and decisions may be conscious, they cannot be said to be *due* to consciousness. Nor, as has been suggested, can they be equated with consciousness. They spring from a variety of cognitive and affective processes. Their implementation is the product of *will*, which again is conscious, but is itself not consciousness.

Like consciousness, will was a central concern for early psychologists, the study of which was aborted by the advent of Behaviourism. It has remained an actively debated topic for philosophers but, unlike consciousness, has not yet invited reconsideration by psychologists. Indeed, the last authoritative psychological study was, once more, that of William James. As usual, James's discussion was insightful, acute, and elegant. But his much-cited *fiat* can scarcely be ranked as an explanatory construct. He used the word merely as a synonym for 'consent' or 'resolve'. Thus, despite the respect that has been accorded the term, it is hard to see how its introduction has advanced our understanding of violition or cognitive control.

ANOMALIES IN THE AVAILABILITY OF IDEAS

In response to good or exciting news, people often experience a surge of ideas, images, and conjectures. 'I hadn't really dared to believe that I would win a scholarship. When the news sank in, I couldn't think straight at first—my mind was in a whirl. . . .' 'When the prize was announced, I was so excited; I just stood there with my mouth open. I didn't know what to say, but I was swamped with all sorts of ideas.' This is not to say that such ideas are richer or more novel than usual, or that the quality of thinking is enhanced. On the contrary, elation often results in a stream of inchoate images and fragmentary thoughts. What is noticeable in retrospect is not the flexibility of associations or the clarity of cognition, but simply the rapidily with which ideas, images, and hopes succeed each other in the stream of consciousness.

The pathological equivalent of the above is the 'crowding of thoughts' often reported by schizophrenic patients. This is usually classified as one of the 'formal thought disorders' associated with the psychosis. Sufferers complain that thoughts press in upon them with speed and confusion that is actually painful. Ironically, the opposite affect accompanies the similar experience of *'flight of ideas',* which we will discuss shortly. Far from being accompanied by discomfort or distress, the classical flight of ideas is experienced as cheery and ego-enhancing, in the context of mania or hypomania. It is, in fact, one facet of the exuberance central to those disorders.

In Chapter 4, we discussed stage fright and examination dry-up as anomalies of recall. Under stressful conditions, we are all liable to find that we are temporarily unable to recall information or actions that we have carefully learned, especially for regurgitation in the theatre or examination room. Very often, we despairingly discover that it is not only the learned material that absents itself at the crucial time. We find ourselves unable to summon up any ideas of relevance whatsoever, so that we cannot even 'wing it'. Our minds, we complain, are a total blank. No helpful associations seem to be available. Now, this regrettable experience is not limited to the recall of formally learned material. Mind-blankness can smite us when we are requested to make a short, informal address, or even merely to engage in civil conversation. 'And now', announces the master of ceremonies affably, 'it gives me great pleasure to ask our old and respected friend, Mr. Higginbotham, to say a few words.' And Mr. Higginbotham, although the situation is seemingly without threat, finds himself quite unable to think of any words at all. Despite the minimal verbal responses demanded of the central protagonists in the marriage ceremony, how many nervous grooms have found themselves incapable, until prompted, of capturing and enunciating those two tiny words: 'I do'?

A similar mind-blankness can assail individuals where there is no immediate stress, and no question of concurrent public exposure. The best-known example of this is 'writers' block', about which thousands of words have been written, presumably by unblocked writers. On occasion, they complain, most writers simply dry up. Despite hours, days, months, even years of struggle, they find themselves incapable of writing. Usually, it is reported, this is because they are unable to think of anything—or, at least, of anything worth writing. The experience brings frustration and then anguish in its wake, according to how protracted it is. The student battling with the production of a thesis sees her chances of attaining the degree fading. The professional writer begins to fear that she is burned out, her literary career at an end. Amateur poets and novelists, while not depending upon the pen for a livelihood, nevertheless may be miserable in concluding that they have been deserted by the Muse. This interpretation of the problem reflects the widely held belief that writers' block is due to a failure of 'inspiration'. The well-spring of creativity, it is assumed, has dried up. The metaphor, of course, betrays assumptions about the nature of creative activities, which have about as much validity as explanations of the aging process in terms of the 'Fountain of Youth.'

'Mind-blankness' described above is common among healthy people, given appropriate situations, and must have been experienced by most of us. A pathological form of the experience is sometimes suffered by the mentally disordered and termed 'thought blocking', which was described as one of the schizophrenic formal thought disorders in Chapter 6. Patients report brief stoppages of their thought processes, the observable correlates of which are the cessation of attention and speech. These short interludes are reminiscent of *petit mal* attacks; they do not involve loss of consciousness, as do major epileptic seizures. The victims often attempt to explain the experiences subsequently in terms of delusional 'thought withdrawal'. Some external, malignant power has siphoned the thoughts away. As we saw earlier, the resultant vacuum may be left empty, or may be replenished by alien thoughts ('thought insertion'). Thought blocking is usually momentary, but occasionally may last for hours. In either case, a noticeable feature is that the normal cognitive continuum is broken. After the blockage, the sufferer's thoughts have no apparent connection with those which led up to the lapse. Metaphorically, the train of thought is not simply brought to a halt and then restarted, but taken out of service, to reappear on a different line.

Whereas 'thought blocking' refers to an intermittency of conscious thinking, there is another pathological phenomenon that involves cognitive deceleration. This is 'retardation', a term whose technical use in psychopathology differs from its more common one, which refers to subnormal intellectual and social development. In its more specialized sense, retardation refers to the slowing down of thinking and the stream of consciousness. The rich network of associations that contribute to normal thinking diminish drastically. The vestiges may include only limited fragments ('poverty of thought') or, indeed, only a single, often distressing idea ('monoideism'). Patients complain that whatever flow of thought remains has become slow and sticky 'like wading through mud'. Thinking is laborious, demanding considerable effort. Ideas do not come spontaneously, imagery becomes sketchy, application to a problem is agonizing, and recall is exceedingly difficult.

ANOMALIES IN THE FLEXIBILITY OF ASSOCIATIONS

So far, we have been concerned only with anomalies in the perceived speed of cognitions, the rate at which thoughts and images seem to present themselves in consciousness. Let us now turn to a closely related topic—anomalies in the spread and flexibility of associations. It may well be that this is the other side of the same coin, and that to distinguish between them is an exercise in pedantry. However, the relationship is not constant. It is possible to experience a rapid series of thoughts which have little discernible connectedness. They appear in consciousness in a speedy but disjointed sequence, like the bullets from a machine gun. And it is also possible to experience a stream of thoughts, whose appearance in consciousness seems to be the result of the fluidity of associations between them. Unlike the series of individual bullets, they seem to be links in a chain, or nodes in a net, each one triggered or elicited by its predecessor.

In everyday life, people may be described as 'grasshopper minded' because their thoughts (as reflected in attention and speech) flit about from one topic to another. Sometimes, this betrays an inability to maintain a logical sequence of thinking, verging on incoherence. The individual loses track of his original line of thought, and flies off at a tangent, as though his threshold for distraction is too low. His associations are said to be too loose, and his cognitive efficiency suffers as a result. This impairment is often the result of shock or undue stress. But in some individuals it is a cognitive style, a characteristic of the regular personality pattern. A more organized version of this flexibility of associations is *circumstantiality,* where the theme or line of argument is not lost, but a variety of associated ideas are considered and elliptical excursions made before return to the original topic is effected. Here, the problem seems to be one, not of simple 'grasshopping', but a failure in the hierarchical ordering of material. The circumstantial raconteur fails to see the wood for the trees, giving the same consideration to every detail of his account as he does to the key features. This, of course, destroys the rhythm and thrust of the account, and brings a lingering death to any artistic or dramatic recital. The flattening and bathos usually engender tedium, if not irritation in the hearer. But the reaction can be recruited to good purpose where the intention is comic.

In the brilliant British television comedy series, 'The Two Ronnies', a regular segment consists of Ronnie Corbett recounting a joke. There are no props, no chorus or colleagues, no film clips. Corbett simply sits alone, centre stage, and tells his story. The stories are amusing in themselves, but the major contributor to the comic effect is the fact that every phrase triggers off another joke, or sidetracks the raconteur into wry reminiscences. However, he invariably manages to return intermittently to the original story line. No matter how complicated the network of associated red herring diversions, the theme is always recovered. And this resolution, in the context of surprise and schematic shifts, is arguably at the heart of our enjoyment of the comic. Corbett's technique, of course, is the diametric opposite of the 'one-liner' approach followed by most stand-up comics. Here, a rapid series of short quips is rattled off, the comedian aiming to win over his audience by the cumulative effect of many small jokes, rather than by the more leisurely development of a humorous ethos. The former attack might be compared to a string of firecrackers, the latter to a long fuse, followed by a complex display. The 'one-liner' technique is more effective, or at least safer, in cabarets and clubs, where the entertainer has to contend with noisy and inattentive audiences, whose attention span is likely to be very limited. Only very talented or 'name' comedians like Ronnie Corbett or Woody Allen can hold their audiences long enough to risk the more extended, developmental technique.

The classical pathological example of both rapidity and over-loose associations is 'flight of ideas', which is most common in people suffering from *mania* and its milder form, *hypomania,* although it may be manifested in other psychotic disorders. The term is applied to an incessant, rapid stream of thought and speech, where the theme is lost in a welter of associated words and images. Most commonly, these are expressed in word-play, punning, and rhyming. 'The name of the President? Sure, the name's the game. He's a resident. In the White House, but it could be yellow, right? Whatever you tell the painter'. Manic patients are readily distractible, so that a chance word, or the sight of some object in the vicinity, can trigger off another chain of associations. The apparent richness of the ideas expressed is fallacious because the flow does not reflect chains of meaning so much as surface characteristics. The associations are determined by superficial features of what is heard or seen. This is readily apparent if the flow of speech is transcribed. It may not be immediately discernible in face to face encounters, where the listener is diverted by the energy and bomhomie of the patient. The latter's affability serves to discourage objective assessment of what he is saying.

Although in the flight of ideas the original point is rapidly lost, an underlying theme may be tenuously retained. But in extreme cases, the flow of ideas becomes so extreme that the speech cannot be articulated rapidly enough to express them, and there is a deterioration into incoherence. The flow of speech becomes fragmented, so that the associations between words and phrases disappear, and connected speech is replaced by isolated words and expressions.

So far in this section, we have been looking at cases where associations seem to be unduly flexible. What of those where associations are readily available but across a limited range? The best example from everyday life is *preoccupation,* when our minds revolve around a single topic. This is different in kind from blocking, or the mind-blankness of stage fright or examination nerves. Far from there being any conscious diminution of mental activity, preoccupation often involves furious thinking—but the thinking revolves around one particular theme. Commonly, this theme has to do with some matter of significance. It may be a past event and its implications, ranging from the contemplation of some gratifying achievement right through to such sad happenings as a bereavement or the sickness of a loved one. But often the focus of preoccupation possesses little personal significance or affective tone. For instance, we tend to become preoccupied by unresolved problems or puzzles, which represent cognitive challenges rather than emotion-chargedness. They are characterized by their incomplete, unfinished nature. It will be recalled that Gestalt psychologists emphasized our tendency toward completion, exemplified by responses to perceptual tasks. Subjects tend to round off or complete incomplete figures by ignoring gaps and distortions. Similarly, the 'Zeigarnik effect' is the term applied to the reported propensity of subjects to recall unfinished tasks more readily than completed ones. This Gestalt 'Law' may be of high relevance to our present topic, for when we become preoccupied with an unsolved problem, the preoccupation usually ceases as soon as we arrive at a solution or reconciliation.

In the mnemonic sphere, the 'puzzle' may simply be the recall of a name or piece of information. In Chapter 4, we looked at the 'tip of the tongue' (TOT) phenomenon. A TOT state is often accompanied by prolonged attempts to recover the material in question, and these attempts in themselves become preoccupying. (Ironically, the TOT experience is usually best dissipated by a refusal to continue conscious striving to remember. The elusive material may then 'pop into consciousness'.) A very common example is the failure to match a melody with its title. We find that we are unable to recall the tune of a song, although we know its name. Or, conversely, we are haunted by a melody, but cannot recall what it is called. That this is a common experience is attested by the continuing popularity of radio and television games of the 'Name that Tune' variety.

A certain type of preoccupation is usually referred to as 'brooding', a term which carries derogatory connotations. Brooding is preoccupation accompanied by such negative feelings as jealousy, suspicion, vengefulness, or hostility. A person is said to brood when he is preoccupied, for instance, by suspicions as to a spouse's fidelity, by failure to win a promotion, by awareness of one's unpopularity, by a belief that life is treating one unfairly, or because one has been the victim of a slight (real or imagined). Here again, the key to brooding seems to be the (negative) affective capacity of the preoccupying theme.

As noted above, preoccupation does not imply restricted, repetitive, or stereotypic cognition. The theme, topic or question dominates consciousness. But it is attacked and worried from a variety of viewpoints. The question is actively gnawed at, the topic is analyzed and re-analyzed. Preoccupation, in fact, is a consciously willed activity, which involves attempts to resolve a dilemma, solve a problem, or come to terms with a threat. Its end result may be constructive, signalling a resolution, adaptation, or schematic incorporation.

Preoccupation is usually triggered by a particular event or problem. But the same sort of delimitation of cognitive energy may in certain individuals be such an habitual pattern as to be classifiable as a personality characteristic. At the opposite extreme from the person we describe as having a 'grasshopper mind' is the one with a 'one track mind'. This is somebody who tends to 'harp on' about one topic, to worry interminably about some difficulty, or to give protracted consideration to an idea that does not seem to merit such close attention. Where the grasshopper-minded person is accused of failing to apply himself to problems, and to be too easily distracted from the question at issue, the one-tracker may exasperate his fellows by his inability to accept a situation or realize that a subject has been exhausted. The first individual displays an over-fluidity of associations, the second either a paucity of associations or a fixity of focus. This latter propensity is more than *preoccupation,* which, as noted above, is a common reaction to the receipt of significant news, the witnessing of a dramatic event, or frustration in the solving of a problem. One-track-mindedness seems to reflect a cognitive style of handling information. This is often not the optimal mode, but a lot depends upon the nature of the task or situation. Certain problems may lend themselves to solution by a tenacious, reiterative, detailed approach. But generally, more problems yield to a flexible, innovative approach. Most types of input are neither assimilated more readily nor appreciated more richly by being hashed over repeatedly. And, certainly, social interchange is stunted by continual repetitions of inquiry or discourse. The inveterate one-track-mind is liable to be regarded as a bore, to be avoided at all costs. At social gatherings, he is likely to be a 'party pooper', not by intent or malice, but simply because his conversation is earnest, circumscribed, repetitious, and generally tedious. His inability to abandon his topic of choice, or even to approach it from fresh viewpoints, impedes the spontaneous flow of conversation and deadens the lightness of tone associated with an enjoyable party. Furthermore, even the most well-intentioned of one-trackers will display a fiendish ability to turn the line of talk back to his focal theme, should attempts be made by others to change the subject.

What we have just described is a characteristic of certain normal, healthy people. They are boring, but their mental functioning and stability are not in doubt. Their reluctance to abandon a given topic until its every detail has been scrutinized from every angle seems to be under conscious control. We have little doubt that they are capable of turning to other subjects. Given some cataclysmic disaster or the offer of a substantial monetary reward, they certainly would do so. However, a more extreme version of their problem does exist, being termed *perseveration*. Although this has been measured experimentally in the responses of normal subjects, it is associated with several mental disorders, including those resulting from brain injury and senility. The term 'perseveration' is to be distinguished from 'persistence', which, of course, describes determination in the face of obstacles. Such resolution is under volitional control, and is regarded approvingly as one aspect of character strength. Perseveration, on the other hand, refers to the continuance or repetition of behavior after its purpose (or the stimulus or cue in experimental terminology) has disappeared. It is taken to be beyond conscious control.

For many years, perseveration was the darling of experimental psychologists, being particularly favoured by factor-analysts. The data from vast batteries of tests were analyzed in an enthusiastic quest for the grail of a 'factor of perseveration'. The great factor-analyst, Charles Spearman, was convinced that he and his associates had demonstrated such a group factor, which formed all behavior but was possessed in varying degrees by individuals. He claimed this 'p' factor as perhaps one of the 'greatest conquests of experimental psychology', and went so far as to elevate its status to that of a law—his 'mental law of inertia'. Unhappily, psychology does not seem to lend itself to universal laws, and knocking this particular contender became something of an academic mini-industry during the 1930s. Critics pointed out that the correlations that provided the underpinning for Spearman's factor were pathetically low, although they were often technically significant in the statistical sense. The raw data were results derived from performances on a number of tests, such as writing digits backwards, which, it was pointed out, had never been shown to measure perseveration. And in any case, many test results could be explained in terms of speed or motor ability without the postulation of any independent factor. By the mid-1940s, interest in *p* as a factor operating as a functional unit in normal subjects had all but disappeared. Perseveration survived, however, in its original sense, as a clinical symptom.

THE RESISTANCE TO SHIFT

As experimental studies of perseveration were diminishing in number, interest was increasing in an associated topic, that of *rigidity,* which appealed not only to personality theorists and factor-analysts but to clinicians as well. The concepts of perseveration and rigidity overlap, and have sometimes been judged to be synonymous. Neither has been satisfactorily defined, or at least defined in a way that has received general agreement. In particular, the task of pinning down what is meant by rigidity has excited the inventiveness of both psychiatrists and psychologists, and dozens of different definitions have appeared in the literature. But in general terms it is fair to say that rigidity refers to resistance to shifting from an habitual pattern of thought or action to a more effective, economical, or rewarding alternative. This represents a change in emphasis from the concept of perseveration, which refers to the continuance of the line of thinking or action. Perseveration focuses upon *inertia,* whereas rigidity draws attention to a failure to exploit possible alternatives. This view was promoted in an authoritative article by Cattell (1935), who distinguished between perseveration and 'disposition rigidity', while the second is manifested when a subject is required to perform a familiar task in a new way. Ironically, however, having made this distinction, which sounded the death knell for Spearman's 'perseveration', Cattell subsequently changed his definitions, and totally completed the circle by 1949, when he was referring to disposition rigidity as 'classical perseveration'. Meanwhile, his factor-analytical extraction of a 'rigidity factor' proved to be as vulnerable to criticism as had Spearman's p.

From a welter of confusing and contradictory statistical studies only one finding emerges with any clarity, and that is that there appears to be no single factor to explain rigidity. On the contrary, over thirty different factors have been invoked by various investigators. One reason for this unsatisfactory situation is the nature of the tests that have been used, many of which seem to have little or nothing to do with rigidity. A second, closely related reason is that nobody has ever been quite sure what *does* test rigidity. There has been a dire shortage of any valid measures of rigidity that could be inserted as 'anchors' in test batteries. The only test that still commands acceptance is Abraham Luchin's test of 'Einstellung' rigidity. In its usual form (the 'Water Jars' problems) the subject is presented with a series of problems that he is encouraged to tackle in a particular way. He is then given similar problems that are amenable to a different, simpler method. He is assumed to manifest 'Einstellung' rigidity in the degree of reluctance shown to abandon the original 'set'.

Despite the conceptual and semantic confusions that have bedeviled experimental approaches to rigidity, and the debacle of the factor-analytic studies, the idea of rigidity has retained its importance in clinical work. And it is not generally doubted that there does exist a cognitive characteristic, personality trait, mode of response or impairment that may appropriately be termed 'rigidity'.

Perhaps the most mystifying of anomalies in the stream of consciousness, and a prime example of the inability to shift, is the *obsessional experience*. An obsession is defined as a thought (idea, doubt, image, or impulse) which, although unwanted and resisted, is preoccupying to a degree that causes the individual extreme anguish. There has always been agreement as to what constitutes an obsession. Unlike many other psychopathological phenomena, although different authorities have emphasized different components, their definitions all revolve round the same three criteria:

(a) An obsession is characterized by the flavour of *compulsion*. The sufferer is reported to feel in the grip of the thought, as though he is the victim of an invader, and is compelled to harbour it. It dominates his consciousness at the expense of his 'natural' train of thought. He is fully aware that the intrusive thought originates in himself. But it is *ego-dystonic;* it does not feel natural or desirable to him.

(b) The thought is recognized by the sufferer as being *senseless,* absurd, odd, or irrelevant. This is one aspect of the dystonic character mentioned above. The sufferer's recognition of his obsession's absurdity betokens the fact that, unlike the psychotic person, he has insight.

(c) At least in the early stages of being gripped by his obsession, the sufferer *actively resists* it, fighting to oust it from his consciousness. But by definition the struggle is unavailing.

The intrusive thought commonly takes the form of an *obsessional doubt;* the sufferer is plagued incessantly by a nagging worry of the 'What if . . .?' or 'Did I . . .?' kinds. At its most prosaic, this uncertainty may depend on whether a domestic routine, such as locking the front door, has in fact been completed. The attempts made by the individual to reassure himself are called *compulsive checking,* which differs from ordinary checking in the accompanying flavour of compulsivity and the fact that the obsessional person is seldom fully satisfied. His checking of household switches, for instance, may take several hours each day; his attempts to assure himself that he has in fact switched off all the lights may keep him awake half the night. At the other extreme of content bizarrerie are cases where the obsessional doubt is in regard to some grotesque implausibility, possibly reflecting the sufferer's ambivalence or self-insecurity. For example, a young mother could not part from her baby, however briefly, without wondering whether it was possible that she had inadvertently dropped it on its head as she left.

Sharing many of the features of obsessional doubts are *obsessional ruminations*. The individual is unwillingly subjected to a protracted, picayune, and totally inconclusive internal debate. This very often revolves around an abstruse, metaphysical topic, or one that is clearly not amenable to rational debate. The sufferer recognizes this, but is unable to desist. He is so preoccupied that his normal mental effectiveness may become seriously impaired; he may even find it necessary to leave his employment in order to devote himself to his ruminations. Thus, one young man found it necessary to abandon a promising career, in order to spend his days ruminating about what might have happened to the Jewish people if the Red Sea had not opened.

Clearly, an experience marked by the criterial attributes outlined above shares certain features of some of the anomalies of consciousness that we have already considered. But in one or more ways, the obsessional experience stands alone. It differs from everyday preoccupations and the one-track-mindedness of healthy people because of its compulsive quality and the fact that it is ego-dystonic. It cannot be classed as one of the 'formal thought disorders', because the sufferer is in full possession of his faculties and retains insight, while realizing the personal source of his obsessions. It differs from perseveration and rigidity for the same reasons, and because the sufferer actively resists the experience.

It will have been noted that the definition of obsession is restricted to the *form* of the experience. In theory, the *content* could be anything at all. But in practice, although the contents of obsessions vary enormously, they are not of a cheerful nature. The most common obsessions have to do with morbid or depressing topics, such as death, sickness, disasters, degradation, contamination, or personal inadequacies of various types. In everyday life, we may be preoccupied by happy thoughts, hopes, or the possibility of good news. There have been no reports of obsessions of this kind, nor of merriment, self-gratulation, or sanguine optimism. But, of course, nobody is likely to complain of joyous thoughts, or to fight to eject them. And unless this is done, then by definition the experience cannot be classified as 'obsessional'. In lay parlance, individuals are often said to be 'obsessed' by their work, their ambitions, their sweethearts or their stamp collections. Technically, this is an incorrect use of of the term, unless the preoccupation in question is ego–dystonic, regarded as senseless and struggled against. Even though the preoccupation seems excessive to the impatient observer or the irate spouse, even though it betrays a lack of balance in the judgement of priorities, if it affords the individual some comfort or gratification, then it is not an obsession.

The obsession represents at least an intermittent failure in a core process that we take very much for granted. Normally, we can cease to think about something at will. We routinely turn our attention away from an on-going topic, or abandon a line of reasoning. This ability is essential if we are to adapt to the continual shifts and variations in the problems and demands with which an active life bombards us. But the individual trapped by an obsessional experience is unable to do this, struggle as he may.

The other side of the equation is that we normally do not simply stop thinking about something—we immediately start to think about something else. The cessation of the original thought does not produce a cognitive void. As William James emphasized, the stream of consciousness does not come to a halt, even temporarily, if we are in normal health. An integral part of stopping is that we *shift*. We do not stop a train of thought—we change trains. Perhaps, instead of fighting in vain to oust their obsessions, a more hopeful strategy might be for sufferers to focus upon potential alternatives, to aim for changing, rather than stopping.

A point of some theoretical significance springs directly from the above suggestion. Traditionally, obsessions have been described as 'invaders'. Indeed, the very word derives from the Latin *obsidere,* to besiege. As we saw earlier, during the Middle Ages the psychotic person was assumed to be 'possessed' by a demon or evil spirit. The person plagued by an obsession was not as yet 'possessed'—in other words, he was not a lunatic or maniac. In his case, the evil force was taken to be still striving to gain admittance to the citadel. The victim was under siege, but not yet possessed. After the 'evil spirit' assumption had been abandoned in the face of more rational scientific approaches, it was realized that the source of the experience of compulsion was within the victim himself. But the idea of an 'invader' persisted, although now only as a metaphor. Standard texts of psychiatry and abnormal psychology stress that the obsessed individual feels compelled to undergo his undesired experience. The problem, we are told, is that the compelling force is too powerful for the defender to repel successfully. This account accepts the personal nature of the 'force', but emphasizes its intensity. The problem is regarded as one of morbidly augmented cognition. However, as the present writer has argued, this traditional view may represent some misunderstanding of the phenomenological flavour of the compulsive experience. Patients do not, in fact, emphasize the strength of the obsession so much as their own weakness in failing to shift from it. The problem, therefore, may not be one of increased excitation, but one of reduced or faulty inhibition.

If the above argument is valid, it would suggest that the heretofore unsolved problem of obsessionality might be amenable to a cybernetics-type approach. The continuance of an obsession can readily be conceptualized in terms of an impairment of negative feedback, and the development of an information loop with feed-forward characteristics. In other words, experiencing the thought reinforces its continuance, and raises the probability of its recurrence on a subsequent occasion. The choice of the cognition to be thus recirculated is presumably determined by its personal significance and affective loading. In the absence of regulation by a negative feedback 'governor', the obsessional thought will continue to preoccupy the individual by reemerging and dominating his consciousness.

10

ENVOI

At one time pupil teachers were expected to abide by a pedagogic precept which said:

'(a) Tell 'em what you're going to tell 'em.
(b) Tell 'em.
(c) Tell 'em what you've just told 'em.'

A concluding chapter demands that it all be told again. Perhaps one can be content with a re-statement and re-emphasis of the book's main themes and emphases.

FORM VERSUS CONTENT

The study of the *content* of experiences is a perfectly valid activity which can afford illuminating insights into both the experience of the individual and the values and presumptions of his society. But as Jaspers and his followers have stressed, structural analysis can only be undertaken after the *form* of an experience has been examined. The fact that a man goes about with a goldfish bowl over his head, announcing that he is a visitor from outer space and of indeterminate gender, can tell us something about him and his particular culture. But before we can undertake any precise psychological analysis we must conduct a phenomenological investigation. We need to know, for instance, whether he thinks he really *is* a visitor from outer space or merely 'as though' he were such a being. Does he perhaps believe that his body has been taken over by some astral force, or is it that he feels that he *is* the astral force who happens to be occupying a human cadaver? Or is he just an inveterate science fiction reader who happens to like dressing up? In other words, we need to know not only precisely *what* he is experiencing, but *how* he experiences it. We require this sort of information before we can uncover the underlying form of his experience. The content of his experience—his description of himself as a denizen of outer space—enables us to determine the form, but itself can be very misleading if we are interested in psychological (or psychiatric) analysis. Another individual may have the same basic disorder, but experience and express it through different content. He may perch on a fence, believing that he is the reincarnation of the Great M'Gombo. Yet another may manifest no such bizarre behaviour, going about his affairs in a quiet and orderly manner. But privately he may be uneasily aware that his thoughts are being manipulated by some outside agency. In each case we must abstract the basic form from the manifest content. And this, let it be noted, cannot be done merely by observing the individuals' actions. Our first man may stand, run, jump and twiddle his goldfish bowl with startling dexterity. We may record all that meticulously for months on end; but we will not have acquired a jot of evidence about the form of his experience.

COGNITION AND AFFECT

Many of the anomalous experiences considered in this book are referred to in textbooks of clinical or abnormal psychology. Typically, they are only *described*. What approach is used when they are *discussed*? It is fair to say that, apart from those authors whose concern is with learning, the standard approach has used or implied the postulates of psychoanalysis or some other 'affect' approach.

The main assumption of 'affect' approaches is that anomalous experiences are due to the individual's emotional state, or represent his defence reactions to stress. It is true, of course, that many unusual experiences occur in highly affect-laden situations. But this is not to say that they are necessarily due to, or even explicable in terms of, emotion alone. Indeed, the latter may be the result rather than the cause of the experience. Furthermore, 'explanations' which attribute experiential phenomena to affect may inadvertently suggest that certain types or intensities of emotion bring into play cognitive structures and processes which are somehow different from those we employ 'normally'. Now it is clear that on any given occasion the way we feel will colour what and how we think. But it must be equally clear that what and how we think will determine the way we feel.

There are a number of ways of studying thinking. The approach in this book might be placed under the heading of 'information processing' because it is concerned with the vicissitudes of information—

how it is sampled, synthesized and stored. As well as processes, cognitive *structures* have been discussed. We have emphasized their dynamic aspects and their hierarchical organization. This simple model is drawn directly from the work of Sir Frederic Bartlett, though it owes much to contemporary cognitive theorists such as Neisser (1967). The approach stresses *organization*; it presumes that we do not store intact and unaltered gobbets of information, but incorporate them into what is already stored. Subsequently it is not the gobbets which are utilized, but the structures into which they were incorporated. These structures, which we have referred to throughout as 'schemata', are themselves under continual modification as they accommodate to new information. And schemata necessarily include emotional and attitudinal components reflecting, like the other components, the life experience of the individual. It could be argued, then, that precise affective responses are themselves a matter of cognitive attribution. Each of us learns to load with affect certain objects, people, experiences and thoughts, because these loadings are included in the schemata in question. But even those psychologists who would be reluctant to accept this argument would agree that thinking and feeling are inextricably interdependent. And of central relevance to the present discussion is the fact that this interdependence applies across the board, to 'regular' experiences as well as to anomalous ones. To attempt to consider any experience in terms of affect alone or in terms of cognition alone may be suggestive but must be artificial This makes it even more ironic that for many psychologists affect seems to be an irrelevant consideration in the study of most 'normal' experiences, but after a certain point in the spectrum it suddenly becomes central, as though some sort of conceptual cut-off mechanism is activated. It would seem inappropriate and conceptually restrictive that so many students of anomalous experience have concentrated on the affect component. The argument of this book is *not* that affect should be ignored, but that concentration upon it has led to the ignoring of cognitive aspects, just as the emphasis on content has diverted attention from the consideration of form.

ANOMALOUS EXPERIENCES AND 'PROBLEM-SOLVING'

Much of the perplexity with which we react to anomalous experiences is due to 'camera'-type assumptions about perception—that a percept is a facsimile of what is being perceived. This approach is reflected in the various 'cupboard' or 'tombstone' assumptions about memory —that a memory is a stored facsimile of an original experience. Most of the discussions in this book have involved denial that we function in such an objective, mechanistic manner. It is not a question of 'real' events and 'true' perceptions or memories of them. We seem to function by selecting cues—a tiny sample of those available—by matching, comparing and synthesizing them to make a working model of the world. It would be convenient if we really did record outside events objectively, though the study of psychology would then be much less intriguing and challenging. But all the evidence suggests that this is not the way in which we function, whatever the external 'realities'. Note that in arguing this we can prudently by-pass philosophical problems, drawing our material almost entirely from the field of psychology.

Perhaps the crucial point is that it has become more and more apparent that all our commerce with the world is *constructive, interpretative and tentative*. At all levels of cognitive activity we seem to operate by setting up and testing hypotheses, by problem-solving and by selecting strategies. As we have seen, this applies to attention, perception, imagery and memory as well as to the more conscious weighing of evidence involved in judgment and belief. Once this view is accepted, many of our 'anomalous' experiences suddenly seem much less sinister and inexplicable. For if cognitive processes are constructive, interpretative and problem-solving in nature, then there can be no question of objectively 'correct' or 'identical' perceptions and memories. It is no longer mystifying that our recollections of a place or a person may turn out to be sadly amiss. We need not invoke reincarnation to explain why we 'recognize' something we have not previously encountered. We need not rely upon spiritualism to explain why we occasionally 'see' somebody who is not there or 'hear' our name called when no living person has called it. Our cognitions are dynamic, and each of us is continually constructing his own models and arriving at decisions according to his experiential history and his personal schemata. It is to be expected that discrepancies will occur—both between and within individuals.

Throughout this book we have noted the 'problem-solving' element in all cognitive activity. The interesting point is that the 'problems' posed do not have 'right answers'. Most of the intellectual puzzles that are usually classified as 'problems' are designed as closed entities. All the necessary information is presented to render them amenable to the application of formal logic. This leads to one correct solution or at least to a finite number of alternative solutions. And the solution itself can be checked to ensure its correctness. The 'problem-solving' involved in cognitive activity is not like that. The situation is open-ended, the data are seldom sufficient, the criteria are never absolute and there are no ultimate solutions. Most of these cognitive 'problems' are therefore insoluble in any formal sense.

Their 'solutions' can only be tentative and relative to the working models we construct. Yet we engage in such 'problem-solving', often at various levels concurrently, throughout our waking lives. It is small wonder that our 'solutions' occasionally surprise us or others. What *is* surprising is that so much of our experience strikes us as being orderly and appropriate, and that our reports of it can be shared or at least accepted by those around us.

SUGGESTED FURTHER READING

Chapter 1. Anomalies of Attention

Broadbent (1971). Reviews the mass experimental findings subsequent to his earlier classic and modifies his original model.

McGhie (1969). A good review of the experimental literature on attention deficit, particularly with regard to schizophrenia.

Moray (1969b). An excellent summary of contemporary developments in the field of selective listening and vision.

Norman (1976). Covers a wider field, and is a crisp and elegant introduction to the information-processing approach.

All of the above are primarily concerned with one type of attention (selective) from one point of view (the information-processing approach). No recent psychology book about other types of attention is known to the author.

Bakan (Ed.) (1966). A good historical overview.

Chapter 2. Anomalies of Imagery and Perception: I

McKellar (1957). Contains interesting accounts of the topics discussed here.

Neisser (1967). A stimulating and provocative book that discusses imagery and perception in terms of the author's own information-processing model.

Segal (1971). A sound discussion with a cognitive slant.

Chapter 3. Anomalies of Imagery and Perception: II

Descriptions of the content of hallucinations are to be found in most textbooks of psychiatry and abnormal psychology.

Brownfield (1965). Very readable introductory account of SD.

Cohen (1964). Readable account of the effects of hallucinogenic drugs.

Fish (1967), Jaspers (1923), Anderson and Trethowan (1967). Discussion of their formal qualities and those of allied phenomena.

Reed (1979b). Provides a retrospective summary of the SD movement.

West (Ed.) (1962). For more advanced study, reference may be made to this collection of readings.

Chapter 4. Anomalies of Recall

Clinical accounts are to be found in most standard textbooks of psychiatry.

Baddeley (1982). Up to date and very readable coverage of most aspects of memory.

Freud (1960). A classical discussion of anomalies of recall.

Kihlstrom and Evans (Eds.) (1979). Good accounts of amnesia and other memory disorders.

Talland (1968). A most authoritative introductory account of the mnestic (or amnesic) syndrome.

Chapter 5. Anomalies of Recognition

The phenomena discussed in this chapter are discussed in most standard textbooks of psychiatry. The author is unaware of any full discussion in the psychological literature, though introductory descriptions abound.

Reed (1979a). Discusses some of the phenomena.

Sacks (1984). A highly readable and often moving series of essays on agnosia and other neurological dysfunctions.

Chapter 6. Anomalies in the Experience of Self

The phenomena are described in most textbooks of psychiatry, and are discussed in detail in many advanced psychoanalytical and philosophical works. No readily available account of the *whole* area from the psychological viewpoint seems to have been published.

Alcock (1981). An excellent discussion of ESP and credulity.

Wapner and Werner (Eds.) (1965). Some relevant material in this collection of readings.

Chapter 7. *Anomalies of Judgement and Belief*

The content of delusions is described in all the standard textbooks of psychiatry and abnormal psychology.

Bannister and Mair (1968). Applications of Kelly's ideas.

Eysenck (1960) and Buss (1966). Offer reviews of some relevant psychological experimental findings at a fairly advanced level. No introductory psychological discussion is known.

Fish (1967) and Jaspers (1923). Examine the distinction between primary and secondary delusions, and between those and over-valued ideas.

Chapter 8. *Anomalies of Consciousness*

The disorders are described in most standard textbooks of psychiatry and psychopathology.

Tart (1975). A widely read discussion of states of consciousness.

Wallace and Fisher (1983). A readable and succinct introduction to the psychology of consciousness.

Chapter 9. *Anomalies in the Rate of Flow of Consciousness*

Again, some of the disorders featured here are described in standard psychiatry texts. But no full discussion is known, whether from the psychological or the psychiatric viewpoints.

Reed (1985). A modern coverage of obsessional experiences; to date, the first book to discuss these in terms of cognition.

BIBLIOGRAPHY

Ackner, B. (1954). Depersonalization, *J. Ment. Sci.,* **100**, 838–52.

Alcock, J. E. (1981). *Parapsychology: science or magic?* Oxford: Permagon.

Anderson, E. W., and Trethowan, W. H. (1967). *Psychiatry,* 2nd ed. London: Ballière, Tindall and Cassell.

Baddeley, A. (1982). *Your Memory: A user's guide.* New York: Macmillan.

Bakan, P. (Ed.) (1966). *Attention: An enduring problem in psychology.* Princeton, N.J.: Van Nostrand.

Bannister, D. (1962). The nature and measure of schizophrenic thought disorder, *J. Ment. Sci.,* **108**, 825–41.

Bannister, D., and Mair, J. M. M. (1968). *The evaluation of personal constructs.* London: Academic Press.

Bannister, H., and Zangwill, O. L. (1941). Experimentally induced visual paramnesias, *Brit. J. Psychol.,* **32**, 30–51.

Bartlett, F. C. (1932). *Remembering.* Cambridge: Cambridge Univ. Press.

Beaumont, J. G. (1981). 'Split brain studies and the duality of consciousness', in G. Underwood and R. Stevens (Eds.) *Aspects of consciousness,* Vol. 2. London: Academic.

Belbin, E. (1950). The influence of interpolated recall upon recognition, *Quart. J. exp. Psychol.,* **2**, 163–9.

Brain, Lord (1965). *Speech disorders. Aphasia, apraxia and agnosia.* London: Butterworth.

Broadbent, D. E. (1958). *Perception and communication.* London: Permagon Press.

Broadbent, D. E. (1971). *Decision and stress.* New York and London: Academic Press.

Brown, R., and McNeill, D. (1966). The 'tip of the tongue' phenomenon, *J. Verb. Learn.,* **5**, 325–7.

Brownfield, C. A. (1965). *Isolation. Clinical and experimental approaches.* New York: Random House.

Bryan, W. L., and Harter, N. (1897). Studies in the physiology and psychology of the telegraphic language, *Psychol. Rev.,* **4**, 27–53.

Buss, A. H. (1966). *Psychopathology.* New York: John Wiley.

Byrd, R. E. (1938). *Alone.* New York: Putnam's.

Cameron, N. (1946). 'Experimental analysis of schizophrenic thinking', in J.

S. Kasanin (Ed.) *Language and thought in schizophrenia*. Berkeley: Univ. of California.

Cattell, R. B. (1935). Perseveration and personality: Some experiments and an hypothesis. *J. Ment. Sci.*, **81**, 151–67.

Cohen, S. (1964). *Drugs of hallucination*. London: Secker and Warburg.

Deikman, A. J. (1963). De-automatization and the mystic experience, *Psychiat.*, **29**, 324–38.

Downing, J. (1969). 'Attitude and Behavior change through Psychedelic drug use', in C. A. Start (Ed.), *Altered States of Consciousness*. New York: Wiley.

Ellson, D. G. (1941). Hallucinations produced by sensory conditioning, *J. exp. Psychol.*, **28**, 1–20.

Enoch, M. D. (1963). The Capgras Syndrome, *Actia Psychiat. Scand.* **39**, 437–62.

Eysenck, H. J. (Ed.) (1961). *Handbook of abnormal psychology*. New York: Basic Books.

Federn, P. (1952). *Ego psychology and the psychoses*. New York: Basic Books.

Festinger, L. (1957). *A theory of cognitive dissonance*. New York: Harper & Row.

Festinger, L., Riecken, H. W., and Schachter, S. (1956). *When prophecy fails*. Minneapolis: Univ. of Minnesota.

Fish, F. (1967). *Clinical psychopathology*. Bristol: John Wright.

Fisher, S. (1962). 'Body image boundaries and hallucinations', in West, L. J. (Ed.), *Hallucinations*. New York: Grune and Stratton.

Fisher, S., and Cleveland, S. E. (1958). *Body image and personality*. Princeton, N.J.: Van Nostrand.

Foulkes, D., Spear, P. S., and Symonds, J. D. (1966). Individual differences in mental activity at sleep onset, *J. Abnorm. Psychol.*, **71**, 280–6.

Freud, S. (1960). *The psychopathology of everyday life*. Standard ed. VI (1901). London: Hogarth.

Galambos, R. (1956). Suppression of auditory nerve activity by stimulation of efferent fibres to cochlea, *J. Neurophysiol.*, **19**, 424–37.

Gardner, R. W., Holzman, P. S., Klein, G. S., and Spence, D. P. (1959). Cognitive control: a study of individual consistencies in cognitive behavior, *Psychol. Issues*, **1**, No. 4.

Gregory, R. L. (1970). *The Intelligent Eye*. London: Longmans, Green.

Harriman, P. L. H. (1947). *The new dictionary of psychology*. New York: The Philosophical Library.

Head, H. (1920). *Studies in neurology*. London: Oxford Univ. Press.

Hebb, D. O. (1949). *The organization of behaviour*. New York: Science Edition.

Heron, W., Bexton, W. H., and Hebb, D. O. (1953). Congnitive effects of decreased variation to sensory environment, *Amer. Psychologist*, **8**, 366 (abstract).

Hoenig, J., Anderson, E. W., Kenna, J. C., and Blunden, Ruth (1962). Clinical and pathological aspects of the mnestic syndrome, *J. Mental Sci.*, **108**, 541–59.

James, W. (1890). *Principles of psychology*. New York: Holt, Rinehart and Winston.

Janet, P. (1903). *Les obsessions et la psychasthénie*. Paris: Alcan.

Jaspers, K. (1923, trans. 1963). *General psychopathology*. Trans. by J. Hoenig and M. Hamilton. Manchester: University Press.

Kelly, G. A. (1955). *The psychology of personal constructs.* Vols. I and II. New York: Norton.

Kihlstrom, J. F., and Evans, F. J. (Eds.) (1979). *Functional Disorders of Memory.* Hillsdale: Lawrence Erlbaum.

Luria, A. R. (1969). *The mind of a mnemonist.* London: Jonathan Cape.

Luria, A. R. (1978). 'The human brain and conscious activity', in G. E. Schwartz and D. Shaprio (Eds.) *Consciousness and Self-Regulation,* Vol. 2. Chichester: Wiley.

Mackworth, N. H. (1950). *Researches in the measurement of human performance.* M.R.C. Spec. Rpt. 268. H.M.S.O.

McGhie, A. (1969). *Pathology of attention.* Harmondsworth: Penguin.

McGhie, A., and Chapman, J. (1961). Disorders of attention and perception in early schizophrenia, *B. J. Med. Psychol.,* 34, 103–16.

McKellar, P. (1957). *Imagination and thinking.* London: Cohen and West.

Moray, N. (1969a). *Listening and attention.* Harmondsworth: Penguin.

Moray, N. (1969b). *Attention: selective processes in vision and hearing.* London: Hutchinson.

Neisser, U. (1967). *Cognitive psychology.* New York: Appleton Century Crofts.

Norman, D. A. (1976). *Memory and attention: An introduction to human information processing.* (2nd ed.). New York: Wiley.

Payne, N. (1961). 'Cognitive abnormalities', in H. J. Eysenck (Ed.), *Handbook of abnormal psychology.* New York: Basic Books.

Perky, C. W. (1910). An experimental study of imagination, *Amer. J. Psychol.,* 21, 422–52.

Piaget, J. (1926). *The language and thought of the child.* London: Kegan Paul, Trench, Trubner.

Potter, S. (1947). *The theory and practice of gamesmanship.* London: Rupert Hart-Davis.

Proust, M. (1954). *À la recherche du temps perdu.* Vol. I. Paris: Gallimard.

Reed, G. F. (1979a). 'Everyday anomalies of recall and recognition', in J. F. Kihlstrom and F. J. Evans (Eds.) *op. cit.*

Reed, G. F. (1979b). 'Sensory deprivation', in G. Underwood and R. Stevens (Eds.) *Aspects of Consciousness,* Vol. 1. London: Academic.

Reed, G. F. (1985). *Obsessional Experience and Compulsive Behaviour.* Orlando: Academic.

Sacks, O. (1985). *The Man Who Mistook His Wife For a Hat.* New York: Harper and Row.

Schneider, K. (1959). *Clinical psychopathology.* Trans. by M. W. Hamilton and E. W. Anderson. New York: Grune and Stratton.

Seashore, C. E. (1895). Measurements of illusions and hallucinations in normal life, *Stud. Yale Psychol. Lab.,* 2, 1–67.

Segal, S. J., and Nathan, S. (1964). The Perky effect: Incorporation of an external stimulus into an imagery experience, *Percept. Mot. Skills,* 18, 385–95.

Segal, S. J. (1971). *Imagery: Current Cognitive Approaches.* New York: Academic.

Seitz, P. E. D., and Molholm, H. B. (1947). Relation of mental imagery to hallucinations, *A.M.A. Arch. Neurol. Psychiat.,* 57, 469–80.

Shakow, D. (1962). Segmental set: A theory of the formal psychological deficit of schizophrenia, *A.M.A. Arch. Gen. Psychiat.,* 6, 1–17.

Slocum, J. (1900). *Sailing around the world*. New York: Century.

Spearman, C. (1927). *Abilities of Man*. New York: Macmillan.

Sperry, R. W. (1964). *Problems Outstanding in the Evolution of Brain Function*. New York: American Museum of Natural History.

Sperry, R. W. (1973). 'Lateral specialization of cerebral function in the surgically separated hemispheres', in F. J. McGuigan (Ed.) *The Psychophysiology of Thinking*. New York: Academic.

Talland, G. A. (1968). *Disorders of memory and learning*. Harmondsworth: Penguin.

Tart, C. T. (1975). *States of Consciousness*. New York: E. P. Dutton.

Tooth, G. (1950). *Studies in mental illness in the Gold Coast*. London: H.M.S.O.

Treisman, A. (1960). Contextual cues in selective listening, *Quart. J. exp. Psychol.*, **12**, 242–8.

Wachtel, P. L. (1967). Conceptions of broad and narrow attention, *Psychol. Bull.*, **68**, 417–20.

Wallace, B., and Fisher, L. E. (1983). *Consciousness and Behavior*. Boston: Allyn and Bacon.

Wapner, S., and Werner, H. (Eds.) (1965). *The body percept*. New York: Random House.

Warren, H. C. (Ed.) (1935). *Dictionary of psychology*. London: George Allen and Unwin.

Watson, J. B. (1913). Psychology as a Behaviorist views it. *Psychol. Rev.*, **20**, 158–77.

West, J. J. (Ed.) (1962). *Hallucinations*. New York: Grune and Stratton.

Witkin, H. A., Dyk, R. B., Faterson, H. F., Goodenough, D. R., and Karp, S. A. (1962). *Psychological differentiation*. New York: John Wiley and Sons.

Woodworth, R. S., and Schlosberg, H. (1955). *Experimental Psychology*. 3rd ed. New York: Holt, Rinehart and Winston.

INDEX OF NAMES

INDEX OF SUBJECTS